Boston Tabloid

Charlies
ENTERTAINMENT
COCKTAILS

SHOW

DEPARTMENT
MASSACHUSETTS

POLICE DEPARTMENT
BOSTON, MASSACHUSETTS

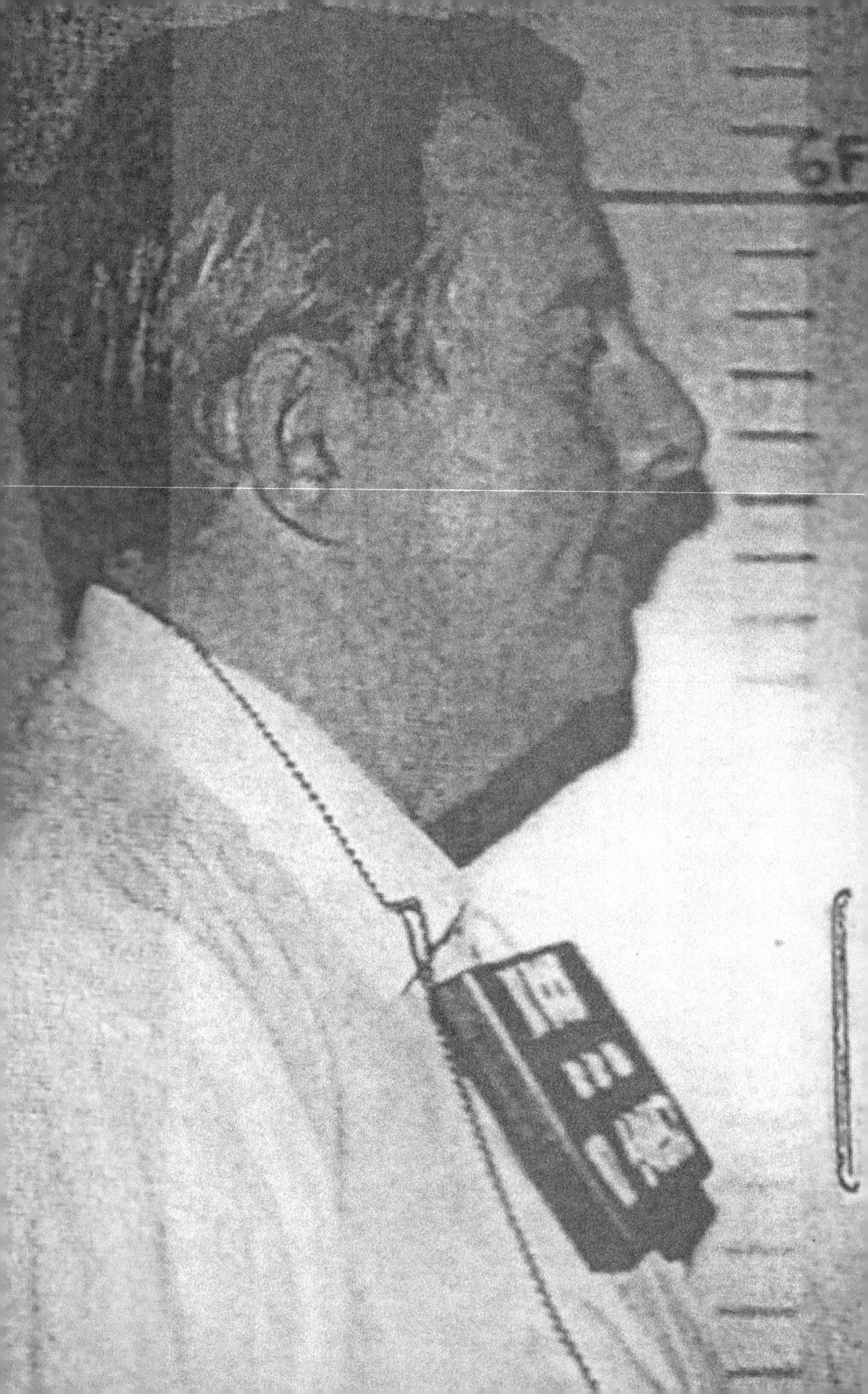

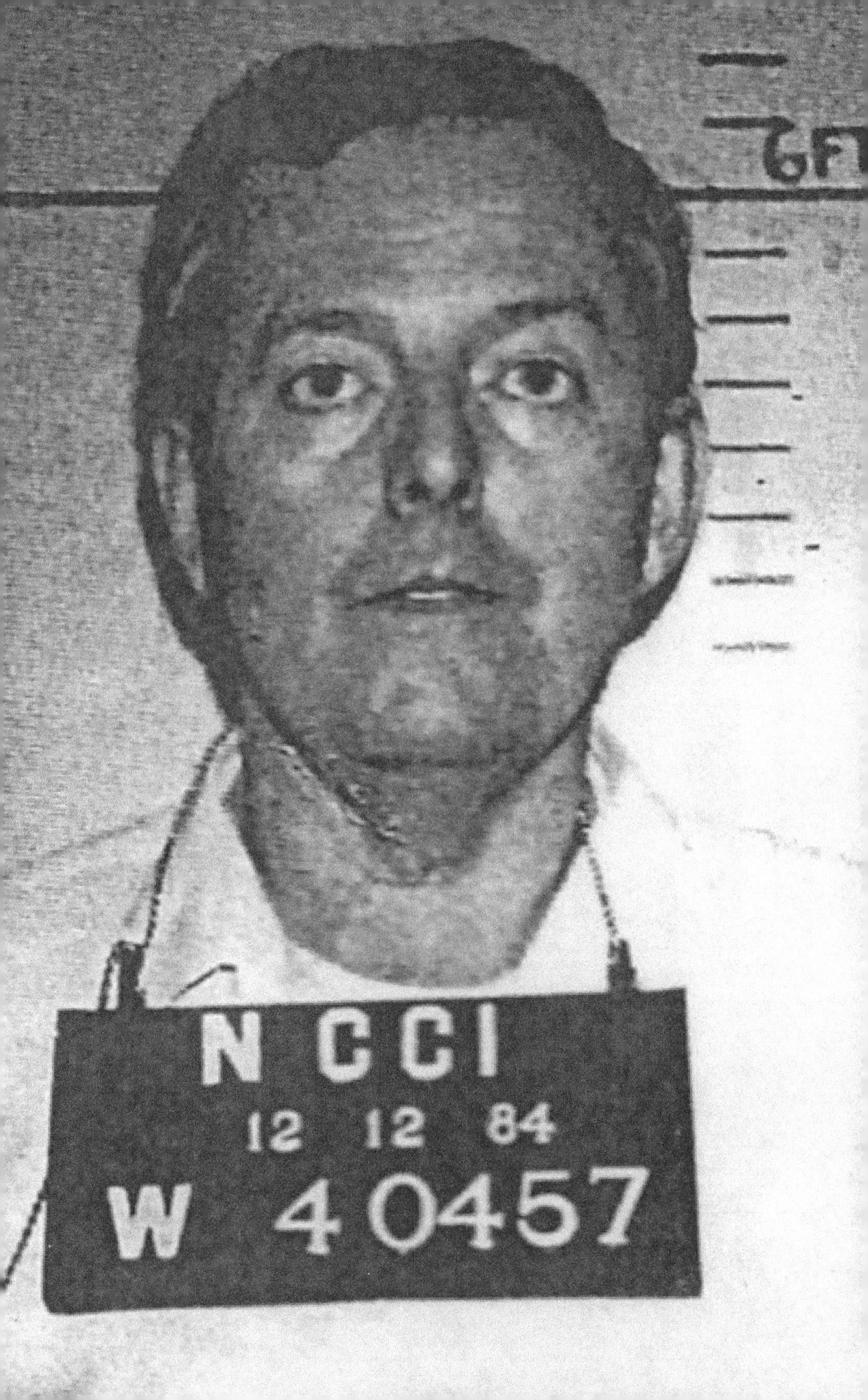
6FT
NCCI
12 12 84
W 40457

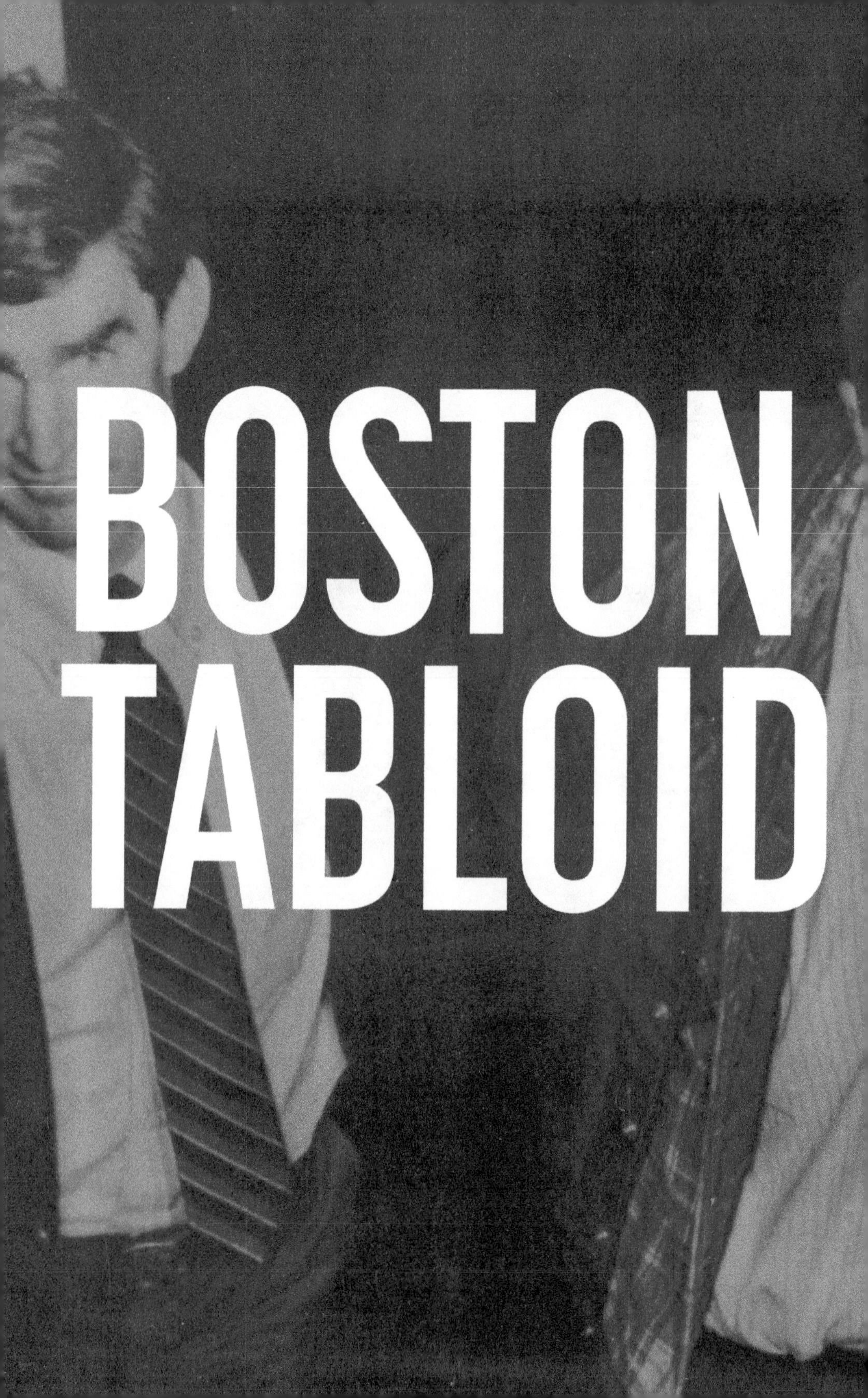
BOSTON
TABLOID

THE KILLING OF ROBIN BENEDICT

DON STRADLEY

HAMILCAR
PUBLICATIONS
Boston

ISBN: 978-1949590-55-5

CIP data is available.

hamilcarpubs.com

Aut viam inveniam aut faciam

"Knowing you has made my life brighter and happier.
You are a remarkable, wonderful woman, and being with
you makes me a very fortunate man."

—William Douglas, in a letter to Robin Benedict

"You can never tell what we are going to do next.
It's been wonderful and will be more
wonderful in times to come."

—Robin Benedict, in a letter to William Douglas

If it bleeds, it leads. . . .

—Television news axiom

ALSO BY

DON STRADLEY

THE WAR: Hagler–Hearns and Three Rounds for the Ages

"There are books about boxing. There are books about the 1980s. But I've never been transported into those worlds quite like I have for *The War*. In Hagler and Hearns, Stradley has two powerful—and underexplored—protagonists that he utilizes expertly as the book moves inexorably toward the greatest ten minutes in the history of sports. A total triumph."

—Dave Zirin, author of *The Kaepernick Effect: Taking a Knee, Changing the World*

Berserk: The Shocking Life and Death of Edwin Valero

Slaughter in the Streets: When Boston Became Boxing's Murder Capital

A Fistful of Murder: The Fights and Crimes of Carlos Monzon

CONTENTS

PROLOGUE

Dedham, Massachusetts, is an affluent town southwest of Boston. Along with being the archetypical "bedroom community," Dedham is known for the Endicott Estate, a glorious mansion built in 1904 by Henry Bradford Endicott, one of the richest men in the world. Nowadays it's a tourist attraction, advertising itself online as a perfect place for wedding receptions. Just eight miles from the Endicott Estate is the Norfolk County Courthouse, a grand building declared a National Historic Landmark during the Nixon administration. With its Greek revival architecture and a simple but handsome courtroom, it is an austere setting. On April 27, 1984, spectators settled in for what promised to be one of the most notorious murder trials in New England's history. Yet the elegant old courtroom seemed unlikely for a case concerning a prostitute and a bloody hammer.

The man on trial seemed unlikely, too. He had once been a revered associate professor at Tufts University. The newspapers constantly reminded us that he was a sort of academic superman. Yet to look at William Douglas, one saw an oversized, clumsy geezer behind horn-rimmed spectacles, his pale face washed out by months of anxiety.

Though standing over six feet tall and weighing more than 300 pounds, Douglas took his place in the courtroom like a shamed child. There was something cartoonish about him—his head seemed too small for his enormous frame, a tiny cherry atop a massive mound of vanilla ice cream; he was a parade float of a man. Indeed, Douglas's physical appearance had been fodder for reporters since the earliest days of the case. Those in a rush to meet deadlines simply called him "the portly professor." To more highbrow types, he had been "a turtle in disarray" or "a great penguin."

The story of Douglas and the woman he'd murdered was a tabloid sensation that year. Though the sordid case inspired books, a movie, and a few documentaries, nothing quite captured the electricity of reading about it each morning. Every day there seemed to be some new development in the case, some revelation to keep the story alive and the horror unfurling. Even the *Boston Globe*, that stuffy fortress of good taste, benefitted from articles about bloodstains and prostitutes, giving more space than ever before to the Combat Zone, the neighborhood of sleazy bars and porn shops where Douglas met his victim.

It was impossible to not see Douglas as a symbol of something, an emblem of our decaying moral values and our preoccupation with sex. In Douglas there was the scary suggestion that unchecked desire conquered all else, that God, family, and social status wilted before the charms of a beautiful whore. The sheer insipidness of Douglas made him all the more fascinating. He was the killer mope.

And what of Robin Benedict, the woman who was murdered? The media seemed split. Was she a conniving sex worker, or just a nice girl who had made some mistakes? What had any of us really known about prostitutes before seeing her picture in the newspaper? As we learned more about her, our image of prostitutes lurched away wildly. We took it all in, a city full of 1970s kids adjusting to adulthood in the 1980s. We'd grown up on *Sesame Street* and the Fonz. If any of us had ever seen a real "working girl," she was probably stumbling past the old Boston Garden as a Bruins game was letting out. Whatever else we knew about prostitutes came from old episodes of *Barney Miller*, where they always had frizzy hair, chewed gum, and spat out punch lines with impeccable timing. Prostitutes on TV shows or movies looked nothing like Robin Benedict. An attractive woman with syrupy brown eyes, she might've starred in commercials for hair conditioner.

We hadn't known prostitutes could look so wholesome, any more than we'd known professors could be homicidal.

On this first day of a trial that many believed would last months, Douglas stepped before Judge Roger J. Donahue. The judge was sixty years old but seemed much older, having mastered the slightly sour look of old-time movie judges.

"Did you kill Robin Benedict?" asked Donahue.

Douglas blinked. He seemed nervous, out of breath. In a weedy voice, he gave an answer that few were expecting.

"Yes, sir."

With those two words, Douglas deflated what many had hoped would be the trial of the decade.

In short order, Douglas confessed that he had killed Robin Benedict and had disposed of her body. He agreed to help the authorities find the corpse, and then made brief apologies to the Benedict family and his own. When the dramatic moment ended, guards led him out of the building in handcuffs. He stopped briefly on the courthouse steps to be photographed by the media.

As he stood humbly before the photographers, Douglas appeared exhausted. His attorney assured the press that Douglas felt relieved at having confessed and was looking forward to helping uncover the dead woman's body. It had been thrown in a dumpster and was by now in a landfill somewhere in Massachusetts or Rhode Island.

"That's the first time in my life that I ever hit anybody," Douglas said in his official confession. "I was never in a fight in grammar school or high school or college and I never ever laid a hand on anyone."

Robin Benedict was supposedly a savvy operator when it came to the men who paid her for sex. But in a seedy Boston bar called Good Time Charlie's, during the plain, pleasant days of the Reagan era, she encountered a slumming professor with a shy manner. During the day, his colleagues knew him as a bright but awkward man, the sort who seemed unable to dress himself but could write groundbreaking articles for scientific journals. They knew nothing about his frequent visits to the city's infamous Combat Zone, or his collection of pornographic material, the sort that featured people being tied with ropes and tortured. A lover of prostitutes, a compulsive ogre who wasn't above stealing from his employer or being unfaithful to his oblivious wife, he'd pursued his covert activities for many months without being discovered.

Throughout the early accounts of Douglas's journey from revered professor to killer, he's depicted as a callous and senseless figure: his colleagues are trampled on, his wife is cast aside, other prostitutes are sampled like so many snacks at a buffet table. Yet we were to believe that this man who was fascinated by prostitutes had no idea that Robin was working for a pimp or that she would never return the feelings he had for her. The general conclusion was that the connection between William Douglas and Robin Benedict was pure fantasy on his part, and that he was fueled by deluded dreams where dull professors could turn beautiful young sex workers into loving girlfriends.

But as time passed, the story was flipped. Douglas was depicted as less a fiend than a helpless man duped by a hooker. Even some of the investigators would admit to feeling sorry for Douglas. They saw him as a silly, middle-aged man who had somehow fallen in love with a cocaine-addicted young scammer. Forty years later, investigators who are still living hear his name and laugh. The fool had fallen into a hellish trap, and the only escape he saw involved violence. They chuckle at Douglas's folly.

For what he did to Robin Benedict, Douglas was a monster. Yet many also perceived his victim as a villain. Even the most liberal publications presented her as an unfeeling streetwalker; some readers may have felt she had in part even deserved her fate. The journalists who covered the case then know the tone would be different now; we are a bit beyond such blaming of the female victim now, in the era of #MeToo. At the time, though, a prostitute garnered only so much sympathy, even if Douglas had beaten her to death.

Douglas's appearance and personality may have made it easier to shift the blame. Overweight, bespectacled, soft-spoken, he didn't resemble the killers we knew, the smooth-talking psychopaths and cunning drifters we occasionally saw on the nightly news. This was evil not born in the gutter, but from a university setting. For once, we couldn't blame rock music or the economy or hippie cults. The madness came from a suburban family man who drove a Toyota.

The uproar in Massachusetts nearly forty years ago had little to do with the murder of a young prostitute. What grabbed the people was how the case exposed a man's double life, how a respected scientist could possess a cruel mind worthy of the lowest criminal. And as more of Douglas's secret life was revealed, we may have thought about our own secrets and all that we kept hidden. We may have been relieved. Compared to William Douglas, what we did during our own dark hours was nothing.

Part ONE
BLOODY
HAMME
AT RES
ON I-9

R FOUND
STOP

1.

Thirteen months earlier . . .

Sunday, March 6, 1983. It was one of those damp, chilly mornings that made New Englanders feel springtime would never come. It would've been a nice morning to sleep in, but some folks were out and about.

Two unemployed men were checking out dumpsters along Interstate 95 near the Mansfield exit. Freezing temperatures be damned—there were empty bottles and cans to find and cash in. Massachusetts had just passed the bottle bill on January 1 that year, but it was already common to see people scrounging around at rest stops along the highway. Grab enough empty bottles at five cents per deposit, and you could keep yourself in cigarettes and lottery tickets for the weekend, or maybe a six-pack of Pabst Blue Ribbon, just enough to drive the new concept of bottle returns.

The two men, Joseph Plotegher and Robert Jewell, approached a trash barrel that looked promising. On Sundays, the rest stops were always full to bursting with empties, all a result of the Saturday night traffic. They rooted around and lifted out a mysterious bundle. It was a brown plastic kitchen bag, tied at the top with a knot. Inside was a woman's tan corduroy blazer. It was folded around something hard and lumpy.

Wrapped snugly inside the blazer, which smelled of expensive perfume, were two items: a man's blue shirt and a small sledgehammer.

The hammer was sticky. The men saw dark traces on the handle, like two large freckles, of what they guessed to be blood. Stuck to the hammer was a single strand of long dark hair. The clothing also had traces of what appeared to be blood. It was enough to send a shiver dancing up the men's spines. They debated calling the police but decided against it. Why get involved with the cops?

They put the bag back in the trash barrel and moved on. There were more dumpsters to check along the highway. Maybe they could be done by noon, home in time for some Sunday sports on TV.

But Plotegher was bothered. Had that really been blood on the hammer? Had someone been whacked on the head? And it had been one mean mother of a hammer, the kind you usually see on demolition sites, the kind that smashes plaster out of walls.

Within a few hours, Plotegher called the Massachusetts State Police in Foxborough and described what he'd seen.

Later, a police lab identified the blood type on the jacket. It matched that of a missing woman named Robin Benedict. In Boston's adult entertainment district, she was known as "Nadine" and was rumored to make $1,000 per night as a prostitute.

• • •

On average, two Boston prostitutes were killed per year in those days. The corpses turned up in the strangest places: one body was found in a pond in New Hampshire; another was stuffed in a car parked outside a church in Lawrence, a city north of Boston. Some turned up in grassy areas along the highway; some were found in their apartments. They died in different ways. Some were shot. Some were strangled or beaten to death. In 1979, a twenty-six-year-old shoe salesman from the Boston suburb of Everett, Glenn Breese, received a life sentence for the murder of twenty-two-year-old prostitute Karen Bloomenthal. He'd stabbed her forty-three times with a serrated steak knife.

Unlike the Bloomenthal case, most of the murders went unsolved. Although the term "Combat Zone Killer" wasn't being used, Boston's homicide division wondered if a maniac was seeking victims in the Zone. Or maybe a variety of men were killing prostitutes and slipping out of town like phantoms. Detective Lieutenant Arthur Kelley felt it was unlikely for these prostitute murders to ever be solved.

"Look," he told the *Boston Globe* during the Blumenthal investigation, "say a john leaves the Zone with an intended victim. You have to find someone who saw them leave, a witness who can definitely place the victim and the suspect together—and then get the evidence to prove that this guy is the one who committed the crime. No guy visiting the Zone wants to get involved for fear of publicity. And the prostitutes have not been willing to talk because they have been scared of being singled out and slain themselves."

Four years later, it appeared Robin Benedict had joined the list of Boston's murdered prostitutes. Had she known about those other unfortunate women and their unsolved murders? A few of the bodies had actually been dumped in the Greater Lawrence area, only a few miles from her own childhood home. Had she ever imagined that she, too, would come to such a grisly end?

But how could she have known that one of her clients was capable of killing her, or that his name would be forever synonymous with nightfall, obsession, and sickening violence?

2.

William Henry James Douglas was born November 1, 1941, in Saranac Lake, New York. Known for its dry atmosphere and fresh air, Saranac Lake was where Dr. Edward Livingston Trudeau established the Adirondack Cottage Sanitarium, a top location for recovering tuberculosis patients. Trudeau's great-grandson, Garry, was a Saranac Lake boy. He went on to create the beloved *Doonesbury* comic strip. Albert Einstein spent summers in the town. So did Mark Twain.

Despite the town's bucolic and sophisticated reputation, William Douglas's early life was decidedly lower crust. His dad, Bill Sr., was a plumber, while his mother, Eleanor (née Wintz) occasionally earned money as a maid. They struggled to get by. When William was five years old, they moved thirty-six miles south to Lake Placid. William later described Lake Placid as "God's place."

By all accounts, William was a clumsy boy and socially inept. The investigators who spent time with William would later describe him as a familiar type, the hapless kid on the playground who always dropped the ball, a boy whose mother had to rescue him from bullies. Lake Placid was a jock town known for ice skaters, rowers, and hockey players; such a healthy, outdoorsy environment was difficult for the plump and uncoordinated William. Childhood neighbors and teachers remembered him as a lonely boy unable to make friends. That his mother had a thick German accent during the years just after World War II probably made it doubly hard for William. Along with hearing jokes about his size, he was probably teased about Eleanor sounding like Hitler and Goebbels.

William was encouraged to embrace the American dream of the postwar years, a time of prosperity and optimism in the country. Bill Sr. put in many hours on plumbing jobs and hoped his work ethic would inspire his son to better himself. But the American dream of the Douglas home was filtered through the neurosis of William's mother. Eleanor was a fussy woman who put a premium on politeness and decorum. She took jobs cleaning houses and hotel rooms and was often disgusted by the manner in which people lived and behaved. Eleanor stressed graciousness and modesty to her young son.

As an only child, William was probably saturated by the constant influence of Bill and Eleanor. They doted on him, spoiled him to a degree. Doctors had told Eleanor that having children would be difficult for a woman her age—she was in her forties—so William was a kind of miracle child.

As one might expect, Eleanor sheltered the boy. She also preached to William about the importance of self-control and of being a clean and decent citizen. To keep William from picking up bad habits, she isolated him from other children his age. This overprotection denied him the chance to socialize. It may also have planted a seed in his mind that he was different from other children, and that the world outside the home was somehow dangerous.

Though he was basically well mannered, William would sometimes misbehave. His biggest thrill was to sneak out of the house without permission. Eleanor would blow these minor incidents out of proportion and scold him. Though he was never beaten, the verbal reprimands were so severe that the little boy would break down into sobs and apologize for whatever he'd done; he'd promise to be good from then on. Then Eleanor or Bill would pat him on the head, call him their "Little Man." This pattern went on throughout his upbringing, with William breaking a house rule and then begging forgiveness. This drama was always followed by more isolation.

The shape of William's childhood was set. Eleanor appeared to offer a stable environment, but her isolation and pampering of William kept him immature. Eleanor became a sort of mother-manager, a concierge holding off the outside world, guarding William from scrutiny. In the interim, he stuffed himself with Eleanor's German meals and snacks and grew into a little oddball.

That was how William spent his formative years in Lake Placid. Imagine a claustrophobic home and the sense that you're not part of society. Sometimes his sleep was interrupted by nightmares, scenes of bullies prowling in the shadows, ugly hands reaching out to harm him. Children in such tight mental pressure cookers are given few ways to cope. Our future killer had two choices: He could be open and unafraid, or he could learn to do things furtively. In time, he developed an instinct for the latter.

• • •

The family relocated again when William was in seventh grade. This time they moved fifty miles north to a Plattsburgh trailer court. Though some children can flourish in a new environment, being the new boy in school was probably difficult for the shy and sheltered William. And though he was bright, his grades were only average. Despite the coddling and the assurance that he was special, Bill and Eleanor's miracle child was rather unremarkable.

By his teen years, when other kids of the 1950s were listening to rock 'n' roll records and watching monster movies at the local drive-in theaters, William had developed an interest in science, particularly biology. This was promising; he might actually live up to his father's hopes and make something of himself. Like his dad, William showed a strong work ethic, taking jobs throughout high school. He gave the appearance of a regular kid, bagging groceries at a local market, keeping his grades up. He was blending in.

Yet he remained mystified by the young girls in his class. Now and then he'd try to approach them, but too many years of isolation had left him awkward around other teens. To make things worse, his voice was high and girlish.

Mastering his science classes gave him an identity and improved his confidence, but William remained an outsider. In the meantime, there was not much he could do but be a good little man and do as his parents said.

• • •

There's no telling when William Douglas discovered pornography. He came of age during the 1950s and '60s, a boom time for smut in America with the arrival of *Playboy* and its various imitators. Ted Bundy, probably

America's most infamous serial killer, and born the same decade as William, told stories about finding porn magazines in garbage cans. It isn't likely that Eleanor's boy would be digging around in the trailer-court trash, but it is possible. Maybe, like Bundy, he saw a magazine in a bin, an image of a sultry woman with red lipstick gazing up at him from underneath the rubbish, the pouty lips calling out to William. It was easy for him to just reach in and . . .

Maybe his father had some porn. In those days, long before people could find porn online, most men had a private stash of "adult" magazines or sexy postcards hidden somewhere. Maybe the teenaged William stumbled upon his father's stash. In any case, at some point, William was introduced to pornography and it became a part of his life. Over the years, he acquired a taste for the most brutal kind of imagery.

In that era, there was a raft of magazines depicting scenes of bondage, with such titles as *Torment* and *Bondage Life*. They were marked by disturbing covers that featured women hog-tied or chained to walls, exaggerated looks of horror on their faces as they were being menaced by ominous figures. Even nonpornographic magazines such as *Detective Files* often featured a bound woman on the cover; such was the demand for images of women in distress. The scenes were obviously staged by a photographer, but were no less unsettling. Perhaps this was a reaction to the growing women's movement, with publishers tapping into the frustrations of men who couldn't handle the new breed of enlightened women. Whatever the reason, there was an audience for these vulgar scenarios. William was in that audience.

William's constant isolation as a child may have hurt his self-esteem, laying the foundation for his future transgressions. At the very least, William was learning to escape into a world of fantasy. He was creating the sort of internal dungeon that C. S. Lewis, a Christian author who often dealt with themes of sin and desire, termed a man's "prison of himself, there to keep a harem of imaginary brides." If only William had been searching for a bride. What he liked were cheap paperbacks about innocent young women being forced to take part in orgies; he was especially interested in publications about people, men or women, being tied up and humiliated. It seemed the preaching he had heard about self-control resulted in a man with serious control issues.

3.

William was accepted to New York State University, a small, government subsidized teachers college in Plattsburgh. Eleanor and Bill Douglas could say their son was a college man, though Bill didn't get to see the boy receive his diploma; in 1963 he died in a construction accident just months before William graduated.

Eleanor's mental health declined dramatically after her husband's death. Only in her sixties, she was increasingly confused and was reportedly seen mumbling and slobbering. She would sit unattended in the trailer, while William studied his schoolbooks and ignored her. In fact, William was often unpleasant to his mother during this period. She'd been leery of his scientific pursuits; she was a Christian Scientist and had no use for her son's interests. To be mean, he'd read aloud from his textbooks, knowing the scientific jargon irritated her.

There was a cruel streak in William. When his father died, William had an opportunity to be the so-called man of the house and to be helpful to his mother. But when Eleanor was ill and had only her miracle child for company, he treated her badly. Visitors to the trailer were occasionally shocked at how rude William would be to her. One guest even recalled that when Eleanor tried to speak, William told her to shut up.

• • •

The college setting was good for William. He learned to socialize. He enjoyed drinking beer with his fraternity brothers at Pi Alpha Nu, and he even attracted some young nursing students who found him interesting.

Though still immature in many ways, his intelligence gave him an air of sophistication. Crash diets and exercise regimens had helped him lose weight. Though not handsome, he evolved into an average young man with an angular face and peculiarly large ears. William's yearbook photo in the *Plattsburgh Cardinal* shows him to be a generic college graduate of 1963, a bland young man offering a half-smile. He's wearing a dark suit and tie, his hair carefully combed, looking more or less like the other fellows in his class. The caption next to the photograph is simple: *William Douglas—Plattsburgh—Secondary Science.*

This new and improved William won the heart of a nursing student from Rhode Island named Nancy Boulton. Many have described Nancy as plain, heavyset, and prim, a stoic type. Like William, she had lost her father at a young age. She saw William as a classroom marvel destined for success. As for him, he tended to be interested in any woman who paid attention to him. William and Nancy were married shortly after he graduated.

Newly married and educated, William established himself as a small-town high school science teacher in upstate New York. Frustrated with the limitations of his job, he applied for and was granted a National Science Foundation fellowship for a year of postgraduate study at Yale. This turned out to be pivotal in his life.

William flourished at Yale. He rose to the challenge academically and thrived in the atmosphere. Having succeeded at this level, he imagined himself as no mere high school teacher, but as a researcher, a full-fledged professor.

His next step was postgraduate work at Brown University in Providence. This was a lively environment, with campus protesters engaged in the issues of the day, from civil rights to the war in Vietnam. But William, already planning a family with Nancy, focused only on his studies. He had little in common with the long-haired student body, and so remained absorbed in studying. By now his mother had passed away, and just as William's father had missed his graduation from Plattsburgh, so too did Eleanor miss his graduation from Brown in 1970.

After earning his master's and doctorate in biomedical sciences, William secured a teaching position at Edinboro State College in Pennsylvania. Within a year, he landed a research job at the W. Alton Jones Cell Science Center, a private institution in Lake Placid. He became director of the center's electron microscopy facility as well as associate director of education. He made his name known in research circles, specializing in tissue culture. His particular talent was the exacting task of cutting tissue into thin sections and mounting it on slides. Those who saw him do it were amazed by his ease and dexterity. He was something special.

In the coming years, his studies involved the new procedure of isolating cells and growing them *in vitro*, outside the body, as well as extensive research into surfactant, a waxy substance that allows the lungs to inflate but is absent in premature babies.

William was also a family man with three children, Billy, Pammy, and Johnny. He presented himself as a good modern father, bringing the kids to skating lessons and becoming the local Peewee hockey coach. He cut a ludicrous figure on the ice—the weight he'd lost in college had come back—and onlookers were surprised by his high voice, but he was doing his best to be a supportive hockey dad. When Nancy decided to return to work, William made himself useful by helping with household chores. He certainly gave the impression of being a kind and caring partner, once taking a week off from the center to help Nancy after she'd miscarried.

Throughout his early years of being a father and husband, William's work output was extraordinary. He published numerous articles in scientific journals and was soon serving on various editorial boards. He was also on the review panel at the National Institute of Health to assess the work of his peers and served as a consultant for the American Cancer Society and for the Department of Medicine at Memorial Hospital in Pawtucket, Rhode Island. He also took teaching jobs at both his alma mater in Plattsburgh as well as North Country Community College in nearby Saranac Lake. He hadn't come from a background of academic strivers, but he was scratching his way to the top of his field, returning triumphantly to the towns he'd lived in as a child to take teaching jobs.

In 1978, William received an offer from the Tufts University Medical School in Boston. His work at Alton Jones had caught the attention of Dr. Karen Hitchcock, an esteemed cell biologist from Tufts. Hitchcock saw William as the sort of laboratory wizard who could elevate the medical school, especially in acquiring grants. He was offered an assistant professorship with the promise of supervising his own lab.

The opportunity came at the perfect time, for William had created problems at Alton Jones. It seemed the mild-mannered William had started a feud with the center's director and created an upheaval among the scientists. This dispute, which stemmed from William's disapproval of how the center was being run, indicated that underneath his high voice and soft figure was a hard character, one who demanded things be done his way. He would leave Alton Jones under a cover of controversy, but no matter. He was off to bigger things. Tufts University was highly regarded and growing.

The medical school was also near Boston's Combat Zone, where William would meet the woman he would eventually kill.

4.

When William Douglas arrived in Boston in 1978, the Combat Zone was at the height of its sinister glamour. Although the neighborhood's reputation had been risqué since the 1960s, city officials formally centralized the bawdy three-block area during the 1970s. This roping off was an effort to keep prostitution out of the other Boston neighborhoods, namely the financial and shopping districts. This coincided with the government relaxing its obscenity laws, which meant a flare-up of porn theaters and sexually oriented entertainment.

Located on Washington Street between Boylston and Kneeland, and extending up Stuart Street to Park Square, the Combat Zone was Boston's forbidding Oz. Rising up among the elegant movie palaces that had been built in the 1920s, the Zone was visible to people traveling through the city by bus or on foot, the billboards and arc-sodium lights beckoning. For a city mostly known for blue-collar sports fans and provincial politics, the Zone provided a shadowy alter ego. A State Street accountant on his lunch hour could walk through the neighborhood, stop somewhere for a drink, flirt with a stripper, and be back at his desk by 2 p.m. But at night, as the *Boston Globe* once reported, "the area turns into a Coney Island for the emotionally scarred . . . the place for the emotionally and sexually deformed."

Columnists from the city's newspapers made annual visits to the Zone. They reported back on the rancid atmosphere or commented on the emaciated strippers. Some of the coverage was tragicomical, like the arrest of a hooker in Chinatown who revealed her age to be seventy. Yet some of the stories were just plain tragic, like the tale of a Vermont woman who shot and killed her own daughter to prevent her from working as a Boston prostitute.

It was inevitable that the neighborhood's ugly tone would bust through the designated parameters. Families coming into Boston to do their Christmas shopping would see drug-addled prostitutes arguing with pimps right outside Filene's Basement, the most popular department store in the city. If you drove through the Zone and stopped at a red light, a prostitute might run out to your car, reach in through the window, and grab for your crotch; before the light changed your wallet was gone.

Sometimes street entrances were blocked so unwitting tourists wouldn't end up in the Zone, where they might see anything from a murdered prostitute to a mob hit. Now and then dead bodies were dumped in various Zone locations, tossed out of speeding cars. One story, possibly an urban legend, involved a woman's body found in a parking lot on Essex Street. She'd been burned and was unrecognizable, so badly charred that she couldn't be fingerprinted.

Yet the Zone also bustled with campy entertainment. Burlesque superstars Chesty Morgan and Blaze Starr performed at the old Pilgrim Theater on lower Washington Street. Exotic dancers such as Panama Red and Princess Cheyenne developed loyal local followings. Many of the Zone's retired strippers and musicians recall with affection the Mousetrap, the Pink Pussycat, the Sugar Shack, the Tam, the Two O'Clock Lounge, and a dozen other places where middle-aged men, college kids, hippies, and prostitutes wasted away the wee hours. For many years, Roger Pace and the Pacemakers, an amphetamine-fueled R&B group, provided the Zone with a jumping soundtrack. Billed as "the white James Brown," Pace was known both for his high-powered dance moves and for the time some local wise guys stuck him pompadour-first into a barroom toilet.

At times, venturing into the Zone was a bit like entering an old county fairground, though one geared toward adult entertainment and vices. You parked your car in a parking lot littered with broken glass, and when you stepped out onto the sidewalk, you were slugged with a variety of odors: gas fumes from city traffic, clouds of chemicals from nearby restaurants, marijuana smoke, frying peppers and hotdogs from street vendors who shamelessly overcharged for what they advertised as "genuine Italian sausage." You'd see the sort of bright electric signage that you only saw in movies like *Blade Runner*, and bleary-eyed prostitutes staring out from inside coffee shops, their hard faces reflecting their miseries. You heard the hollering of barroom touts, aggressive and slightly stoned, all promising nude girls and cheap drinks. You heard rock 'n' roll music from somewhere, everywhere, and a kind of long-distance, persistent rumbling, which may have been from the enormous arcade on Washington Street that housed hundreds of the loudest pinball machines you'd ever heard, probably the same ones the sailors used to play after the war, but now electrified and with more gimmicks, wired for a new generation of drunks and delinquents. It was a boisterous, scary neighborhood, but there was always the sense that, if you didn't get mugged or lose your wallet, you might win a prize or get felt up by a nasty lady.

Male students from Boston area colleges often took jobs in the Zone. They'd be seen tending bar or clerking at adult bookstores. It wasn't uncommon for the Harvard football team to celebrate a win by heading to the Zone and downing a few beers. In November of 1976, Harvard Crimson defensive back Andrew Puopolo was partying in the Zone when a prostitute picked his friend's pocket. Puopolo chased the woman into the street only to be stabbed by one of her male friends. Puopolo died as a result of the attack, inspiring a massive police crackdown on the neighborhood. That it took the death of a white man to alarm the locals, rather than the death of several women, says much about Boston in the 1970s.

The year before William Douglas's arrival, police arrested ninety-seven girls under the age of seventeen for soliciting men in the Zone. Some were as young as twelve; many had been in the city for only a short time. Tufts psychiatrist Dr. Arthur Z. Mutter, who spearheaded a movement to counsel young girls rescued from the Zone, told the Associated Press in 1977 that these girls were insecure and easily manipulated by pimps. "These kids become susceptible to these guys who say they care," Mutter said.

Among the Zone's most active spots was LaGrange Street, which was little more than a crowded alley connecting two of Boston's busier streets, Washington and Tremont. LaGrange Street was the Zone's boiling point, and the home of Good Time Charlie's, a bar known to all Bostonians as the spot to meet prostitutes. In those days, simply entering the place involved pushing through a crowd of thirty or more streetwalkers, gathered near the bar's entrance and along the sidewalk.

In 1975 alone, there were thirty complaints against Charlie's registered at the city's licensing board, mostly for liquor license violations. A new manager, Willie Moses Jr., was brought in after the owner's brother, Charles Sicuso, was found guilty in Boston Municipal Court of "knowingly allowing a café to be used for immoral solicitation." A veteran restaurant manager, Moses decided to make the place seem less like a nest for hookers; he put a jazz band upstairs, and demanded the prostitutes follow a dress code. If they came into Charlie's, they had to look clean and presentable, not obvious. Despite Moses's mild efforts to change Charlie's image, the bad reputation remained.

In 1977, the bar's license was revoked for being a center of prostitution, with vice detectives reporting that ninety percent of the female patrons at Charlie's were prostitutes. *Globe* columnist Mike Barnicle once visited several bars in the area, including Charlie's, and came to a gloomy conclusion. "Boston does not have a town dump," he wrote. "It has the Combat Zone." He added, "You risk buying more than a drink or a few minutes with a girl along here. You risk your life."

The presence of pimps, annoyed by recent police interventions, had dwindled in the Zone. Many prostitutes of the day felt pimps would soon be a thing of the past, with more-liberated prostitutes working on their own and keeping the money they'd earned. There were even editorials written that imagined prostitution would someday be legalized in Massachusetts. Yet despite the fleeting optimism in the sex trade, there was more danger than ever for a woman working in the Zone. During a seven-month period in 1978, more than thirty prostitutes reported to police that they'd been beaten or mugged.

A prostitute known as "Donna" told the *Globe* in 1976 that the neighborhood's volatile atmosphere was at least part of the attraction. "This is a weird business with a great deal of danger because of all the cuckoos that you run across," she said. "But I guess at the time those are the very things that attract most girls into prostitution—besides the money, which most of the girls never saw anyway."

If the Zone girls wanted a dangerous cuckoo with money, they were about to meet the gold standard. He was just up the street working in a lab.

5.

William Douglas and his family settled in Sharon, a pretty suburb twenty-five miles south of Boston. Sharon was part of Norfolk County, the wealthiest county in Massachusetts, and among the wealthiest in America. The county of Norfolk would come to be known as "The

County of Presidents," as it was the birthplace of four U.S. presidents: John Adams, John Quincy Adams, John F. Kennedy, and George H. W. Bush. For William Douglas, he'd finally netted the American dream he'd heard about since sharing a cramped trailer with his parents. Now he lived in a green Dutch colonial on Sandy Ridge Circle, a comfortable cul-de-sac where each split-level house appeared identical to the one next door. Some of Sharon was undeveloped; the Sandy Ridge area touched swampland that would be drained in the years to come, as well as a gravel pit.

Though they had found an ideal location to raise their three children, William and Nancy Douglas's relationship had cooled. Nancy was content to be a good suburban mother, but William would later claim Nancy refused to have sex with him. Some sources claim Nancy had undergone an operation that made any sort of physical contact unbearable, and that she blamed her husband for her discomfort. Nancy had also taken a new job at the Ellis Nursing Home in Norwood, which left William feeling neglected and unhappy. The pair tried to maintain a façade, occasionally inviting William's colleagues from Tufts over for dinner, but visitors to the house in Sharon described a boring atmosphere, where Nancy said nothing and William talked only about work.

The most likely reason for the collapse of the marriage was William's secret life. He had been at Tufts only a short time when he began exploring the porno palaces of the Combat Zone. Wandering those brightly lit streets, William let the high-risk, high-octane atmosphere overwhelm him, like a kid sniffing glue for the first time. Against Boston's most oversexed neighborhood, plain and stolid Nancy didn't stand a chance.

• • •

Douglas's troubled home life had no impact on his day job; he was doing superb work at Tufts, teaching at both the dental and veterinary schools, earning accolades from staff and students alike. He remained the most distinguished professor in the university's Department of Anatomy and Cellular Biology. Students found him to be patient, concise, and considerate. Bryan Toole, chair of the department, would later tell the press that Douglas was extremely popular. When students voted, Toole said, Douglas "was always the highest-rated teacher."

Douglas's career apex may have come on April 8, 1981, when the New England Anti-Vivisection Society (NEAVS) presented Tufts Medical School with a check for $100,000, the first of two, for Douglas and his team to develop an eye irritancy test using cells taken from human corneas.

This was a time when radical but dedicated groups were defending the rights of lab animals—one task force had recently held a protest outside of Revlon headquarters in New York, many dressed in rabbit costumes to demonstrate against animal testing. One of the leading lights of the animal rights movement, Henry Spira, had been in league with Douglas for several months as the professor formulated a plan to grow cells obtained from an eye bank. When Spira successfully lobbied NEAVS to fund Douglas's research, the NEAVS newsletter described the moment as "historical," for no animal rights group had ever joined a research institution to develop an alternative to using animals in product testing. Douglas later sat on the NEAVS editorial board and contributed articles to a new bulletin sponsored specifically to report on alternative methods in toxicology.

Douglas's peers respected him but found him eccentric. He'd gained considerable weight and was well over 300 pounds. His shoes tended to be on the raggedy side, his shirts usually marred by perspiration stains and rips under the arms. Nancy was busy at her job; she had no time to sew on buttons or make sure her husband's pants were pressed, tasks she would've once done. To some, Douglas's shabby look added to his reputation as a brilliant professor, too consumed with his work to consider such things as personal grooming. His office at Tufts was also a mess, which contradicted his compulsively detailed lab work.

Some of his colleagues would describe Douglas as shy, and others simply felt he was uninterested in anything but the lab. But some were uncomfortable around him. For instance, Douglas's coworkers learned to never question him about anything. He reacted badly to criticism and was easily riled. Most didn't dare approach him. In fact, in a show of deference, his colleagues took to calling Douglas "The Man." This was a long way from when his parents had called him "Little Man."

He also had a few unfounded fears, such as the notion that his assistants talked about him behind his back and even stole his belongings. At one point he complained that students had ransacked his office; he took to labeling everything on his desk with his initials: WHJD. At times Douglas could become angry. Ronald Sanders, a research professor who worked alongside Douglas for years, had witnessed genuine temper tantrums. "If he got upset, he'd slam doors, throw pencils, and swear," Sanders said.

Colleagues also noticed Douglas's behavior around women. He was prudish. Sanders even described him as "asexual."

"There were plenty of women in our lab," Sanders told the *Miami Herald*. "But as far as I know, Douglas never made any advances or innuendoes, or even personal remarks, to any of them." Even when the conversation turned to the nearby Combat Zone, Douglas refrained from joining in. "There are four bachelors in the lab who were always discussing it," Sanders said, "but when the subject came up, he never participated in any of the comments."

Douglas probably ignored the chatter because he wanted to be perceived as a family man. To share what he knew about the local scene would hurt his image. But at the end of a school day, Douglas would put on his old coat and head out into the night, a gawky, unkempt man leaning into a twilight world where people did lowdown things for money.

• • •

Douglas had probably heard about the Combat Zone dating back to his days at Brown University in nearby Providence. The neighborhood was already known on a national level as a rough, dangerous place, having earned its name in the 1950s when brawls between local biker gangs and sailors frequently spilled out of the bars along lower Washington Street.

The Zone was edging past its prime by the time Douglas started trolling the neighborhood. The clubs and topless dancers were in decline, and the advent of videocassette recorders meant customers no longer had to sneak into dilapidated theaters to see X-rated action. Yet there were still cheap thrills to be found. Drug dealers roamed the sidewalks, and the sex trade was still strong.

To Douglas's delight, the medical school abutted this world of sleaze. How did an ungainly professor navigate one of the shaggiest neighborhoods in the country? He might've been an inviting target for rowdy teens awaiting a bus to Roxbury or Dorchester, and he may have felt the burn of a cigarette butt flicked at him for laughs. For Douglas, certain aspects of the Zone must've been bothersome, even scary.

What helped Douglas move freely in and out of the Zone was the area's dichotomy. Despite the neighborhood's reputation, it wasn't merely a community of creeps and drifters. It was common to see elderly women and conservative businessmen cutting through on their way to a bus or subway station or strolling the neighborhood to buy a slice of pizza somewhere. The Zone maintained a few nice eateries and was adjacent to Chinatown; if Douglas's colleagues happened to see him on Washington or Kneeland Street, he could say he was merely sampling a local restaurant and was on his way back to the lab.

The Zone had a way of getting into a person's blood. Though there were dangers, many of the regulars were linked by a common good-humored attitude. Some of the strippers were friendly to customers, and even some of the area prostitutes were known by their first names. The bookstore clerks got to know the customers and might even let you know when a new magazine had arrived that might appeal to your particular interest.

Still, Douglas's fascination with prostitutes would perplex many. His acquaintances remembered him as a killjoy. In his younger days he had avoided rowdy barrooms, discouraged vulgar talk, and hated to spend money. Was the pious cheapskate routine only an act? Or did Douglas's hunger for the X-rated life supersede all else?

Others have wondered if Douglas's obsessive behavior would've blossomed if not for the proximity of Tufts to the Combat Zone. Without such easy contact with prostitutes, would he have maintained his regular suburban life in Sharon?

Douglas never revealed how he first entered the Zone or how he first met Robin Benedict, but chances are he came to the neighborhood because of his interest in pornography. Douglas's taste had become more aberrant, now including material about gang rape and outright sadism. In those pre-internet days, a man like Douglas satisfied his porn interest by seeking out adult bookstores. Granted, one could find "dirty books" in a supermarket bookrack or any big city bus station, usually wrapped in plain brown paper, but Douglas knew he could explore the Zone and not be seen by his Sharon neighbors. Plus, the Zone had mystique, its storefronts practically vibrating with deviancy.

As the market for "erotica" grew in the 1980s, the Zone bookstores did a booming business, whether hole-in-the-wall shops or massive places such as the Liberty Book Shop on Washington Street. The Liberty was a Disneyland for perverts. The layout was like a maze, and one could get lost wandering the long, overstocked aisles. Clerks were stationed everywhere like sentries to prevent shoplifting, behind counters and along the walls. Crammed onto the racks were apparently every pornographic movie and magazine ever produced, catering to every sort of fetish. There were sex toys and furry handcuffs and life-size inflatable love dolls; there were a variety of dildos, endless dildos, lined up on shelves like the stone statues on Easter Island. The mixture of heavy clear plastic that wrapped the magazines, the leather masks and bondage gear, and daily douses of super-strength cleaning products created an unmistakable scent. One whiff and you knew you were in the catacombs of adult entertainment. Visually and aromatically, it was dizzying; to stay there too long was to risk nausea. These shops were likely Douglas's entry to the Zone. From the bookstores it was a quick hop to the bars.

Ultimately, Douglas's love for the neighborhood was no deep riddle. He had developed an overwhelming addiction to all things carnal or pornographic. To be enslaved by such sexual hysteria was like having a wolf in his brain. In the Combat Zone it could be fed.

6.

When not burning away the nights at Good Time Charlie's, Douglas returned to the solitude of his room in Sharon, away from Nancy and the kids. He purportedly loved to load up on junk food, still with the appetite of a spoiled child. (He was also a glutton for pizza; colleagues recalled him dusting off an entire pie in the privacy of his messy office.) Perhaps he slurped up his snack while reading his books. His collection now included such titles as *Illustrated Gang War Torture*, *Little Sarah's Slave Training*, and *Wanda and the Whip*. Douglas hoarded them like a kid collecting comic books.

Another of his hobbies involved scanning newspapers for articles about the local sex trade. The gold mine for Douglas was in Boston's two weekly publications, the *Boston Phoenix* and the *Real Paper*, alternative newspapers available from any college bookstore or newsstand. The back pages were a boon for horny men, relying heavily on ad revenue from sex workers and private escort services. There were also dodgy personal ads placed by married men looking for mistresses or couples looking to swap partners. When an item intrigued Douglas, he'd clip it with scissors and save it in a folder. Most of the stories he collected were about Boston prostitutes.

The Combat Zone was under fire in those days. There was talk during 1981 that nude dancing would be banned in venues where alcohol was sold, while Governor Edward J. King signed a bill outlawing the sale of drug paraphernalia. There were rumors that Wang Laboratories Inc., representatives from Chinatown, and even Tufts were planning to buy property along Washington Street and chase out the old porn shops and "Live Nude" emporiums. Meanwhile, five people were convicted that year of trafficking obscene material into the Zone, including magazines depicting bestiality and sadism.

There was also an increased effort to deny operating licenses to various porn-shop owners to make way for new building projects, which resulted in several lawsuits filed against the Boston police commissioner and Mayor Kevin White.

And as usual, there were killings. In July of 1981, prostitutes Lucille Reid and Lisa Odell went on trial for the stabbing death of a Canton man. Reid was already serving a life sentence in Walpole for killing a neighbor in Cambridge. One year later, two Zone regulars, Kevin Roach and Arthur "Butchie" Brown, received life sentences for stabbing a Cambridge man to death during an early morning robbery. Their victim had been Carl Lobig, a part-time announcer at classical music station WCRB.

Douglas didn't let the Zone's reputation deter him from visiting. He continued drifting through the neighborhood like a slow blizzard, always returning for more.

• • •

Douglas's behavior grew stranger by the middle of 1982.

He started arriving late to work by as much as an hour or more. He offered fanciful excuses, anything from crashing his car to being mugged. His stories sounded like lies, but no one questioned him.

He had a couch delivered to his office, saying he planned to start taking midday naps, but it was eventually learned that he was spending nights on it. He often greeted colleagues looking sleepy and disheveled, explaining that he occasionally "had to" stay all night in his office. Sometimes he showed up for a class looking pale and sick, perspiring heavily. He missed meetings and would sometimes disappear in the middle of the day.

Increasingly, he engaged colleagues in petty arguments. Once, when some grad students were playing their radio loudly, Douglas hurled a book at the wall and shouted, his shrill voice echoing across the lab.

Douglas's associates felt he was overworked. Some suspected that he and Nancy were having troubles at home. He still called Nancy several times a day, but a man who slept in his office couldn't be having a happy home life. His weight was dropping, too, and some were certain he'd started coloring his gray hair.

Most puzzling about Douglas at this time was his preoccupation with a mysterious grad student named Robin Benedict. No one could recall ever meeting the woman, but he'd put her on the medical school's payroll for $1,000 a month as an "assistant." He described her as an illustrator who drew sketches for his projects. Douglas explained that the young woman once worked for a colleague at MIT, but this unnamed colleague could no longer afford to pay her. Douglas insisted that he needed her help. In an unusual gesture for a mere grad student, he even pushed to get her overtime pay.

Douglas's associates at the lab joked that he was having an affair with this obscure grad student, though most still thought of him as rather sexless. What created the most curiosity was when Douglas presented a list of people allowed to call him at his office, no matter how busy he might be. His staff expected to see the names of his family members or a few department heads. To their surprise, Robin Benedict's name was near the top. Douglas demanded that she get through to him any time she called.

It was unusual for a mere grad student to appear on such a list. But who would question "The Man"?

7.

March of 1982 was a bleak and rainy month in Boston. It was the type of late winter where the last remnants of dirty slush seemed to never melt off. Good Time Charlie's was, if nothing else, a place to come in from the cold. Maybe the patrons talked among themselves about the recession or the mayor's recent announcement that Boston was about to get the most advanced cable TV system in the nation. Or maybe they just stared vacantly into their drinks.

Compared to the honking car horns and flashing neon outside, the atmosphere inside Charlie's could be downbeat. Forlorn male customers, as many as a hundred or so, sat on high wooden stools around a circular bar; they showed only vague interest in the nearly nude dancers, slowly gyrating to the loud music coming from two enormous speakers mounted on a wall. Dancers were continually climbing down from the "runway," needing to insert more coins into the jukebox between sets.

The idlers at the bar—blue- and white-collar types, local businessmen, their neckties loosened after a day at the office, sailors and scruffy immigrants from nearby rooming houses—sat like dazed victims of some secret poison, while the prostitutes lingered along the walls. If the women saw a guy who seemed to have a few extra dollars on him, they would approach him and ask, "Want to party?" Though the place was often described as bleak, at least one reporter from the *Globe* once noted the venue's strong lighting: "The lights are bright so you can see what you're buying. These ladies don't want you to buy them a drink. They want you to buy them."

No one remembered exactly when Douglas started showing up, but he'd become a fixture at the place. He'd arrive in the afternoon and stay all night. He'd tried other bars on the block, but Charlie's was his favorite. He could sit silently, unobserved, a lone frog in a fetid swamp. Best of all, Charlie's was only a minute's walk from the medical school.

During one of those drab March nights, as disco music blared from the jukebox, a charming young woman began flirting with Douglas. Her name was Robin Benedict. She went by her middle name, Nadine.

There was probably nothing unusual about their first meeting. The surprise was that Robin spoke to Douglas at all; she was known to dislike overweight men because they perspired too much. When she finally sidled up to Douglas, it was the kind of scene that played out at Charlie's every night: another pretty young prostitute talking to a lonely forty-year-old man.

Still, it is tempting to imagine the first time Douglas saw her. Charlie's was known for having red and pink track lighting over the stage where the dancers performed, providing the entire room with a flush of warmth. When she first appeared in front of Douglas, it may have seemed she was emerging from the ether, bathed in a rosy glow, a fantasy come to stunning life.

8.

She was only twenty, and though myth would have her as among the highest-paid prostitutes in the Combat Zone, the truth is that Robin Benedict met William Douglas when she was relatively new in the neighborhood. Reporters would make a point of her charging fifty dollars for half an hour of her time, as if that indicated her lofty street status, but fifty bucks for the length of a sitcom was the going rate in those days. They'd write of her little address book, filled with the names of over 250 clients willing to pay for her services. Yet that client list was still months in the future. How many names were in it when she met Douglas? A few, perhaps. She really was just getting started.

Still, Robin had enough experience to recognize a sucker when she saw one. Douglas was nervous and smiled like an idiot. Yet he was gracious. Despite his immense size, he seemed gentle as a cow. She probably found him preferable to the typical customer at Charlie's. Some hideous characters came into the place, the loneliest and lowest of the city, men who could only find a woman's touch right there on LaGrange Street. Then there were the rough, arrogant types who might belittle a woman, even after she'd given him what he'd wanted. Douglas appeared meek. And he had money.

What took place during their first meeting was probably similar to what transpired between Robin Benedict and all of her customers. She introduced herself as Nadine, and gave a well-rehearsed spiel about herself, how she was only working at Charlie's for the time being, that she had plans to go on to college someday and study graphic arts. There was actually a morsel of truth here; she had an artistic background, having briefly attended the Rhode Island School of Design. She'd taken courses in airbrushing and artist's anatomy. She was somewhat unusual for Good Time Charlie's.

"What was really neat about her was she was so fresh-looking, the clean-cut type," one of the other prostitutes would later say.

Douglas, we can guess, listened raptly to this fascinating young woman, getting lost in her deep brown eyes, wanting to touch her raven-colored hair. He may have tried to hold his own in the conversation. Or maybe he was tongue-tied in the presence of such a beauty. Sure, he'd known other prostitutes, but in comparison to Robin Benedict, the others were all rough and burned out; she could've been running for senior class president.

Could Douglas take in everything that was happening? Did it all go by in a blur?

Was he already obsessed?

• • •

Legend has it that Robin refused to perform oral sex on her customers. When a client asked for this particular service, she would pass him along to one of the other prostitutes at Good Time Charlie's.

It was said that Robin ended her first few conversations with Douglas by introducing him to other women. Not only was she unwilling to give him oral sex, but she was put off by his weight. By April, however, she agreed to bring him to Beacon Street for the full Robin Benedict treatment, whatever that may have been. It was as if Douglas had passed some sort of initiation, proving himself a compliant trick who behaved and paid without questions. Once he had proven himself worthy, she took him on as a regular client. She began meeting him once or twice a week. His name went into her little book. She would call him at his office and say, "What's up, Doc?"

The other women at Charlie's recognized Douglas. "I remember seeing him in here a few times," said one of the prostitutes to the *Miami Herald*. "He was pretty hard to miss because he was so big, but he stopped coming in after he met her."

There was a rumor that Douglas had once been a regular at another nightspot, the Two O'Clock Lounge at 642 Washington Street. That place had since been closed down and reborn as an all-night juice bar, but it had been one of the seediest spots in the city; lights were kept so low that one needed a flashlight to get around. Unlike Charlie's, the Two O'Clock Lounge was where women allegedly serviced men right there in the darkness. Douglas had been so enamored of one particular woman that he became something of a pest. She eventually left the city for Vermont to take a job as a dog groomer. Since then, Douglas had tried unsuccessfully to glom onto other girls.

It was not unusual for prostitutes or exotic dancers to be hounded by one or two loyal admirers. Sometimes, if the guy was persistent and seemed harmless, the woman would have him running errands. As one regular remembered those days in the Zone, "A stripper wouldn't think twice about sending some guy down to Providence for a slice of her favorite cheesecake."

These sorts of men could become bothersome, but Douglas was extraordinarily polite and had money to burn. Robin was soon suggesting they spend more than the usually allotted half hour together.

• • •

Robin's base of operation was a Beacon Street studio apartment within a few minutes of the Zone. The apartment, or "trick pad," was sparsely furnished, just a bed and some robes in the closet. The place was meant for quick and dirty business.

One night at the trick pad, Douglas asked some personal questions. Was this apartment where she lived? It didn't seem classy enough for a girl like her.

She told him that her real home was in Natick. Douglas said he would like to see her home someday.

"Maybe," she said.

She didn't tell Douglas that she shared her Natick home with a man named Clarence Rogers. He was her boyfriend and, for all intents and purposes, her pimp.

At some point Robin was comfortable enough with Douglas to joke around with him. During one of their evenings together she asked, "Does your wife mind you going out every night?"

Douglas assured Robin that his marriage was dead. He said Nancy was "an android," and that they hadn't touched each other in years.

Their talks grew more engaging. This beautiful twenty-year-old enchanted Douglas. Old enough to be her father, he felt like a boy in high school. In time he didn't even go into Good Time Charlie's to meet her. He'd simply park his car nearby and wait for her. They'd drive off together, away from the clamor of LaGrange Street.

Robin soon stopped appearing in the Combat Zone altogether. Douglas was paying her so well that she didn't need to work those long shifts at Charlie's, which sometimes lasted from four in the afternoon until four in the morning. Now, thanks to Douglas, she was able to take weekends off. Perhaps out of a sense of obligation, she even started performing oral sex on Douglas, though she insisted he wear a condom.

According to the Combat Zone gossip that would come out in the months ahead, the real treat for Douglas was for Robin to climb on top and straddle him so he could gaze up at her face. For a man who read sadomasochistic porn, this was mild. It appeared he was creating a new category for Robin in his mind. She wasn't a wife, she wasn't a dominatrix from a magazine, and she wasn't some "dirty hooker" from the street. She was a kind of holy vision hovering over him, blessing him with her beauty, and peering into his soul with her warm brown eyes. The lonely overweight boy from the trailer court, the overworked teacher and husband, was utterly beguiled.

The other women at Charlie's knew what was happening. They suspected Douglas was in love with Robin, and she was playing along. They all thought this was a mistake on her part. Of course, they understood that it was easier to have one steady client than to spend every night of the week servicing a variety of men. Still, it was a risk to let a customer think he meant anything to you. All prostitutes knew this.

The arrangement quickly escalated. Douglas went from meeting Robin once or twice per week to having nightly encounters lasting as long as two hours. He was spending as much as $200 per night on Robin, sometimes more.

There were also nights where Robin would say that she was tired and didn't want to go back to Charlie's to pull more customers. Douglas would quickly give her another $200 to $300, just so she could make her nightly quota and knock off early. Her true feelings about the man would never be known, but there had to be nights where she looked at Douglas and thought she'd won the lottery.

9.

Robin Benedict was from Methuen, a mill town thirty miles northwest of Boston, along the northern banks of the Merrimack River. Methuen had been home to a short list of lesser-known athletes and politicians and was known as the birthplace of the famous American poet Robert Frost. Looking at a map of Methuen, it is shaped like a bow tie, or perhaps a butterfly.

She grew up in a world of shopping malls and high school sports, a place that presented itself as a town, though its population was nearly 35,000 and growing. In the summer, one might enjoy a concert in the Methuen Memorial Hall, usually an organist playing classical pieces. During the winter months, Leone's Furniture usually offered discounts on suede couches. The autumn months were beautiful, worthy of any tourist wanting to celebrate the colorful New England foliage.

Robin's father, John, was from Trinidad, with ancestors hailing from Spain and Venezuela. This accounted for what journalists would later describe as Robin's vaguely Hispanic features. John's original surname was Lopez, but after a stint in the navy he changed it to Benedict. While stationed in Virginia, he met and married Ellen Shirley Menzies, a New Englander, which is what led them to a small, five-room house on Lowell Street in Methuen.

The town had some rundown areas, and the polluted river and nearby factories created an unhealthy atmosphere of fog and foul air, but Methuen fit John's vision of wholesome Americana. He tried to be a typical American father, upbeat and patriotic. He worked at Raytheon, hosted backyard barbecues, and filled scrapbooks with pictures of the family.

Like any father, John wanted the best sort of life for Robin and her four siblings. He encouraged the brood to work hard at school; he also enrolled them in a local marching ensemble called the White Eagles Drum and Bugle Corps. This became such an important part of the family's life that John became the group's codirector.

The White Eagles took part in competitions throughout the state. Robin joined at age eleven. She knew how to strut in front of a crowd, and even as a teen knew how to cut a commanding figure as a member of the color guard. The White Eagles won their share of accolades, but their high point may have come in July of 1976 when they marched in the Chelmsford bicentennial parade. Nearly 70,000 people turned out that afternoon to see marching bands from all over the region. John's kids were standing tall and looking proud. Robin, marching along in her tasseled boots, shined like new money.

Robin was her dad's special girl from the start. Indeed, a massive sign unfurled from the Benedict's roof heralding her birth on July 19, 1961, announcing: IT'S A GIRL!

Robin wasn't especially attractive as a child, but even in her most awkward phases she could steal hearts with her smile. As happens with some girls, she blossomed during her teen years. She became an eye-catching, olive-skinned beauty, the sort of girl that everyone noticed, including the teachers.

Her interests were on the creative side; she took flute lessons and displayed a talent for drawing. She signed her sketches with her first name followed by a little drawing of a bee, to signify Robin B. Of course, there were thousands of talented girls just like her across the country, but John and Shirley were proud of their lovely and uncomplicated daughter.

"Robin was the glue of the family," said her brother Robert in 2016. "She always had a smile on her face and was very energetic." With her good looks and good grades, Robin was the household's little star.

When her father began moonlighting as a wedding photographer, Robin would accompany him and help set up his equipment. She also enjoyed posing for John, with a precocious understanding of how to stand and tilt her head just right. Though not tall enough to be a model, she had an instinct for posing. She also had a more mature fashion sense than that of her schoolmates; she carried herself in a way that made her seem older than her years.

Kelley Bartlett was a Methuen classmate of Robin and also a member of the White Eagles. She still remembers Robin for her kindhearted nature.

"I had a younger sister," Bartlett recalled, "and Robin was always very nice to her, almost like a role model. Many, many years after all of the sad news about Robin, my sister would still break out into tears thinking about her, just missing her so much."

Robin's kindness was accompanied by a magnetic quality. A simple nod from her could make your day.

"She had that long black hair and dark eyes; very pretty," Bartlett said. "Speaking generally from a woman's viewpoint, she was probably the envy of the other girls.

"I don't remember her having a big circle of friends," Bartlett continued. "She was a bit of a loner, though she had her family, of course. I found all of her siblings to be nice, normal. Can't say a bad thing about them or her."

The Benedicts often invited members of the White Eagles to their house on Lowell Street. In those days, Robin was content with ordinary fun.

"I remember being in her bedroom," Bartlett said. "She played the flute. Then we sat on her bed and chatted. She was just a sweet, quiet girl."

• • •

John enrolled Robin in the Greater Lawrence Regional Vocational and Technical High School where she pursued her interest in commercial art. She had perfect attendance, received top grades, took part in candy sales, won the Presidential Certificate of Merit, played her flute in school talent shows, and was voted "Best Dressed" for the class of 1979.

She also was a member of the yearbook committee, coyly inserting photos of herself throughout the book, turning it into a personal showcase. This was one of the rare instances where Robin's bold personality showed itself; she was a girl who wanted to be front and center. This could be seen as comical, of course, just a case where a brash girl took advantage of the situation, but it could also suggest a burgeoning ego. How many photos were rejected so Robin could include another picture of herself? Her official yearbook photo was accompanied by a rather ironic quote: "Robin Benedict leaves behind her flashy wardrobe and goes stark naked into the world."

Though she appeared to be straightlaced, Robin developed a wild, fun-loving streak. She allegedly ran with a rowdy crowd, and her taste in boys veered toward unruly and unsophisticated types. She wasn't interested in white boys. She claimed they didn't know how to treat girls. Her boyfriends tended to be black and much older.

It has been said that John objected to Robin dating black boys, but he later denied this. The fact was that he simply didn't like the boys she brought home. As far as John could tell, Robin's boyfriends tended to be lazy, arrogant, without prospects. They weren't good enough for his favorite girl. Eventually, John and Shirley expressed their feelings, but their sweet daughter had a stubborn side and wouldn't listen.

It was clear that a smart and energetic girl such as Robin found Methuen boring. There was little for teenagers to do, and the nearby cities such as Lawrence and Lowell offered little more than crime and squalor. She and her friends began running up to Salisbury Beach on the weekends, or to nearby Manchester, New Hampshire.

"It didn't matter what crowd you were in," Kelley Bartlett recalled. "Fast crowd or regular crowd, Methuen kids went to New Hampshire as soon as somebody had a car. We couldn't go to Lawrence, because there was nothing there. At one time it was a beautiful city, but it had been destroyed."

Though the Benedict kids were generally well-behaved, Robin's older brother Ron had a reputation as a rowdy teenager who liked fast cars and motorcycles. Sean Sullivan, who grew up in Methuen at the time of Robin and her siblings, remembers Ron having some uncouth friends. "He was an outlaw type," Sullivan recalled. "Crazy. You could describe a lot of Methuen kids that way; we had all kinds. But I do remember Ron and his friends being Methuen outlaws."

Perhaps sharing her brother's rebellious streak, Robin craved more action than could be provided by dreary Methuen. One way that Robin escaped her boredom was by going to dance clubs with her new friends. A vision under the flashing strobe lights, she won her share of dance contests, sometimes winning cash prizes.

At seventeen, however, Robin became pregnant and had an abortion. It must've stunned John and Shirley to see their golden girl in such a condition, but by now they knew there was more to Robin than marching bands and flute lessons. John would later tell *Penthouse*, "I'd like to read a book about Robin someday. Maybe I'll know then what kind of daughter we raised."

Robin's love for her parents and siblings was strong, but she wanted out of Methuen. She yearned for a glitzier lifestyle.

She kept her fantasy about doing commercial art for a living. Even when she first got into prostitution, she still told the other girls about her plans to be a commercial artist.

10.

How she became involved with a New England Patriots linebacker, and where it led her, was one of the sad ironies of Robin Benedict's short life.

One evening Robin and her then boyfriend attended an event at the vocational school that saw the faculty playing against members of the Patriots. It was a charity fundraiser—this was long before the Patriots became the Super Bowl–winning dynasty team of the 2000s, so the players were willing to take part in such unglamorous events—and she made the acquaintance of Ray Costict, a Pats player, at a postgame dinner. Later, they all went to a nearby club for some dancing. Costict wasn't a superstar, but in comparison to the other young men Robin knew, he seemed worldly. They hit it off.

Costict was still involved with a woman back in Mississippi, who was the mother of his child, and Robin was involved with someone, but there was an attraction between them. He revealed that he was often lonely in New England, missing his Mississippi home. Through Robin, he was soon a frequent guest at John Benedict's weekend barbecues. He became enmeshed with Robin and her friends.

When Robin happened to walk in on her boyfriend having sex with another woman, she drove to Costict's apartment and practically cried on his shoulder. Their affair didn't happen right away, but in time Costict and Robin were living together in Quincy.

Costict took Robin to great parties and expensive restaurants. It was just the sort of cut-rate splendor a kid from Methuen would view as the big time. Thinking she had found the gateway to a better life, Robin worked hard to be a good girlfriend, even running errands for Costict when he was laid up with an injured knee. John Benedict thought Costict was low class, however, which resulted in more fights between Robin and her dad. To Robin, it was just her dad once again objecting to her having a black boyfriend.

Yet John had been correct to question Costict's character. Costict was a former drug user, he had fathered a son who he rarely saw, and he mingled in some dirty circles. At one of the many parties Costict attended with Robin, a short black man known as J. R. approached him and asked about his pretty girlfriend. J. R. was known as a small-time pimp, a lowlife who mysteriously appeared at parties or nightclubs where local athletes or businessmen were hanging out. He'd ingratiate himself to the most powerful people in the room and ask if anyone was looking for "female entertainment."

What J. R. said about Robin has been the subject of some debate. To one interviewer, Costict claimed J. R. said, "That's the kind of child you put out on the street." Yet when Costict spoke on another occasion about J. R., he claimed he had said Robin was "the kind of girl you marry."

Either way, J. R. stared at Robin all night.

• • •

To prove her devotion to Costict, Robin abandoned her Catholic upbringing and promised to join his church. He'd been a semi-devout member of the Jehovah's Witnesses and sometimes felt guilty about not being more serious about the church's teachings. For Robin, becoming a Witness was just part of her mission to make herself indispensable to Costict. She was so committed that she even began going door-to-door to hand out pamphlets with other Jehovah's Witnesses.

Yet their relationship remained rocky. While living with Robin, Costict was taking trips to Mississippi to visit his former girlfriend and his young son. At one point, Robin suggested Costict bring his child up to Massachusetts where she'd help take care of him. Then she said she wanted to have a baby with Costict, which surprised him. His own son was nearly four, and Costict barely knew him. To have another child with Robin was out of the question.

When Costict's Mississippi girlfriend came up north to visit him, he asked Robin to stay away for the weekend. But when he took the unsuspecting woman to a Patriots game, he saw that Robin had finagled tickets in the same location for her and her brother Rick. Robin caused no trouble, but her presence made Costict uncomfortable.

Costict felt Robin was becoming pushy and territorial. One day she even screamed at him to make a commitment. That December, Costict informed Robin that he'd be spending the off-season in Mississippi to be closer to his son. The news leveled her. Robin tried to make Costict stay, but he showed more willpower than she'd counted on. The charms that had always worked for her in the past were suddenly useless.

She maintained an upbeat appearance, though, and continued taking her religious instruction. She was also working a steady job as a graphic designer at a company in Wilmington called Screenprint. She even organized a major anniversary party for her parents, and during the holidays she appeared to be her usual, cheerful self. But when Costict eventually informed her that he was leaving permanently for Mississippi to marry his ex-girlfriend, Robin was stung.

Showing a venomous side, Robin contacted the church elders and informed them that she and Costict had snorted cocaine together and had been fornicating. Costict smoothed things over with his church, but he was alarmed by Robin's attempt to ruin his reputation.

There was one moment when Costict almost capitulated, but it took a tragedy. Merely a week after he'd gotten married, his mother-in-law's house caught on fire; his little boy died of smoke inhalation. Devastated after losing his son, he also learned the Patriots were trading him to another team. Down and out, he returned to Massachusetts to see Robin. They spent the night crying together, but when the sun came up he said he was going back to Mississippi. Robin had to accept the fact that Costict was out of her life.

She discontinued her religious studies. She stayed on at Screenprint but appeared depressed, her old energy gone.

By late 1981, Robin was seen in the company of another man. He was short, wore jewelry, and drove a new Mercedes.

It was J. R.

11.

Clarence Rogers told people he was a hairdresser. Indeed, he could cut and style hair. He could cook, too.

Known as J. R., or Junior, or, as Robin called him, "Junie," he was somewhere in his early thirties, the sort of character who had tried to toughen himself up by taking karate lessons but was still easily intimidated by cops. He had a few minor criminal charges: receiving stolen credit cards, unarmed robbery. Punk stuff. The Boston vice squad knew him as a pimp.

His girlfriend was an undocumented migrant from Trinidad named Savitry Bisram, or Savi. She was a prostitute. They had a child together, a little boy named Taj. They lived in a small apartment on Howe Street in Natick. Savi was tall and striking in appearance; she was known in the Combat Zone as "Indian Debbie." She didn't like the name. Savi was an emotional sort. She liked getting high and having fun but was also known to lose her temper and raise her voice. She'd been a prostitute for seven years or so. It was believed that J. R. used Savi's fear of being deported as a way to keep her hustling on the street.

J. R. had roots in Mattapan, a poor black neighborhood south of Roxbury. He and a pimp named Walter "Chink" Martin owned a grubby piece of property that appeared to be an abandoned barbershop, which may have led to J. R. referring to himself as a hairdresser. When other pimps came into the area, J. R. and Martin would host them in Mattapan, their shop serving as a kind of headquarters for visiting "players."

Yet even with his reputation and a couple of girls working for him, J. R. was hardly the standard American pimp. Though he flashed a diamond ring and owned a mink coat, he was more likely to be seen in casual clothes. He rarely appeared in the Combat Zone but was occasionally seen tooling around his Natick neighborhood on roller skates, a trendy hobby at the time.

Employees at Screenprint noticed J. R. in the parking lot almost every afternoon waiting for Robin. She didn't keep him a secret but never revealed what he did for work. When a coworker asked about him, Robin said only that J. R. "moved money." When pressed for more information, Robin refused to say another word.

Robin soon quit her job, making up a story about moving to California. Actually, she was moving to Natick to live with J. R., Savi, and Taj. And then Savi and Taj moved out.

As Robin spent more time with J. R., the Benedict family noticed subtle changes in her. One particular visit to her old Methuen home stood out to her brother Rob. He said during a television interview, "She came in wearing this beautiful dress and this fur coat. Her hair was done up and she had on extra makeup. I thought it was so unlike her. She had a natural beauty; she didn't have to put on extra makeup to look pretty.

"Something was wrong."

• • •

How did a small-time, roller-skating pimp turn a nice Methuen girl into a prostitute?

Had Robin been so upset after the breakup with Costict that she was susceptible to J. R.? Had she simply decided that she wanted fast money?

Robin had none of the usual traits of a girl who turns to prostitution. She wasn't from poverty, she didn't have a drug addiction, and she wasn't running away from a bad home environment. Nor was she helpless; she was smart and capable. Could it be that even a girl from a good home can feel so emotionally deprived and vulnerable that she'd fall for a pimp's line of patter? Though she'd always enjoyed sex, Robin had never been promiscuous. Costict would later say that she was not the "sleep around" type.

What she did have was a tendency to do whatever it took to gain a man's approval. For Costict, she took up his religion. For J. R., she took a much bolder step, becoming a prostitute. Her artistic talent and bright personality had impressed Edward Ratyna, the art director at Screenprint, but he suspected Robin was easily persuaded by whatever man she was involved with at the time.

"Six months strong she was reading the Bible every noontime," Ratyna told the *Philadelphia Inquirer*. But once Costict left her, "that kind of threw her nose out of joint. All of a sudden, she dropped the religious angle . . . and she was going out again." But like others who knew her, Ratyna was stumped by Robin's new career choice. "Maybe she got involved and she couldn't get out," he said.

J. R.'s method was already well tested. He liked to start a girl out in a health club giving massages. His other girls started in Peabody at the Parisienne Sauna on Route 1, near such seedy local establishments as the Golden Banana and the Green Apple. *Playboy* magazine had once dubbed the Parisienne as "probably the largest and best adult entertainment center in New England." The place was also under scrutiny by the Peabody Board of Health for suspect licensing practices. It was a target of undercover vice cops who might arrest as many as a half-dozen women at a time for soliciting money for sex.

As the Parisienne was under siege, J. R. brought his prostitutes out of Peabody to a more upscale venue in the tonier suburb of Newton. It was there that Robin started her career for J. R., giving massages and more at the Newton Health Club. Through some fast-talking and a bit of charm, Robin actually acquired a masseuse's license from the Newton Health Department, a ploy by J. R. in case she was ever caught during a police raid.

After Robin's brief apprenticeship in Newton, J. R. thought she was ready for the Combat Zone. Savi mentored Robin in the ways of the street. Savi could be trippy and erratic because of her drug use, but she was personable; she and Robin became friends.

Just a year or so earlier, J. R. was pimping another girl, Cynthia Plowden. For three years she had been known as the "Queen of the Combat Zone" and reportedly earned more than a million dollars during her time at the top. J. R. had no need for a full stable of prostitutes, because Cynthia was such a moneymaker. Unfortunately for J. R., Cynthia grew tired of the life and moved on, leaving him without a big earner. Savi was loyal, but J. R. needed another one like Cynthia, a fresh-faced girl who could cater to the businessmen who frequented the Zone.

Later, when investigators were learning about J. R., Cynthia explained that he seemed "classy" and could mesmerize a girl with sweet talk. He would even bring his prostitutes to meet his mother in Mattapan, making the girls feel like they were part of his family.

He'd also take a girl to the most expensive clubs on Lansdowne Street behind Fenway Park, places that were cut-rate imitations of New York's Studio 54 but were impressive to a lonely, gullible girl; he'd convince her she was on the verge of having a fun and extravagant lifestyle. Then came the massage parlors, where he'd persuade a girl to get more intimate with customers. When the girl was deep into the business, tired and disgusted and wanting to quit, he'd give her a pep talk, convincing her to get back out there and earn the money. "Do it for us, baby. . . ." He didn't control the women through intimidation. He used finesse and sweet talk.

Cynthia had met Robin toward the end of her own time with J. R. Cynthia had been talking about quitting the business, wanting to return home to tend to her sick mother, and she knew J. R. was bringing around a new candidate, possibly to intimidate her into staying. *You are easily replaced*, he seemed to be saying, *one bitch is as good as another*. . . .

It is very likely that the first time J. R. clapped eyes on Robin, he knew he had found Cynthia's replacement, a new Queen of the Combat Zone.

And as Cynthia later told police, J. R. had a way of making an insecure young woman feel like a star.

Was that all it took? One person who struggled to understand how Robin became a prostitute was her brother Robert.

"I always figured that (prostitution) was for someone who didn't have much of a personality, no brains," Robert told the *Philadelphia Inquirer*. "She definitely had personality and brains." Years later he would say in a television interview, "She didn't go into prostitution on her own. She was coerced."

• • •

Word about Robin's new career path eventually reached Costict in Mississippi. His ex-roommate and teammate, Ray Clayborn, had seen Robin in the Combat Zone near Good Time Charlie's. Clayborn had always gotten along with Robin, but when he tried to speak to her she ignored him. Costict suspected J. R. had gotten to her with cocaine and promises of marriage.

Costict contacted Robin's mother and told her to beware of J. R. By then Robin had already brought J. R. to Methuen and introduced him as her "boyfriend." She'd even brought Taj, J. R.'s son, to meet Shirley, hoping to exploit her mother's love of children.

When Costict told Shirley that Robin's boyfriend was a pimp, she surprised him by saying she felt the same way. But Shirley wouldn't give Robin's phone number to Costict, most likely because she blamed Costict for introducing her to J. R. in the first place.

Stranger still, Costict soon received a phone call from J. R. The angry man told Costict to mind his own business and to stop spreading lies.

Costict eventually tracked down Robin's phone number, but when he finally reached her, she told him that she didn't need any more male friends.

That was the last time Costict spoke to her.

Robin cut ties everywhere. Russell M. Glitman of the *Lawrence Eagle-Tribune* would later interview some of her friends from high school. They'd all lost touch with Robin and knew nothing about her new life. As Glitman recalled, "She left everybody in the dark."

• • •

No single factor steers a young woman into sex work. Generally, there's some sexual abuse in her childhood. Earning money for sex, or turning it into "work," is a way of normalizing it, taking control of it. Prostitutes often speak of being in control, but the irony is that the customers also feel in control because they pay for the service. In most cases, prostitutes come from dysfunctional family backgrounds. There's usually some violence or drug addiction or alcoholism, though none of this has ever been said of the Benedict home.

Why Robin turned to prostitution is unknown, as is when she started. A private detective agency hired by the Benedicts determined that Robin had dabbled in prostitution while still a high school senior. This is unsettling to those who want to blame her downfall solely on meeting J. R. It makes sense, though. The one constant in studies is that adult prostitutes generally start earning money for sex at around the age of eighteen. If Robin had started as far back as her senior year, that could explain why she so quickly joined forces with a Mattapan pimp.

"The family knew what she was doing, but they tried to do the best they could," detective Andrew Palermo told the *Miami Herald*. "Sometimes you close your eyes to what's really going on, hoping it will go away."

Part of the Robin Benedict myth is that she came from a clean, respectable town, yet Methuen wasn't as vanilla as advertised. Methuen in the late 1970s had its share of crime and prostitution, some of it spilling over from Lawrence, a neighboring city with a shockingly high crime rate. (A 1982 survey of 277 American cities by the *Places Rated Almanac* listed Lawrence-Haverhill as dead last for "livability.") Lawrence was rife with juvenile crimes, drug use, barroom stabbings, and unsolved murders, including three prostitutes found strangled to death in 1975/76.

"I considered Robin's neighborhood to be nice," recalled Sean Sullivan of Methuen. "But she was within range of a depressed section called the Arlington District." Known for rundown housing projects and failed efforts at renewal, the area was a haven for drugs and prostitution. Sullivan felt Robin's journey into a seamy lifestyle was almost predictable. "It didn't shock me that it happened to someone from this area," he said.

Certain derelict sections of Methuen became congregation points for prostitutes, some as young as thirteen. Undeniably, there was a sex-trade presence in Methuen. Furthermore, attending high school in Lawrence may have exposed Robin to seedy types. Prostitutes from Lawrence, many of them Hispanic women with heroin addictions, often came to Methuen where they had regular customers. Also, a police crackdown in the nearby city of Lowell during the mid-1970s caused Lowell prostitutes to drift into Lawrence and Methuen.

"She definitely would've seen prostitutes in Lawrence," said Robin's classmate Kelley Bartlett. "In Lawrence, the prostitutes were right there on the street. But I don't think Robin was a product of geography. I think it was her looks more than anything else. Beauty can be an asset, or it can be a downfall. People judge you in an instant. They think because you look a certain way then you must behave a certain way. She was only eighteen or nineteen, and she was with people who were much older, and they manipulated her. She was just a kid; because of her looks she was introduced to people that were *way* over her head."

Russell Glitman felt Robin might have fallen into prostitution in her rush to find excitement. "It probably seemed very glamorous at first," Glitman said. "At least on the surface."

"I never thought of her as a prostitute," said Bartlett. "That's what she was, we can't deny it, but I never imagined her on the street. I thought, maybe she was a high-priced call girl."

By some definitions she was a call girl, a busy one with an address book full of clients. Yet she had a pimp, and she could hustle several men in one night. She was a hybrid of prostitute, escort, call girl, and masseuse, a multi-tool player as comfortable in luxury high rises as the tacky bars of the Combat Zone.

Could Robin have gotten out of prostitution? Her relationship with J. R. was nothing to fall back on. There was no certainty that Robin would stay with J. R., any more than Cynthia Plowden or Savi had stayed. Did she think she might become a sort of whorehouse madam and go to art school on the side? What sort of image of the future did she entertain?

Robin wasn't likely to seek help. She thought she was smarter than the average girl in the Zone, and she may have been. But she was living with a pimp, and at one point Robin was even investigated as a possible drug connection for the New England Patriots. Nothing came of it, but she was keeping some bad company. Even if she hadn't met William Douglas, Robin Benedict seemed destined for a bad end.

She didn't see any problems coming, though, for the one thing she had in common with all prostitutes was a talent for delusion that bordered on the psychopathic.

12.

Whether it was marching in the White Eagles, drawing, or studying to be a Jehovah's Witness, Robin had always excelled at anything she undertook. In only a short amount of time she was fully immersed in the life of a Combat Zone prostitute. She was a bright young nymph in a neon forest.

It was her unspoiled appearance that impressed clients. Yet the other prostitutes knew that Robin's youthful look hid a forceful side. If you weren't quick, she could take your client from right under your nose, bring him to her nearby trick pad on Beacon Street, settle their business, collect her fee, and be back at Good Time Charlie's within an hour. This clean and neat girl was as mercenary as any hardened streetwalker.

Robin was cocky, too. The manager at Charlie's, Willie Moses, insisted that prostitutes had to encourage their trick to buy some drinks before luring them away. Yet Robin would simply breeze into the place, pluck a man from his barstool, and whisk him to Beacon Street.

Robin could also be reckless. She was known to get into a car with four or five guys in it, a stunt that could get a woman hurt or robbed. The more experienced prostitutes knew she was courting danger by being so careless, but they didn't stop her. Because of her links to J. R. and Savi, she was looked upon as a smug young newbie, someone groomed to be the new Cynthia Plowden. The other prostitutes were content to let the arrogant rookie learn things on her own—and were perhaps hoping she'd fall on her face. She was brazen about stealing tricks from other women, which endeared her to no one.

It is likely that Robin was imitating Savi's tough demeanor. Savi may have mentored Robin to be tough, to not take any shit from anyone. But

Savi had been on the street for seven years, and her confidence was hard won. Robin's bravado was mostly an act; she was only briefly removed from being on her high school yearbook committee.

Possibly because she was new in the Zone, Robin immediately caught the attention of Billy Dwyer, a veteran of the vice squad who had patrolled the area for years. Dwyer would say of Robin, "She kind of stood out."

An officer of the Boston Police Department since 1968, Dwyer's reputation included everything from killing pimps to setting them on fire. He laughed at these rumors, but the notion that a brutal Irish cop was patrolling the Combat Zone was probably helpful to his cause. He hated pimps for the way they manipulated young girls and women.

On the night of April 6, 1982, Dwyer and his partner, Sergeant Eddie McNelley, were off duty and hoping to grab a couple of drinks. Over their police radio they heard of a problem in District Four. More specifically, 478 Beacon Street. Dwyer and McNelley knew immediately that this was a building where prostitutes brought their customers. Cocktail time would have to wait.

This section of the Back Bay had once been an upmarket area populated by old-time Bostonians. By the 1980s, the classy brownstones were being divided up into cheap housing for students or young, low-earning professionals. What was once a debutante's bedroom was now a cheap studio apartment for an Emerson theater major or an entry-level State Street paralegal. Prostitutes turned the tiny studio spaces into rough-and-ready trick pads. Sometimes the prostitute whose name was on the lease would rent out the pad to other women for a percentage, usually ten dollars per trick.

When they arrived at the address, Dwyer and McNelley saw a typical scene. In a scruffy room with a single mattress on the floor, three men were arguing with three women. One of the men claimed his wallet had been stolen.

Dwyer recognized all three women. One was a local prostitute known as "Silver." The second was Savi, whom Dwyer knew as "Indian Debbie." Wild-eyed and probably high, Savi started yelling at Dwyer that she hadn't taken anybody's wallet. Standing off to the side was Robin. Dwyer and McNelley calmed the scene and brought the women to the nearest station house.

Robin was charged with accepting money for "unlawful sexual intercourse." Though she appeared almost tranquil in her mug shot, Dwyer recalled her having a condescending attitude. In what would be a recurring motif, Robin insisted she was not a typical prostitute. "I found her somewhat annoying," Dwyer said.

The arrest led nowhere. The charges were dismissed because the witnesses failed to show up in court.

• • •

Detective John Ridlon had also become familiar with Robin. A veteran cop with many underworld connections, "Big Bad John" was affable, friendly, but he always got the job done. While Dwyer had a reputation for setting pimps on fire, Ridlon was the sort of lawman that even the wise guys liked.

One day Ridlon spotted Robin coming out of Good Time Charlie's with a trick. When he questioned her, Robin confessed to being a prostitute. He brought her into the Vice Control office where she puzzled him with her mix of cooperation and stubbornness. She had proper identification and seemed fairly intelligent. Yet she wouldn't reveal the name of her pimp and, as she had done with Dwyer, insisted she wasn't a typical prostitute.

Though she wasn't a minor, Ridlon called Robin's parents.

When John and Shirley arrived at the police station, Shirley began wailing that Robin was a disgrace. She explained to Ridlon that her daughter had been fooling around with a New England Patriots player and through him had come into contact with a pimp. Robin protested, calling her mother a liar. It was a wild, highly charged meeting with lots of raised voices and denials.

The visit reached a crescendo when the detective showed the Benedicts a stack of gruesome photos. They were of murdered and mutilated prostitutes. Robin and her parents began crying together, but she refused to go home with them.

Despite the histrionics, the meeting between Robin's parents and the police amounted to nothing. Ridlon advised Robin to find another line of work, otherwise she'd end up in prison or a drug addict.

Robin assured him that she had everything figured out.

Sergeant McNelley happened to be in the office that day and recognized Robin from the Beacon Street incident. He took her aside and advised her to get a tattoo.

Robin didn't understand.

He explained that a tattoo would make her easy to identify when the police had to drag her out of a river.

• • •

Though Robin exuded confidence, it is possible that she had doubts about her new profession. In a matter of months, she had gone from being the girlfriend of a Patriot's lineman to being busted for prostitution. She had already posed for a mug shot. Detectives knew her name. She'd also tested positive recently for a venereal disease.

But what else could she do? The Newton Health Club had been closed under suspicion of being a "house of prostitution," so she couldn't return there to earn money.

The best thing she had going for her was the professor.

Of course, there were nights when Robin was tired and didn't feel like dealing with William Douglas. On those occasions, she turned him over to Savi. This was easy, since Savi shared Robin's trick pad on Beacon Street and seemed to have her own magnetic hold over Douglas. Still, Douglas preferred Robin. He was content just to be in Robin's company. There was sex now and then, but sometimes he paid just to sit and talk with her or to take walks around the Boston Common.

He probably wasn't prepared when Robin introduced to him cocaine. Within weeks of their first meeting, she laid out a long fluffy line for him to try. Douglas loved the stuff immediately and began using it regularly with Robin. He would later claim that after an afternoon together, before Robin returned to Good Time Charlie's, she "would always check her nose and my nose very thoroughly because she didn't want to go back to the bar and have anyone see any traces."

Cocaine hits the brain in a way that makes everything seem more interesting. Douglas probably found the combination of a beautiful prostitute and a pile of cocaine overwhelming. By snorting with her, Douglas was also showing that he wanted to be just like Robin. His obsession was such that he'd started mirroring her. He'd never had much of a personality; it may have made him feel good to absorb hers.

13.

Douglas's feelings for Robin intensified.

He rearranged his schedule at Tufts so he could be with her in the afternoons. He would try to see her before she started work. They might meet for a light meal at a Howard Johnson's. They might sit together on a park bench or take a stroll through the Public Garden. Then, hours later, he'd arrange to see her again, meeting her as late as two or three in the morning. He'd stay with her until five or so. These late meetings satisfied some romantic notion that he was the last man she'd see. Douglas wanted to feel that he was Robin's most important and favorite customer.

The cocaine and the attention of a young woman probably made Douglas feel like a superhero. Indeed, the early throes of obsession can make a person feel empowered, as if taking off on a new and exciting adventure, as if life has been shot through with new meaning. Over time, the obsession may leave a person miserable and frantic, in some cases unable to function, but in its earliest form, an obsession has a decidedly positive feel. Douglas in those early months with Robin was excited, vibrant, his mind like a child turning cartwheels on a freshly mowed lawn.

He wanted to do things for Robin. He wanted to buy furniture for her and take her to nice places. They graduated from the cheap Naugahyde booths of Howard Johnson's to the swanky Pier Four restaurant on the South Boston waterfront, feasting on expensive seafood. He imagined taking her away on a vacation, to Europe or the South Seas. He wanted to impress her, to make her think of him as something other than a trick she'd met at Charlie's.

Now and then Robin indulged him in ways that were unusual for a prostitute. One night when J. R. was out, Robin invited Douglas to Natick and made dinner for him. She charged him not only for the time it took to prepare the meal but also for the groceries she'd had to buy. As usual, Robin charged him by the hour. He happily paid. He even talked about bringing Robin with him to Tufts functions instead of dull old Nancy. Clearly, he liked the idea of having Robin for his wife.

Sigmund Freud recognized the fantasy of men wanting to rescue whores as a twist on the Oedipal complex. According to Freudian psychology,

Douglas's ultimate goal may have been to remake Robin into a chaste mother figure. Freud would've noted that Robin was cooking dinner for Douglas and wiping his nose for him, both motherly actions. That the relationship was becoming less sexual would've also fit Freud's theory.

Psychologists who looked into the case after the fact believed that Douglas was showing signs of delusion, perhaps thinking that he would only have to pay for a while before Robin agreed to be with him for free. Some felt Douglas was simply naïve, thinking that a prostitute would eventually like him and not charge him. But Douglas was neither delusional nor naïve. He'd been reading about prostitutes for years and knew exactly what they were about. Spending money on Robin seemed to be part of Douglas's thrill. It is also likely that Douglas simply relished the control. He liked knowing that Robin belonged to him for a certain amount of time; the passing of money to a prostitute was in itself a kind of erotic activity.

Perhaps the strangest moment of their time together was when they went to Boston's Exeter Street Theater for a showing of *The Rocky Horror Picture Show*, which played every Friday and Saturday at midnight. By the early 1980s, *Rocky Horror* was already a late-night cult attraction, with audiences dressing up as the outré characters onscreen, shouting out the dialog and singing along to Richard O'Brien's glam-rock musical score. The Exeter was a cavernous place, with seating for a thousand or so customers; it had originally been built as a temple for nineteenth-century Spiritualists prior to being turned into a movie house in 1914. The old venue was chilly on certain nights. Douglas may have yearned to put an arm around Robin to keep her warm.

Or maybe he was happy to just sit there with a beautiful girl at his side, while all around them were leather-clad transvestites and bisexual musclemen and aliens and hunchbacks, singing in unison, hurling rolls of toilet paper through the air, firing off squirt guns, while Tim Curry minced around onscreen, pursing his lips and growling. It was costing Douglas hundreds of dollars, but a night out had never been so interesting.

• • •

In late May of 1982, Douglas sent a note to Robin outlining a plan to put her on the Tufts payroll, where she would assist him on an "image analysis project" and something he dubbed "the U.S. Naval Submarine Project." He was going to backdate her "employment" to April 1982, which is when they'd started seeing each other regularly. What is most telling in the memo is when he writes, "I would like you to have some form of documentable income/employment. When you retire from 'business' your resume will not have a five-year gap. . . . This will help in April 1983 when I do your tax return. . . ."

It's a fascinating document in that Douglas understood Robin's plans to quit the "business" (prostitution) and appeared to be taking an almost fatherly interest in her future. Yet there is something devious here. By accepting her story that she would only be a prostitute for a while (five years, apparently), and promising to help her "retire," he was making himself integral to her life and dreams. At this point, she probably trusted this older man who seemed to know what he was talking about. If they were discussing Douglas helping with her tax forms a year in the future, she must've felt he was a suitable ally.

The memo—which J. R. later found under a sofa cushion—would be used by legal experts trying to prove Robin had actually done illustration work for Douglas. Yet it is more interesting for another reason. It shows Douglas insinuating himself into Robin's existence, making himself crucial after knowing her for less than eight weeks.

14.

She told him he was gross.

She'd always had a teasing, sarcastic sense of humor—she used to poke her chubby mother in the belly and call her "doughboy"—but when Robin told Douglas that she was disgusted by his rotund figure, he decided to do something about it.

His colleagues at Tufts noticed the pounds dropping off of him, though Douglas was still eating his usual diet of hot dogs, pizza, and pastry. They assumed he was using Benzedrine. He also kept little dumbbells in his office and was sometimes seen grunting through a bit of exercise. One day a faculty member saw Douglas outside, his enormous body stuffed into a jogging suit, huffing and puffing right at the tip of the Combat Zone.

Was he jogging past Charlie's, hoping Robin would see how hard he was working to lose weight?

Eventually, Douglas resorted to pure starvation. The result was a quick weight drop of more than forty pounds. He would sometimes claim to have lost 100 pounds for Robin, though one source has him dropping from 317 pounds to 230. Yet Douglas was spending so much money on Robin that he couldn't afford to buy a new wardrobe. He had to keep wearing his old clothes, which now hung loosely from his frame; he looked unhealthy. He lost weight in his neck, face, and shoulders but remained large in the hips and buttocks. If possible, Douglas looked even more bizarre than before, his outline taking on a sort of fun-house-mirror effect.

And his behavior was bizarre too. He kept talking about *The Rocky Horror Picture Show*, asking colleagues if they had seen it. He seemed more scatterbrained than usual, fuzzy-minded and forgetful. At this point, Douglas was probably bored with the lab and his dreary staff. He much preferred being in Robin's world of late nights and clandestine meetings.

He'd spoiled her with gifts, anything from new music albums to expensive perfumes and clothes. He took her to concerts and shows, including back-to-back performances by Air Supply and Olivia Newton-John at the Boston Common summer concert series. (Douglas had to be the only forty-year-old man at the Air Supply show, though he probably liked their big hit, "Every Woman in the World," with the line "You're my fantasy, you're my reality.")

Because he was nearly broke, Douglas had to get creative when it came to paying for these nights out. When he wanted to forgo a night at the trick pad and splurge on a hotel room for the two of them, he would create a phony expense account for a nonexistent visiting professor. When Robin wanted business cards printed up, he used a Back Bay printshop to create 500 cards reading NADINE, with one of her many phone numbers underneath. He put the twenty-three-dollar receipt in his desk, marked it "Misc." and later added it to his research account.

There were letters, too. Lots and lots of letters.

If seeing Robin in the afternoons and then after her "shift" wasn't enough, Douglas spent the in-between hours writing to her. Early in their arrangement—he sometimes still referred to her as "Nadine"—he was already declaring her one of the most important people in his life. In a note written while he was in Canada on a school-related trip, Douglas said he missed her as much as he missed his children.

He laid out plans for her to join him on future trips, adding that he would gladly pay her usual rates. Sometimes he referred to having a "grand day" with her, meaning $1,000 for a full day at her side. Sometimes he wrote just to thank Robin for meeting with him that day. He would usually sign the letters, "Your friend, Bill."

He even created certificates that he sent along with the letters:

"A hair permanent at a salon of your choice as often as you wish!"

"One complete set of super expensive cosmetics of your choice!"

"A video recorder and player for your television!"

"One bike of your choice!"

The idea, as surmised by investigators, was for Robin to pick one out of an envelope before they had sex. She'd probably feign excitement, making Douglas feel like the ultimate sugar daddy.

A few of Douglas's letters were loaded with scientific jargon, thanking her for assisting him on one project or another, which was obviously done to help his scam that Robin was his employee. He seemed to be preparing for the day he would be called out on the ruse. Otherwise, the letters were sappy and mawkish.

Though Douglas sometimes included short anecdotes about his past, his setbacks, and his triumphs, the letters showed a man in his early forties who was emotionally stunted, a married father of three who sounded like an unsophisticated college freshman.

When he wasn't praising Robin, he was apologizing for not being good enough for her. The letters were not sexual at all, and his pornographic interests never surfaced. The savage scenes he liked in porn appeared to exist in a different part of his mind, one where Robin never entered. He compartmentalized Robin, as if his image of her was kept in a private vault.

The letters also contained a kind of shorthand from Douglas, including "QH," which possibly stood for "quick hug." (Investigators also wondered if it meant "Quaalude high," or "quick hand job.") As a child might do, Douglas filled the margins of his letters with small, primitive cartoons of himself and Robin.

On the surface, Robin Benedict and William Douglas were merely a prostitute and an obsessed client. But on a deeper level, the relationship was fueled by a kind of juvenilia; he was a middle-aged man acting out teen fantasies, while she was a twenty-year-old not far removed from her teens. She wasn't quite Lolita to his Humbert, but she was young enough to be his daughter and flirted with him like a teenager. In one letter he expressed a fondness for her "Velemint transfers," where she'd transfer a mint from her mouth to his. It is doubtful that the women at Good Time Charlie's taught her this playful stunt. It was something straight from the Methuen middle school. To Douglas, who had never experienced such things during his Lake Placid youth, Robin's maneuver with the mint was every bit as mysterious and amazing as anything else she did to him.

Robin sometimes answered his notes. Her own letters were brief and casual, addressed to her "favorite professor," offering comments about their "friendship." She even drew pictures for him, including one that depicted a beautiful woman surrounded by four tuxedoed men. She signed the back of it in a manner not likely for a prostitute, vaguely describing an encounter they'd enjoyed together in her Natick apartment. "A moment," she wrote, "I do believe you will treasure for quite some time. (Me too.) You can never tell what we are going to do next. It's been wonderful and will be more wonderful in times to come. Always, Robin."

Was the sentiment hers? Or did J. R. encourage her to make Douglas feel special?

At times Robin would even link arms with Douglas as they strolled together. She may have been a prostitute, but as far as Douglas was concerned, he was walking on a cloud with his sweetheart.

15.

Very early one morning in November of 1982, Douglas and Robin were leaving her trick pad when she noticed a familiar car parked nearby. She stiffened. The car was Dwyer's. The old Boston vice cop had become an ongoing irritation for her.

She told Douglas to keep quiet if Dwyer approached them and to say nothing about money passing between them.

Dwyer and his partner, Mark Molloy, corralled them. Dwyer took Robin aside while Molloy berated Douglas.

Molloy taunted the professor, warning him that he'd be in the newspapers soon. Douglas stood his ground. He identified himself and insisted that Robin was his employee at the medical school. Molloy scoffed at him, but Douglas vowed that he knew Robin well and had even been to her family's home.

Dwyer and Malloy escorted the couple back to the trick pad. Observing the bleak condition of the place, Dwyer told Robin that she would have to move out immediately. Douglas put on a show of outrage, insisting that Robin was not a prostitute. Tired of Douglas's back talk, Dwyer produced a picture of J. R. It was a photo that Robin's father had taken and given to the police. Dwyer held the photograph up so Douglas could look at it, practically shoving it under the professor's nose. Dwyer explained that the man in the photograph was a pimp. Douglas looked away, still denying that Robin had done anything wrong.

"This girl is a hooker," Dwyer said, "every cent you give her, she gives to him." He waved the photograph in front of Douglas's face.

Douglas protested, but Dwyer tore into him. "You're a professor at Tufts? Screwing around with her can't be good for your career," he said.

Later, Dwyer would remember Douglas's infatuation with Robin, and how "she had him by the nose." Dwyer sensed that Douglas was lost in some sort of make-believe world. He said of Douglas, "I think he didn't want to know she had a pimp."

16.

The police harassed Robin constantly. Even after Robin found a new trick pad in a different part of Back Bay, the vice squad was there almost immediately to close her down.

It seemed to her that someone was tipping them off.

In fact, she was correct. A snitch was reporting her every move to the police.

The snitch was William Douglas.

Since their earliest days together, Douglas had been playing a strange game: He would follow Robin in his car, watching her with other customers. When he knew Robin was with a trick, he'd contact the police and tell them that a prostitute was in the area, breaking the law. He'd give the exact address, and within minutes a vice squad car was on the scene, badgering Robin and her client. Thanks to her favorite professor, Robin was always on the vice squad's radar.

On the morning Dwyer and Molloy approached Douglas and Robin, the two cops were acting on an anonymous tip from none other than Douglas. He'd called the police from his Tufts office and in a disguised voice told them prostitutes were working out of this new location on 400 Marlborough Street. They were attracting "undesirable elements," he said, and ruining the Back Bay.

Many theories were offered about Douglas and his anonymous tips to the police. Dwyer thought it was basic jealousy on Douglas's part—that he couldn't stand thinking of Robin with other men. If she kept getting arrested, Dwyer guessed, perhaps she'd give up prostitution and be available only to Douglas. Others, such as journalist Linda Wolfe, suggested Douglas had already started to hate Robin for taking advantage of him, and also hated himself for being the very "undesirable element" he'd complained about.

Maybe so, but Douglas was displaying a typical stalker's behavior. He used the police to make Robin feel she was in danger. And on that November morning, Robin wouldn't have suspected that Douglas had made the call. It was ingenious, in a way. And if it seems odd that he risked having his family learn that he was with a prostitute, Douglas probably didn't care. By this point, Robin was foremost in Douglas's mind, not Nancy and the kids.

Ultimately, Douglas's methods seem born of his own unique, twisted logic. He was orchestrating something that only he understood. Maybe Douglas simply liked the idea of getting caught and wanted to put himself in jeopardy, like the arsonist who contacts the fire department. Being reprimanded by the police may have been another of Douglas's weird thrills.

• • •

Even as his game with the police played out, Douglas continued to spend money on Robin and help her in different ways. When she wanted a Mastercard, he accompanied her to a bank and said that he employed her at Tufts. He also rented a safe deposit box so Robin could have a place to store her cocaine. On the paperwork he listed Robin as his "wife."

He claimed to have bought a new silver Toyota Starlet for Robin, which probably cost more than $5,000. Some sources have said that J. R. actually picked up the car at a Wellesley Toyota dealer, but if J. R. bought it, he did so with money that Douglas had given Robin. Indeed, a prostitute would later tell the media that Robin once came into Charlie's that fall bragging that Douglas had given her "five grand in one lump sum." By now, Douglas was hemorrhaging money, having already tapped into his family savings account. (He still managed to buy a Toyota Starlet for himself, so he could be like Robin.)

He'd also become more demanding and possessive. If Robin wanted a night off from him, Douglas would call her a dozen times, pleading with her to meet him at least once, even for a half hour. Her new post office box on Charles Street, one that she used because she was frequently changing trick pads, was being flooded with cards and letters from Douglas. He'd insist that he couldn't live without seeing her.

Douglas also developed a big mouth around Good Time Charlie's. The once mild-mannered professor would now saunter in and ask rather boldly if Robin was around. Then he'd inform Savi or Silver or one of the other regulars that Robin and he were going to get together later and snort cocaine. Such talk was risky. Robin dreaded anyone knowing about her drug use, or that Douglas was spending so much money on the stuff. It might invite other prostitutes to steal from her or give the police more reason to bother her.

She'd reprimand Douglas for talking so much to the other prostitutes and blabbing about their cocaine use. Douglas would nearly cry, apologizing and begging her to forgive him. He'd re-created the routine from his early childhood, getting in trouble, then groveling, promising to be a "good little man."

Douglas's contrite act may have kept Robin from taking a closer look at the man she was bilking for thousands of dollars every month. She failed to see that he was far more than a wimp with money. He'd already broken into one of her trick pads on Marlborough Street. He'd smashed a window in the rear of the building and rifled through her things. The professor had the cunning of an experienced burglar. He stole her phone and an answering machine that he'd bought for her as a gift, hoping to learn about the clients who called her, or just to learn what he could about her personal life. He would later say he stole the items because he feared Tufts would be looking for Robin.

More recently, Douglas had been angry with Robin. He'd spent an hour with her and she'd been unpleasant the entire time. Rather than apologize for her sour mood, she simply demanded her usual payment. It may have been a rare moment where Douglas realized Robin saw him as nothing but a money machine. He decided to settle things with another break-in.

By now Robin had a new trick pad on Commonwealth Avenue. She'd made the mistake of letting Douglas help her move in. He'd been gallant that day, renting and driving a U-Haul truck and helping unload her things, gasping for air as he carried her boxes up the stairs to her new place. But when Douglas offered to go to a nearby locksmith and have copies made of her keys, he had a set made for his own use.

While Robin was in Good Time Charlie's trying to hustle clients, Douglas parked his car near the trick pad and timed her movements. Once he estimated that she would be gone for a half hour between her sessions, Douglas broke into her apartment and staged another robbery. He scattered her things and even stole $300.

Along with the money, Douglas took Robin's new answering machine (which he'd bought for her to replace the other one he'd stolen) and also grabbed her address book. Now he had access to information about all her clients. It was later learned that he was figuring out which clients were married, then calling their homes and informing their spouses that hubby was seeing a prostitute on the side.

The next time she saw him, Robin talked about how terrible she felt at having been robbed twice. Douglas consoled her. This may have been what he'd wanted all along, for her to feel vulnerable and frightened. This way he could pretend to be an authority figure and rescue Robin from her dangerous lifestyle.

In an example of one rat recognizing another, J. R. suspected Douglas was responsible for the robberies. His suspicion stemmed from one of the answering machines Douglas had given to Robin. Douglas may have thought it would be used solely at Robin's trick pad, but she first installed it at the home she shared with J. R. One evening they left the machine on to screen calls. After the calls, however, J. R. heard the sound of a beeper, letting the recorded messages play back. It was obvious that someone with a duplicate beeper was listening in. J. R.'s instincts told him that Douglas was the listener.

It was also around this time that Robin noticed Douglas was following her in his car. It happened more than once, usually when she was with another client. She confronted him about this, but he denied it.

By now J. R. wanted Robin to forget Douglas and find another money-man. Yet the pimp's advice had no influence on Robin.

She still thought she had things under control.

• • •

In an unexpected turn of events, Robin found herself banned from Good Time Charlie's.

She'd broken one of the manager's golden rules: She grabbed a john in the parking lot and took him to her trick pad before he'd even stepped into the bar, something Willie Moses couldn't abide. Billy Dwyer took credit for Robin's exile, claiming to have caught her in the parking lot with a customer and threatening to write up Charlie's for numerous infractions unless she took her business elsewhere. Whether it was Dwyer or Moses who caused it, Robin was now unwelcome at her usual headquarters. The other prostitutes didn't miss her at all. As one of them later told the media, "She always bragged about how much he (Douglas) was spending on her and a lot of the girls were jealous."

Robin stayed busy. She'd been in the business long enough to have cultivated side gigs. By now she was accompanying J. R. to Jason's Restaurant on Clarendon Street in Boston's Back Bay neighborhood. Jason's was an upscale meat market frequented by minor Boston celebrities of the day. Working as a team, J. R. and Robin would try to chat up women they pegged as potential prostitutes. Sometimes Robin would act on her own. She'd approach some young, attractive woman, saying she knew of a rich executive who wanted to have a good time.

Robin had also agreed to doing some private sex shows for clients, usually simulating lesbian acts with another girl. There's never been any evidence that Robin was a lesbian, but compared to hustling men in the Combat Zone, a girl-on-girl pantomime act was probably an easy way to earn quick money.

Around this time, Robin took a one-night gig in Framingham, attending a private bachelor party with another prostitute. Dancing to their own cassettes of disco music, the two women stripped. Later, Robin and her partner took turns servicing a rather long stag line.

Robin decided to return to massage work, taking a job in a health club far from Boston. It may have seemed a nice respite from the city and a chance to leave Douglas behind. But no matter where she went, the professor's hulking shadow was blanketing her like a thundercloud.

17.

In the fall of 1982, a routine audit of the lab's finances turned up several unusual expense vouchers from Douglas. The sheer volume was staggering. He was submitting vouchers against university grants that the entire staff was supposed to share; his expenses were both mind-boggling and cryptic. There were vouchers for out-of-town meetings, trips to New York, Sweden, Canada, Washington D.C., Missouri, Georgia, New Hampshire, Connecticut, Texas, Tennessee, and Pennsylvania. No one could recall Douglas ever going on these trips. There were vouchers for entertainment and housing for visiting scientists, though no one could remember any visiting scientists coming to Tufts. Besides, Douglas wouldn't be responsible for their entertainment or housing.

Mostly, there were vouchers for his assistant, this Robin Benedict from MIT. No one could recall seeing or meeting her.

Douglas had even purchased condoms from a Tufts Medical School supply house, listed on the invoice as "biological fluid collection units." (Robin was selling the condoms to her colleagues in the Combat Zone, but this endeavor backfired; the condoms were so old that they often broke during use. How many diseases or accidental pregnancies occurred because of this little scam?)

Douglas had also listed Savi as another of his employees, putting her name on vouchers for a purported research trip to Chicago. Some of the vouchers were merely written out for Douglas's own spending. In all, it was estimated that Douglas's yearlong swindling of the university added up to more than $67,000 (over $215,000 today).

When university vice president Steven Manos and Tufts comptroller Richard Thorngren called Douglas forward to discuss his outrageous expenses, Douglas put on a great performance. He spent several minutes scanning his appointment calendar, squinting through his thick eyeglasses at dates that were empty.

Douglas agreed with his inquisitors. The invoices, he said, were a "problem." He suggested there might be errors in his record keeping. He was, after all, a notoriously absent-minded professor. But he assured Manos and Thorngren that most of his vouchers were legitimate.

When Douglas was asked about the work of his two unseen assistants, Robin and Savi, he told his interviewers that the two women were well worth their pay. Yet when Thorngren demanded to speak to Robin, Douglas grew tense. He claimed to have arranged meetings in the past between Robin and Tufts, but they'd fallen through because of foul weather. When Thorngren asked for Robin's phone number, Douglas claimed that it was confidential and he couldn't give it out.

To take the focus off of Robin, Douglas promised to reimburse the school himself.

Thorngren and Manos were not impressed with his offer.

The investigation into his expenses continued throughout the fall.

18.

Douglas had other issues to consider as 1982 came to an end. Most had to do with his wife, Nancy.

She'd been patient with him for a long time but was fed up with his behavior. He was spending too many nights away from home, and she suspected he was using drugs. She also wondered if he was having an affair. He'd only been involved with Robin for eight months or so, but Nancy would later claim he'd been spending nights out for years, a suggestion that he'd been haunting the Combat Zone since they'd arrived in Massachusetts.

When she finally confronted him about his late nights, as well as some curious expenses on his credit cards, Douglas admitted that he had a "girlfriend."

Douglas blamed Nancy. Her decision to go back to work left him alone too often, he said.

Then he asked Nancy if she wanted a divorce. She said no. She wanted to work out the problem.

They agreed to work together and solve their dilemma, but Douglas had another matter that was even more pressing, one he didn't share with Nancy: His so-called girlfriend had a pimp.

Douglas had always refused to face that fact. Now, after listening to the messages on Robin's answering machines, he gathered that this man she lived with was really her pimp. In one of her messages to J. R., Robin had actually said, "This is your woman calling. . . ."

The idea sickened Douglas. Was all of his money really going to a pimp? When Dwyer had shoved the picture in his face, Douglas hadn't looked closely, and he wasn't even sure what J. R. looked like. He only knew that his quest to control Robin was becoming even more difficult. A pimp was in the way. And with Tufts watching his expenses, his embezzling days were over.

Robin and J. R. were moving to Malden, a blue-collar town just north of Boston. They found a modest old house in a comfortable neighborhood, away from the downtown Malden bars and riffraff. The neighbors were suspicious of the black man with the diamond ring and the fancy car—J. R. had also taken to wearing purple pants and a fur coat—but they were impressed with Robin. She was friendly and fanatical about decorating her new home.

When it came to Douglas, though, Robin was establishing boundaries. After he had helped her finagle $25,000 from the Medford Savings Bank for a mortgage on her new home—Douglas had involved Savi in a cunning ploy that involved more bloated travel vouchers and three different banks—Robin refused to tell Douglas where she and J. R. would be living. She wouldn't even give Douglas her new phone number.

By now she knew about the investigation at Tufts and was possibly worried about how it might affect her. She decided it was time to put some distance between herself and the professor.

Meanwhile, the Anatomy and Cellular Biology Department staff indulged in secret chatter about Douglas. They all agreed that he seemed to be collapsing before their eyes.

19.

There were no laws against stalking at the time William Douglas and Robin Benedict knew each other. Massachusetts's stalking laws were nearly a decade in the future. The concept was still murky, with some arguing that obsessive love was as old as love itself, while others noticed that stalking incidents sometimes ended in tragedy. Douglas, and others like him, may have believed he was acting out of some romantic need, yet stalkers are not driven by love and devotion; rather, they want to possess and control their victims. And to accomplish this, they use terror tactics.

Douglas never directly threatened Robin, but calling the police on her and burglarizing her trick pads were certainly done to scare her. He created an atmosphere of dread, while still presenting himself as the harmless admirer. It was working so far. Not once did Robin ever say she was scared of Douglas or ask to be protected from him.

Even the fortune Douglas was spending on her could be construed as part of his stalking campaign. Robin would invariably be described as greedy, but Douglas spent the money as a way to maintain control of her. The money in her hand was like a leash around her neck. Or so Douglas thought.

One night, just as he had done in the Back Bay, Douglas staked out Robin's old Natick apartment. She and J. R. were still in the process of moving, and Douglas knew she would be there.

It was New Year's Eve, a romantic night for couples. Douglas had probably dreamed all year of spending part of this evening with Robin, to maybe kiss her at midnight and clink champagne glasses.

At some point in the evening, Douglas left his car and walked to a telephone booth to call Robin. When she answered, Douglas told her he was calling from Boston and began begging for a date. She refused.

He continued to plead with her. It was New Year's Eve, after all. Couldn't they just talk?

Robin explained that she and J. R. would be leaving soon and hung up.

Douglas returned to his car, dejected. It was below freezing. He should've been home with his family. Instead, he was in Natick, spying on a prostitute.

He waited there in the dark, hoping to see Robin come out of the apartment with J. R. If nothing else, he could finally get a look at this pimp. He waited for hours, but they never came out.

• • •

The next day, Robin called Douglas and told him he was a pest. In a firm voice, she said that she wanted nothing more to do with him. He was taken aback. She'd never spoken to him this way.

Heartbroken, Douglas spent New Year's Day, 1983, writing a long letter of apology to Robin.

More anguished letters followed that week. Robin softened long enough to meet Douglas for two hours on January 5, which filled him with optimism. In his next letter he suggested they go see *Rocky Horror* again, or perhaps *Airplane II*, and maybe go for crab legs at Pier Four. But Robin had no interest in regular contact. She claimed she was leaving town and didn't have time for him.

"It tears me apart and brings tears to my eyes to hear you say that," he wrote.

Whether Douglas actually cried is doubtful, but something in his brain was beginning to howl.

20.

The auditors spent weeks going over Douglas's accounts and debating how best to handle the situation.

They determined Robin was earning thousands of dollars for a series of vague services. Auditors and department chairs were astounded that Douglas had dared create such a scam, and that he'd offered such flimsy explanations.

As a tenured professor, Douglas couldn't be fired. He could, however, be prosecuted in court or asked to resign, drastic choices that were likely to taint the school with negative publicity. Manos, in particular, wanted to keep the investigation quiet.

When Douglas received a small grant from Johns Hopkins to study the effects of red tide on marine life, his old champion, Karen Hitchcock, suggested he not accept it until the questions about his expenses were answered. Upset that one of his top supporters was treating him this way, Douglas felt cornered. Suddenly, he divulged a secret: He was seeing a psychiatrist and feared he was losing his mind.

• • •

Douglas had started to see Dr. Peter Randolph, allegedly over "personality problems." Yet it appeared Douglas was less interested in his mental health than in creating smoke screens in the event he was investigated.

A mysterious tape recording made by Douglas in his home mentioned his seeing Dr. Randolph. The tape, one of many Douglas made at the time, sounds as if he were rehearsing a monologue to be given at a later date, perhaps to an auditor. It is also likely that the story on the recording originated in his sessions with Dr. Randolph, since it refers to changes in his personality.

In it, he describes how his workload at Tufts wore him down mentally, to the point where he was becoming "a different person." He claimed on the tape to not know why he had faked the travel vouchers, and that he couldn't remember when or why he had done those things. He said it was "unfortunate and heartbreaking" that no one ever caught him before his stealing got out of control. He claimed to not even know what he did with the money.

He describes going to a restaurant in Kenmore Square where he encountered a woman who resembled an old acquaintance but turned out to be a prostitute. Then, he explains, she took him to her apartment and drugged him. When he woke up, Douglas realized the prostitute's boyfriend had taken pictures of him in bed with her. Douglas claimed this was the beginning of a blackmail scheme.

Abruptly, Douglas stops himself on the tape.

"My idea stinks," he said.

There was someone else in the room as Douglas made the recording. No journalist or investigator has ever determined the person's identity, but there is a second voice on the tape as Douglas practices his monologue. It isn't clear if the voice belongs to a man or a woman. Stranger still, no one ever asked Douglas about it. The mystery person says little but merely acts as a sounding board. At one point, the person says, "We don't have the money," which suggests it might be Douglas's wife, but later on the tape, when Douglas refers to his wife as "poor dear," the person laughs. Is it Robin?

Douglas went on, describing a number of possible scenarios. At one point he describes how his wife was not supportive of him, and that he began seeing a young woman on the side, just to get through this "difficult time." He goes on to say he was living two lives, stealing money to give "to the girl so she would continue to see me." At the end of the tape he says, "Am I crazy? My wife thinks I had a nervous breakdown."

On the many tapes recorded by Douglas in this period, he often sounds like he's rehearsing a speech. He was repeatedly trying to describe his first meeting with this enigmatic girl who plotted to get his money, but rather than say they met in the Combat Zone, he would create elaborate scenes. They usually took place in anonymous coffee shops, with him being exhausted after a day at Tufts. He never wanted to say he had been a horny customer looking for action on LaGrange Street. He wanted to portray himself as an innocent man walking into a trap.

What Douglas said during his sessions with Dr. Randolph is unknown, but chances are he was just giving the doctor a rehearsed monologue, like the ones practiced on his home tape recordings.

Douglas's claim that he was losing his mind made no impression on Karen Hitchcock.

On January 11, 1983, Douglas was suspended from Tufts.

• • •

Douglas's inflated expenses were only part of the reason for his suspension.

Hitchcock had learned some troubling news about the once venerated professor. He was purportedly researching Sodium-22, a dangerous substance with a high level of radium. Complaining that books and other items were disappearing from his office, Douglas planned to add the substance to book bindings and then, if a book disappeared, he could track it down with a Geiger counter. A colleague warned Douglas that Sodium-22 was "hazardous," with a minute's exposure equal to "a lifetime of X-rays." Douglas called off his plan, but when Hitchcock learned about it she was horrified.

Hitchcock was also aware of an anonymous letter circulating at Tufts where Douglas was accused of various indiscretions, including improprieties in the lab and not giving credit where it was due. The letter writer was not identified but was assumed to be a staffer Douglas had mistreated.

There'd also been an incident where Douglas had been profoundly rude to his hosts at a seminar in Saskatoon, ranting and raving about his accommodations. During that same trip he was spotted furtively xeroxing documents concerning cell research in the Canadian lab, odd behavior for a revered scientist.

Then there was a recent paper for a British scientific journal on which Douglas had collaborated, one where "Robin N. Benedict" was thanked for her "expert assistance in these studies."

Hitchcock later admitted to weeping over the Douglas situation. He was supposed to be part of Tufts's growth, but now he seemed like a stranger to her, utterly untrustworthy.

She appointed herself the role of escorting Douglas from the building on his last day, struggling to stay composed as they shared an awkward goodbye. Before he left, he asked her, "Do you think this is fair?" She didn't know how to respond.

The fact was that Douglas had been behaving strangely for months. He was paranoid and short-tempered, and he seemed unwilling to take responsibility for his lapses. Most of his colleagues believed Douglas was no danger to anyone and had hoped that his voucher problems would be solved. He was still the slightly eccentric genius who slept in his office, but some had glimpsed enough of his crumbling personality to agree that Tufts was better off without him.

21.

As the Combat Zone went into decline, the city's adult entertainment business began spreading to other areas. A lucrative new spot was a location in Saugus known as "The Strip." Eleven miles north of Boston, Saugus was now home to some of the area's best-known massage parlors and "men's clubs." The *Boston Phoenix* once declared the joints along the Strip as "swizzle stick heaven." One of the more popular spots where men could meet prostitutes was the Danish Health Club. This was where Robin began working in the early weeks of 1983.

Robin was younger and more attractive than most of the other women at the Danish Health Club. Her new coworkers disliked her immediately. They sensed she was arrogant; they suspected she was a drug user.

She was calling herself "Bobbie Benedict" and carried herself in a way that made the other women suspicious. She treated the clients coldly, always finding ways to avoid full sexual intercourse. Robin's finicky nature is hard to understand—just two months earlier she'd been servicing a line of anonymous men at a Framingham bachelor party—but now she was giving customers a quick hand job rather than a full session. And she still had an aversion to oral sex. Robin's coworkers feared they might lose customers because of this new girl who apparently hated sex work.

Of course, Robin's looks would keep her employed, regardless of how she treated clients. That was another reason the other women at the Danish disliked her; it was clear that management would keep "Bobbie" on the staff. Having a pretty young woman around could only be good for business.

• • •

Douglas started coming to the Saugus club. He used the name "Hank" and asked for "Bobbie." Robin allegedly serviced him like a regular customer and made it clear that she wouldn't see him outside of the health club.

Douglas's most recent letter to Robin revealed that he had been suspended from Tufts.

"I need your help," Douglas wrote. "I am so depressed and sad. Everything in my life is going wrong lately. I truly need a friend that I can talk with and share things with."

Robin couldn't be bothered with an unemployed version of Douglas. She even left a message for him saying that she had quit working in Saugus, just to get him off her trail.

But Douglas was not easily fooled.

• • •

It was during Robin's second week of employment that the phone calls started.

A concerned Saugus citizen who gave his name as "Hank" called the Danish Health Club to warn them about their newest employee. She was a former Combat Zone prostitute, he said.

Of course, it was Douglas. He was teaching Robin a lesson.

Tape recordings were later found by investigators where Douglas was apparently rehearsing the speech he gave to the health club. In one of them he spoke in a falsetto voice and said: "Is your whore from the Combat Zone working tonight? The one who calls herself Bobbie. Robin Benedict. You know we're going to close that fucking place of yours for bringing whores from the Combat Zone back here to our town of Saugus. . . ."

The Danish ignored the call. It sounded like someone disguising his voice.

A second call followed that same week, again warning the health club's management that "Bobbie" was a prostitute from Boston. Again, the call was dismissed.

One afternoon Douglas called and simply said, "Is this the Combat Zone of Saugus?" Then he hung up.

Douglas had also been calling the Saugus police and the Saugus Board of Health, using an alias and complaining that the Danish had hired a Combat Zone prostitute. He claimed she had "propositioned me for sex and money (and) tried to sell me some dope." He vowed, "The good citizens of Saugus are going to rid ourselves of the stench of this place!"

During Robin's third week at the club, a city health inspector showed up. He claimed that a certain "Mr. Schloss" had contacted City Hall to complain that a prostitute was working there and selling drugs.

The owners had to take this seriously. Prostitution and drug charges couldn't be established, but they recognized that Robin wasn't properly licensed to practice massages in Saugus. Even a shady health club has a limit. She was terminated that day.

Sitting in a restaurant across the street from the health club was Douglas. With a plate of food in front of him, he waited for the scene to play out.

Feeling vengeful after being ignored on New Year's Eve, he'd placed the calls that led to Robin being fired. He'd suffered the shame of being fired, all because of the phony expense accounts he'd created to please her. The indignity had been terrible; the same woman who had brought him into the school, Karen Hitchcock, had been the one to usher him out. Douglas could only stand by stupidly as security guards changed the locks on his office door and his desk. Old letters from Robin were still tucked away in the top drawer. He'd never get them back.

Since that embarrassing day at Tufts, Douglas had thought only of Robin. He'd been following her for days, parking his car far away and using high-powered binoculars to watch her every move.

By following her, he'd learned that she had lied to him about no longer working in Saugus. Now she was getting what she deserved. He'd lost his job because of her. It was only reasonable that she lose her job, too.

He watched as Robin exited the health club, got into her Starlet, and drove away.

A while later, Douglas drove away, too. On the way home, he passed a billboard advertising a local businessman named "Mr. Schloss."

22.

John and Shirley Benedict received a phone call one evening late in January. A detective named Sheehan was calling.

Robin was in trouble, he said. She'd be in court the following day because of an arrest the previous year.

As far as Robin's parents knew, she'd left prostitution behind. She was employed by a professor at Tufts and was working hard with J. R. to fix up their new home in Malden. J. R. was allegedly working for a rare car dealer in Weymouth.

When Robin visited her family in Methuen, she was always dressed in fine clothes and expensive jewelry. It was only when they looked at her closely that her parents noticed dark circles under her heavily made-up eyes. Her beautiful hair now looked slightly tangled. She was showing the effects of cocaine use and several months of prostitution. Yet her parents were certain she was changing her life around. Perhaps this was the last arrest she'd have to deal with.

The Benedicts arrived at Boston Municipal Court the next morning. The place was buzzing with prostitutes. Robin emerged from the hubbub to greet her parents but was baffled to learn that Sheehan had called them.

Sheehan, in fact, only knew of Robin vaguely. He had been called out to one of her Back Bay trick pads a few months earlier. He remembered seeing a heavyset man waiting outside. He thought the man worked for Robin, because when Sheehan had arrived, it appeared the man sent her a signal. Then Sheehan saw a trick running out of her apartment. He'd seen Robin with the heavy man on other occasions, including court appearances. But that was all he knew of her. He certainly hadn't placed a call to the Benedicts.

As her parents tried to figure out who could've made the mysterious phone call, Robin changed the mood by presenting them to her boss.

Cheerfully, she introduced Professor William Douglas. He ambled over, wearing a heavy green winter coat that made him look even larger than usual. Douglas was charming and polite, using the manners that his mother had taught him back in his Lake Placid days, back before her mental faculties had dipped. Douglas told the Benedicts that he was writing a book and that Robin was his illustrator. He was in court to lend support, as he'd done for Robin's previous arrests.

Robin's parents were glad to meet the eminent professor who employed their daughter, but Shirley was uncertain about him. She knew how men acted around her daughter. By observing Douglas, she could tell Robin's so-called boss had a crush on her. Indeed, Douglas later told the Benedicts that he felt protective of Robin.

Shirley told Douglas about the phone call they'd received from someone pretending to be Sheehan. Douglas told Shirley that he, too, had been receiving crank calls lately. Regarding the calls, Douglas told John that if anyone ever tried to hurt Robin, he knew how to take care of the situation. Douglas explained that he had a special liquid in his laboratory, a poison so powerful that it would take only a single drop on a person's lips to kill them. Douglas dreamily described how it could dissolve an entire human being, including the bones and teeth.

Douglas made John and Shirley uneasy with his talk of dissolving bodies. Yet he seemed to genuinely care about their daughter. When Douglas asked if he could stay in touch in case of more crank calls, Shirley agreed.

As usual, Robin's case was "continued." She walked out of court again, just as she always had in the past.

That same morning, Robin took her mother aside and asked for a favor: If Douglas ever called, Robin said, please don't say anything about

J. R. She explained that her boss knew nothing about J. R. and didn't need to know.

• • •

Douglas had been desperate for a few weeks, unsure of his future. He'd even called Henry Spira, the animal rights advocate who had helped Tufts acquire the massive research funding from NEAVS, and asked him to speak to the dean of the medical school. Douglas had hoped Spira would convince the dean that his research work would override any major expenses he'd accrued. Spira wouldn't oblige.

Still, Douglas could feel his luck changing. Not only had Robin called him to accompany her to court—a sign that she still relied on him—but a few days later Douglas received an offer from his alma mater in Plattsburgh.

As soon as Tufts began investigating him, Douglas sent a resume to SUNY. In 1983, Douglas's reputation was such that there was nothing in the way of a background check; otherwise the hiring committee in Plattsburgh would've rejected a man who had padded his expense account to such a degree as Douglas had. Instead, SUNY was thrilled to offer a professorship to such an esteemed former student.

The new position didn't start until the following September, which gave Douglas seven months to relocate and iron out the problems with his marriage and with Robin.

Later that same month, Douglas was asked to come to Plattsburgh to codirect a weeklong seminar on tissue culture. An exuberant Douglas invited Robin to join him.

This may have been part of a plan to get Robin on the SUNY payroll, just as he'd done for her at Tufts. But from the tone of Douglas's letters, it was clear that Robin hesitated. She didn't want to be with Douglas for an entire week. She eventually agreed to spend just two days in Plattsburgh. Her decision made sense. She needed money, having been fired from the Saugus health club. Douglas was offering to pay her $1,000 a day, which was a nice stipend for a trip to Plattsburgh. She agreed to come on the second-to-last day of the seminar. They established that she would spend the night with him and attend the final day of the seminar at Douglas's side. This would be good for $2,000. Then she'd fly back to Boston.

Robin probably thought this seminar deal would be the last she'd ever see of Douglas. She had to get on without him and find another cash cow.

• • •

She arrived in Plattsburgh on February 17. As planned, Douglas met her at the airport.

The next day she accompanied him to the seminar. He introduced her as "Chris Costello," a graduate student. This, perhaps, was in case SUNY ever heard about the Tufts investigation into Robin Benedict.

Douglas must've enjoyed himself. No one in Plattsburgh knew about his problems at Tufts. Best of all, this was the college where he had once followed his fraternity brothers around like a loyal servant. Now he was an esteemed professor with a beautiful young woman at his side. He told his future colleagues that this Chris Costello girl was going to attend school in Plattsburgh and wanted to see the place for herself.

Yet some of the people at SUNY noticed something odd about Douglas's friend. She was wearing footwear that didn't quite match her otherwise smart ensemble and talking about flying in from Montreal, when there'd been no such flights.

The Plattsburgh secretaries had also noticed that Douglas seemed anxious in the days before her arrival and that he'd taken a number of calls from someone named Robin.

• • •

A series of events took place in the coming weeks.

Douglas and Robin argued over money; at one point the argument grew so heated that he experienced chest pains. Robin took Douglas to a nearby hospital in Lynn where doctors claimed nothing was wrong with him. It was more likely an anxiety attack or something as mundane as gas cramps. (Another possibility: Douglas was faking it. He was losing the argument and wanted to draw attention back to himself.)

Though Douglas was fine, this emergency room visit was significant, for it was there that Robin and Nancy first met. Robin introduced herself as Chris and left.

Nancy later asked her husband, "That's the girl, isn't it?'

The next morning Douglas called the Sharon police and said a woman was trying to extort money from him. An officer arrived and witnessed Douglas and Robin arguing in his front yard.

One week later, on March 2, Robin allegedly called Nancy Douglas at home.

"Bill wants to see me," she said, "but I no longer want to see him. Please keep him away."

Douglas would later say that he spoke to Robin soon after this phone call. He was upset that she had called Nancy, but Robin explained that J. R had forced her to make the call. Yet she was being truthful—she no longer wanted anything to do with him. Douglas pleaded with her to see him again, to "talk over our differences."

She agreed to meet, but only if he paid her $200. Douglas gave her a check for the amount, but when Robin tried to deposit it, the payment had been stopped, either by Douglas or Nancy.

According to a statement Douglas later gave, he spoke with Robin by phone on the afternoon of Friday, March 4. He claimed he was trying to "reason with her."

• • •

Robin spent part of Saturday, March 5, in Malden with J. R. At 3 p.m. she went out to buy a birthday gift for Taj, Savi and J. R.'s son. Robin was fond of the little boy; he was turning four years old the next day.

A witness saw Robin leaving the house that afternoon, wearing a lightweight tan jacket, slightly underdressed for a cold March afternoon.

At 7:45 p.m. Robin stopped by Good Time Charlie's to tell Savi that she would pick her and Taj up the next day for a birthday celebration. The gathering would take place at the Ground Round, a restaurant in the Prudential Center that was known for children's parties, complete with balloons and a mascot named Bingo the Clown.

An hour after planning the party, Robin was in Boston's West End with a new client, a well-to-do real estate entrepreneur named Nichols. It appeared Robin was trying to reinvent herself as a posh escort, perhaps to get out of the bleak arena of LaGrange Street and massage parlors. When Nichols had asked his doorman where he might find a first-class prostitute, the doorman immediately gave him the name of "Nadine," no doubt handing over one of the cards that Douglas had printed for her.

Nichols described Robin as attractive and eloquent, the sort of girl he could've taken anywhere. They didn't have sex; Nichols paid her just to sit and talk for a while, with the idea that they would someday meet for something more erotic. He would later say that he'd liked Robin, but she'd been in a hurry. She had scheduled to meet another client later that night. She explained that this other man was married, and she "had to sneak in between the wife and kids."

The businessman gave her thirty dollars for her time and promised they would meet again.

She left the West End at 9:45 p.m.

That was the last anyone saw of Robin Benedict.

Boston
Bunnies
SHOWS
MOVIES

Pilgrim
NUDES
BOOTHS
FIRST RUN
ULT FILMS
SCREEN COLOR
OPEN
ALL
NIGHT

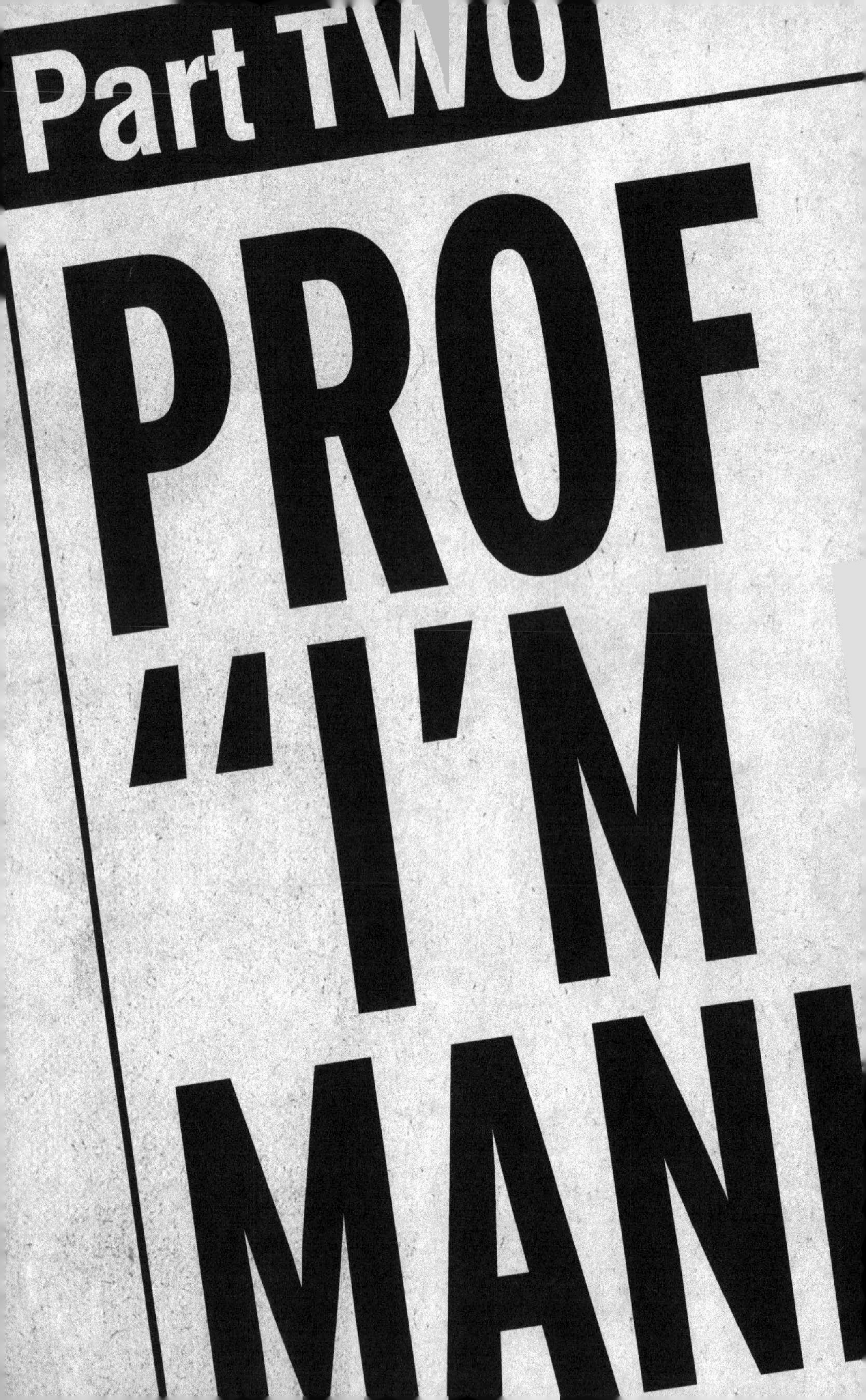
Part TWO
PROF
"I'M
MAN

SAYS:
NO SEX
AC!"

23.

On the morning of Sunday, March 6, 1983, State Trooper Paul Landry was thinking about his upcoming retirement.

He'd loved being a trooper, but he was plagued by headaches, hypertension, and insomnia. A recent divorce added to his stress. He was a young man but scheduled to retire in twenty-four days.

As he sat at his desk in the Foxborough State Police headquarters, absentmindedly eating a sandwich, Landry was given a surprise assignment: Two men had found something bizarre in a trash barrel on I-95; he was asked to go take a look at what they'd found.

At the rest stop, Landry took note of a plastic trash bag containing a tan corduroy jacket that smelled strongly of women's perfume, a blue cotton man's shirt—size seventeen—and a two-and-a-half-pound sledgehammer that was sticky with blood. There was blood on the head as well as the handle; stuck to the head was a single strand of long, dark hair. The clothing, he noticed, was also bloody. What had taken place?

Most telling was that the blood was still tacky, which meant the violence, whatever it may have been, had probably taken place the night before.

He and another trooper, Bud Petrucci, took pictures of the items from every conceivable angle.

Landry wondered if he had stumbled upon the so-called "Big Grab" that all troopers talked about, the high-profile case that created headlines. He'd been a trooper for nine years. Now, because of some guys collecting cans in Mansfield, was this his Big Grab at last?

In the years to come, some would say Landry was the wrong man for the job. He wasn't an investigator per se. He was a state trooper, a proud one, a collector of state trooper memorabilia, but he wasn't suited to a murder investigation. Yet others would consider the amount of work he did in a brief time and proclaim him the case's unsung hero.

• • •

While Paul Landry was beginning his investigation, Billy Dwyer received a frantic call from Savi: Robin was missing.

Dwyer met Savi at the Hotel Bradford, an elegant old Boston landmark not far from the Combat Zone. Savi was a wreck, nervously explaining that Robin had gone out the night before and had not returned. She'd missed Taj's party. Savi emphasized that it was not like Robin to miss a kid's birthday.

Savi claimed Robin was on her way to Douglas's house to get some money he owed her. Savi had called Douglas that morning to ask if he'd seen Robin. Douglas said only that Robin had stopped by but had left his place to go to Charlestown.

Savi was easily excitable, and Dwyer knew it was common for a prostitute to simply take off and never be seen again. He doubted the police would take much interest in Robin not showing up for a birthday party. Still, Savi's suspicion was eating at her.

"It's the doctor," Savi said. "It's gotta be."

• • •

The next day, J. R. walked into the office of private detective Jack DeRosa. He explained that his girlfriend had been missing since Saturday night. She had gone to the home of a man named William Douglas in Sharon to collect some income tax papers he'd been holding for her. She'd never returned.

DaRosa had been with Boston's Central Secret Service Bureau since 1973. Divorced and a bit of a recluse, he liked the hours and legwork that a missing person's case entailed. Tall, strongly built, slightly rumpled, middle-aged, and with a propensity for cheap watches, he could've been a character from an Ed McBain novel. He always carried a Colt .38 Special and took monthly target practice at a gun range, just in case.

He noticed J. R.'s gold jewelry and manicured fingernails. In DaRosa's experience, those were trademarks of a pimp. He was wary. Still, J. R. put down $300 as a deposit and promised to bring in another $1,200 to cover DaRosa's fee.

DaRosa advised his new client to file a report with the Malden police. J. R. hesitated, since he had his own record of arrests, which was probably why he'd come to a private investigation agency in the first place, but he went ahead and followed DaRosa's advice. Indeed, the Malden police immediately understood that Robin was a prostitute and that J. R. was a pimp. Regardless, Robin's name was put into the teletype as a "missing person."

DaRosa and his partner, Jim Smith, spent part of Monday at Tufts, hoping to find information about Douglas. Then they went out to Sharon and snooped around his home. Their efforts at Tufts turned up nothing. No one was home at the Douglas place. DaRosa tucked his card in the door.

Meanwhile, J. R. called Nancy Douglas that night and, pretending to be a detective, asked to speak to her husband. From Nancy he learned that the professor had left for Washington by train and would be staying at the Hotel Washington on Pennsylvania Avenue, in room 742.

J. R. relayed this information to DaRosa on Tuesday morning.

• • •

DaRosa and Smith were soon in Washington, driving a rental car to the hotel where Douglas was staying.

Standing outside Douglas's hotel room, DaRosa could overhear him talking on the phone.

Douglas sounded agitated. He was telling someone that he had not seen Robin since Saturday night at midnight. It was later revealed that Douglas was talking to Savi, who was concerned about her missing friend. DaRosa heard Douglas say Robin had left to go to a party in Charlestown to meet a friend named Joe.

When DaRosa heard Douglas hang up the phone, he knocked on the door. Douglas answered. DaRosa was surprised by what he saw. Douglas didn't look like a professor. He looked like a man on a weekend bender, wearing a dirty white T-shirt, slacks, and no shoes. Completing the disheveled picture was a large white bandage on his forehead.

DaRosa showed Douglas his identification. The professor examined it as DaRosa told him the search was on for Robin Benedict.

"How did you even find me?" Douglas asked. He was more than four hundred miles from Boston.

DaRosa walked into the room and started firing questions.

Douglas admitted that he knew Robin. She was a prostitute, he said, from Good Time Charlie's. Douglas added that Robin had worked for him at Tufts and that he had gone to court with her a few times.

Douglas repeated what he had said on the phone, that he had seen Robin on Saturday, that she had visited his house to drop off some sketches and collect some paperwork, but had left around midnight.

DaRosa asked if Douglas had ever had an affair with this prostitute, and if they'd had an argument on Saturday.

Douglas said no.

"What happened to your head?" DaRosa asked.

Douglas explained that he had bumped into a cabinet door.

This didn't sound right to DaRosa. Douglas looked like he had been in a fight. The bandage on his head, as Billy Dwyer would later describe, looked like a patch on a blown tire.

"Where is Robin Benedict?" DaRosa asked.

Douglas froze.

The detective looked around the hotel room. Jokingly, he pointed to the bed and asked, "Is she under here?"

Continuing in this jokey vein, DaRosa and Smith checked the bathroom and closets. Then they asked more questions.

"Why are you in Washington?" "When did you arrive?" "Why did you take the Amtrak instead of flying?" "Do you have any idea where Benedict might be?"

Douglas had an answer for everything. He'd taken the Amtrak instead of flying because he was behind in his paperwork; he thought a long train ride would give him a chance to catch up. He'd left from the Westwood train station; his wife had dropped him off. He'd needed to go to Washington to take part in a board meeting for the Veterans Administration. As for Robin, he had no idea of her whereabouts. Douglas mentioned that she had said something about a fight with her boyfriend, a guy named Clarence Rogers. Maybe Rogers had something to do with her disappearance, Douglas said.

Well, DaRosa thought, Douglas is blaming Rogers, and Rogers is blaming Douglas.

DaRosa thanked Douglas for his time and then went to his own room to call J. R.

The pimp said Robin might be somewhere in Washington with Douglas, staying at another hotel. He added that Douglas had once promised to take Robin to the Virgin Islands. J. R. felt she might already be in St. Thomas, waiting to be joined by the professor.

"Keep asking him questions," J. R. said.

An hour later, DaRosa visited Douglas again, asking about the bandage on his forehead. Douglas gave a different answer than before, saying he'd been mugged at the Washington Amtrak station. A couple of guys had tried to grab his briefcase, and in the scuffle, he'd been hit on the head. Douglas assured DaRosa that he'd informed the local police about the attempted robbery.

DaRosa and Smith returned to Boston the next morning. They'd learned little about Douglas, but they'd made him nervous. The guy had changed his story about the bandage, which was enough to make DaRosa suspicious of him. During the flight home, DaRosa couldn't forget the way Douglas had stared at him.

There'd been a moment in the hotel room when DaRosa had looked through Douglas's suitcase. He quickly fingered through the contents and found nothing. Satisfied, he thanked Douglas for letting him poke around.

But DaRosa had missed something. Buried within the clothes in Douglas's suitcase was a set of license plates. DaRosa's fingers must've fluttered right over them. Had he noticed the plates and run a check on the number—655HXG—he would've learned that they had been taken from a Toyota Starlet belonging to Robin Benedict.

And he would've had an explanation for the strange look on Douglas's face.

• • •

As soon as Douglas returned from Washington, he called John Benedict.

"Do you know where Robin is?" Douglas said.

"No," Benedict said. "We've been trying to get ahold of her."

Douglas explained that he had seen Robin on Saturday night, but she'd left to go to Charlestown. He added that Robin had given him instructions. If anything happened to her, Douglas said, she wanted John Benedict to keep J. R. from getting her jewelry and furs.

To Benedict, Douglas sounded like he was reading a prepared speech.

24.

The *Boston Herald* was the city's sleazy scandal rag. Previously known as the *Herald American*, the publication had nearly gone out of business a year earlier but was now enjoying a rebirth. New owners converted it to a tabloid-sized newspaper and focused on the trashier aspect of Boston news, namely rape trials and street-corner shootouts. Overnight, the paper had created a scrappy new image for itself.

A few days after Robin's vanishing, John Benedict visited the *Herald*'s office. Among the staff members working that day was Shelley Murphy, a young reporter. Nearly forty years later she still recalled vividly how Robin's father came to the newspaper, "holding a photo of his beautiful, missing daughter, begging us to write a story about her disappearance."

The assistant managing editor, Charlie O'Brien, was intrigued. O'Brien liked stories about missing girls, especially when they were pretty. This one sounded tabloid ready. He gave the assignment to Murphy. "I jumped on the story," Murphy said, "and interviewed many people that first day, including Douglas."

She quickly learned that Robin's boyfriend was reputed to be a pimp. When she spoke to J. R., he suggested Douglas might have harmed Robin. J. R. told Murphy that Robin had actually spoken to Douglas's wife, asking her to tell Douglas to leave her alone.

Murphy drove out to Sandy Ridge Circle and spoke briefly to Douglas's wife, who claimed to know nothing about Robin. As Murphy paused to ask another question, Nancy slammed the door on her.

Later that day, Murphy received a surprise phone call. On the other end of the line was the soft voice of William Douglas.

He gave a brief account of his relationship with Robin. He said she was a graphic artist who worked for him. She'd been to his house on Saturday night, but he knew nothing about her whereabouts since then. Douglas also acknowledged that Robin was a prostitute, but he denied ever using her services. Douglas added that Robin's boyfriend was a problem.

Murphy felt the story made no sense. She didn't understand why Robin had gone to Douglas's house at such a late hour. When she asked Douglas for more details, he went quiet. Then he politely asked Murphy to let him know if she learned anything else.

Douglas said Robin was a nice girl and he wanted to help in any way that he could.

When Murphy explained to her editor that Robin was a prostitute, the story was no longer considered worthy of the front page. Buried in the middle of the next day's edition was Murphy's story about a missing sex worker from Malden.

The article enraged Robin's father. He immediately called Murphy and scolded her, claiming the story was disastrous for the family. How, he asked, could she call Robin a prostitute? Murphy endured John Benedict's anger, but felt she had merely written the truth.

That afternoon Murphy received another call. It was Douglas again. He had liked the story and wanted to talk to Murphy some more.

O'Brien, already bored by the missing girl, told Murphy to leave it alone. He also advised her to stay away from Douglas.

25.

New Englanders got their first real glimpse of Robin Benedict when a Boston television news program aired a missing person's report on the weekend of March 12, five days after J. R. had gone to the police. She was described as a young woman from Malden, but few details were given. Her father had provided a recent picture of Robin. State Trooper Paul Landry didn't see the report but learned about it Monday morning. He overheard two men discussing it, the gist of their talk having to do with Robin's attractiveness.

Landry, thinking of the perfumed jacket found at the rest stop, promptly called the Malden police to see if they had information about the missing woman. Sergeant Charles Borstel informed Landry that Robin had been on her way to meet William Douglas in Sharon. Landry calculated that Sharon was only five miles from where the hammer and jacket were found. Borstel had also learned from the Sharon police about an incident where Robin had been at Douglas's home a few weeks earlier, where they'd yelled at each other on the front lawn until a police officer brought them to the station to cool down.

By this time, DaRosa had already spoken to Borstel, describing his meeting with Douglas in Washington. He told Borstel that Douglas had seemed jumpy. To Landry, Douglas was definitely a person of interest.

Later, DaRosa and Smith went to the Foxborough police barracks where they met Robin's father and Landry. John Benedict was on edge as he met the detectives. He showed them the picture of Robin that he'd been handing out. They were surprised at how pretty she was, but they underplayed the moment. Landry cut to the chase.

"Did your daughter own a tan, corduroy blazer?" he asked.

"Yes," John Benedict said. He explained that Robin had worn a tan blazer to her parent's house the week before, and had even offered to give it to her sister, Rhonda. The sisters had joked about the jacket, Rhonda saying she didn't like the collar. Robin hadn't visited in some time, so her father had taken a special interest in the way she'd been dressed. It had been a new jacket, one he'd never seen on his daughter.

Landry informed Robin's father that such a jacket had been found in a rest area on I-95, along with a hammer and a man's bloody shirt. John Benedict was shaken by the information.

"Maybe it means nothing," Landry said.

When Landry spoke privately to DaRosa and Smith, they were divided on who was the more interesting suspect. Landry leaned toward Douglas, but the detectives thought J. R. was involved.

Landry arranged for J. R. to meet him at the state police chemical lab on Commonwealth Avenue, and to bring some of Robin's perfume samples. John Benedict was invited, too. It was going to be an intense afternoon.

First, John identified the tan jacket as the same kind Robin had worn. Then, fearing what may have happened to his daughter, he began crying.

J. R. grew hysterical, crying to the point where he couldn't breathe. He yelled, "That's it! That's it!"

Not only did J. R. recognize the jacket, but he also noticed the perfume on it was the type Robin wore. J. R. had brought a perfume sample from home, sprayed into a plastic bag, and allowed Landry to smell it. It was a match, for sure.

As J. R. cried, Landry grew skeptical. He thought J. R. was putting on an act. When Robin's father left, Landry took J. R. downstairs and spent the next four hours interviewing him.

J. R. started by admitting Robin was a prostitute. Then he explained that Douglas was a client who had grown obsessed with her. Douglas hadn't wanted much sexual contact; he'd only wanted Robin's companionship, which cost $100 per hour.

According to J. R., Robin indulged the professor at first but was tired of him. She'd actually called Douglas's wife a few days before she disappeared and told her to keep her husband away. The wife seemed to understand, but Douglas was relentless. From J. R., Landry learned about the stalking and how Douglas had tampered with Robin's answering machines; J. R. also suspected Douglas had been calling the vice cops on Robin and breaking into her trick pads.

J. R. also admitted that Robin had encouraged Douglas to steal from Tufts. This was key for the investigation, in that it linked the pair in a criminal activity, one that may have led to a falling out.

One detail J. R. changed was the reason Robin had gone to see Douglas on March 5. He'd originally told DaRosa that she had gone to pick up some tax papers, and that there may have been some sort of trip to the Virgin Islands. Now, as J. R. recounted the story for Landry, he claimed Robin had gone there to tell Douglas she didn't want to see him again.

J. R. also obliged Landry with a timeline of Saturday, March 5. He described Robin as being in a happy mood, leaving Malden in the afternoon. J. R. went to a friend's house in Boston but was back home by 8:30 p.m. He spent the night watching television. Since Douglas appeared to be spying on them via their answering machine, they had since hired an answering service. J. R. claimed a message came in for Robin at approximately 10 p.m. from "Joe in Charlestown," something about an all-night party. A second call came at 11:45 p.m., from Robin for J. R., saying she was on her way to Joe's. Another call came the next afternoon, purportedly from Robin, who claimed to be at "John's at Longfellow."

J. R. heard nothing more from Robin, which was unusual. She was always in touch with him, no matter where she went.

"Why did you hire detectives?" Landry asked.

"Because I love her," J. R. said. "We were planning to be married."

Landry didn't know what to think. He was still suspicious of J. R. Since when did prostitutes go to a customer's house to "break up"?

He started slamming him with questions: "Why did you kill her? Just tell me where the body is . . ."

J. R. looked upset but remained silent.

Then Landry tried to trip him up about the perfume.

"How did you know to bring that type of perfume to the lab?"

"I bought it for her," J. R. said. "Molinard was the only kind she wore."

J. R. slumped in his chair. Landry was starting to believe him.

Throughout the interrogation, J. R. had avoided naming himself as Robin's pimp. When Landry did a background check, he found that J. R. had a few arrests on his record, but no pimping charges. There was, however, a warrant for a traffic violation. In a gesture of goodwill, and to keep him talking, Landry assured J. R. that he wouldn't be arrested but made him promise to go to court and pay his fine.

Perhaps the biggest contribution J. R. made to the investigation was in turning over a collection of Douglas's love letters to Robin. The letters showed Douglas to be a desperate man-child starved for attention. They were full of spelling and grammatical errors unbefitting a professor, as if the words had come tumbling out at great speed. They were probably written in between his classes, or whenever he had a spare moment at home, without his wife or kids around.

Douglas never mentioned anything sexual in the letters, only saying repeatedly that he couldn't live without Robin, that she was his "treasure," his "fantastic lady," his "guiding light." This was apparently based on little more than walks in the park, going to movies, and occasionally sharing a pizza.

Sometimes he addressed her as "Nadine" and took on a businesslike tone, scheduling their meetings like a teacher filling out a daily planner. In one letter he wrote:

"Sunday, July 18th—2–4 p.m. Pier 4 to celebrate your Birthday

Wednesday, July 21st—You work 4 p.m. until 2:30 a.m. We meet 2:30 a.m.–5:30 a.m. at my house in Sharon. We drive down in your car together."

But in other letters, he dripped with cheesy romance, droning on about Robin's "warm, wonderful smile," and "the special things we do and talk about. . . ." He alluded to Robin "squeezing" his hands and arms, and the way she called him on the phone to say, "What's up Doc, would you like to get together?"

There was even a letter where Douglas recalled Robin playing her flute for him—"Amazing Grace"—which had to be a first in the annals of Combat Zone prostitutes and johns. Once a White Eagle, always a White Eagle.

It seemed Robin admired Douglas early on. Eventually, when some of Robin's correspondence was found, it appeared she was playful and even curious about his work. At least she pretended to be interested. Over time, Douglas's letters became more emotional, and Robin started to view him as pathetic.

Robin forbid Douglas to write "I love you," so he would end many of his notes by writing "I love *seeing* you," a way to use the words "I love you" and perhaps tease her a bit in the process. John Brady, editor of the *Boston Globe Magazine*, found this to be a sign of Douglas's passive aggression, and that he "seemed to enjoy irritating Robin, then apologizing afterward as the pleasure of guilt washed over him."

Douglas wallowed in the guilt game, just as he'd done as a child back in Lake Placid.

The letters also showed a downturn in the relationship. Starting in October, Douglas seemed overly worried at having offended Robin, alluding in one letter to having insulted her "house and furniture." He apologized many times, claiming that she had "hurt" him, and he was "striking out defensively." He wrote about being "embarrassed and ashamed for the way I acted," ending the note with "PLEASE FORGIVE ME DEAR!!!!!!!!!!!!!"

The Douglas letters would play a major part in the investigation, with people examining them for clues as to what happened. More letters would be discovered in the weeks to come, with particular focus on a lengthy note written on January 3, 1983. This was Douglas's *chef-d'oeuvre*, a sonic wail from a man under great stress.

Written when his world was capsizing—Robin had cut him off, his wife was wise to his "girlfriend," and Tufts was investigating his expenses—Douglas pleaded with Robin to allow him back into her life. The dense paragraphs were full of remorse at how things had turned out. Douglas apologized for his immaturity, promising to "act like an adult when I interact with you and not some lovestruck teenager." He even wrote about inventing a machine that would take him back in time to fix everything that had gone wrong for them.

The letters were a bombshell. This was not a traditional situation between a lounge lizard and a Combat Zone prostitute. It was a strangely emotional relationship involving two manipulative people, one of whom was missing, the other still at large.

26.

Norfolk County District Attorney William Delahunt always looked his best when he addressed a television audience. Dapper, gray-haired, distinguished in the way of certain Boston politicians, the forty-one-year-old DA spoke before WHDH Channel 7 News cameras and informed viewers that Robin Benedict "might very well be alive at this point in time."

Delahunt was a veteran campaigner, seasoned in the law and local politics. He was, as one journalist recalled, a "tenacious do-gooder." He was also a brazen showboat who loved the media. Appearing on television was typical for Delahunt, but his comments irritated Landry. This was not the time to spread false hope, and such an announcement might soften the investigation. Besides, this was Landry's Big Grab. He didn't want Delahunt to ruin it.

The *Herald* followed up with a similar report that Robin was alive, based on statements from Robin's neighbors at 397 Beacon Street, her last trick pad. Many were certain they'd seen her somewhere, checking her mail or walking down a street. Some were adamant that they had heard sounds coming from her apartment in the days after her disappearance. Some swore they'd heard flute music.

Landry knew better. With keys borrowed from J. R., he and DaRosa had visited the Beacon Street trick pad. The place was abandoned; no one had been there for days.

Yet some of the building's tenants insisted Robin had recently been there. They'd even heard someone singing, someone with a high voice that they assumed was Robin.

One neighbor was convinced he had seen Robin in the lobby, but when pressed by Landry for the exact date, he admitted he'd seen her on Friday the fourth, before she'd disappeared.

Landry wrote off these "witnesses" as mistaken, and the *Herald* as wrong.

Judging by the eerie look of the deserted apartment, he was more convinced than ever that Robin was dead.

27.

John Payton Kivlan was a Norfolk County assistant district attorney. He was in his late thirties, a well-educated local man that some might've called "lace curtain Irish." Based on his unshakable belief in the legal system and a no-frills approach to his job, Kivlan's colleagues had nicknamed him "Johnny America." But despite the joking that went on behind his back, Kivlan had a growing reputation as possibly the best prosecutor in Massachusetts. Delahunt put him on the missing girl case.

One of Kivlan's first steps was to summon Landry to his Dedham headquarters, a decidedly nonglamorous attic office he shared with two assistants. It was a grim old place known as the "Gray House," badly lit and poorly heated. This drab setting was where Kivlan forged his career, one that saw him prosecute a frightening gallery of rogues, from white-collar crooks to such raving heels as William Marguetty, the "South Shore Stabber."

In the dim atmosphere, Landry reported the details of his investigation. Kivlan appreciated Landry's work and gave him his blessing to continue. This was unusual since Landry wasn't an experienced investigator, but the trooper had thus far done an excellent job.

Not all of his work was paying off, though. Along with Sergeant. Charles Borstel of Malden, Landry paid a visit to J. R. at home. They searched the premises but found nothing that might incriminate J. R. Landry also drove out to Sharon and interviewed Douglas's neighbors. No one recalled anything unusual happening on the night Robin disappeared. As far as they knew, Douglas was a decent family man, a respected figure in the community.

Subpoenas for Robin's credit cards and telephone were issued, including all messages taken for her through Americall, the answering service she and J. R. used. Landry learned that someone with a shrill voice had been leaving messages, someone identified as "Mr. Rogers," and was asking for messages left for J. R. and Robin. Employees at Americall felt the person was trying to disguise his identity.

Landry also presented Kivlan with Douglas's love letters. After reading them more than once, Kivlan concluded that Douglas played a role in Robin's disappearance. It was crucial, Kivlan felt, to question the professor in more detail.

Given his instructions by Kivlan, Landry called Douglas at home and asked him to come to Foxborough for an interview.

"I need a little time," Douglas said. "I've got to think about it."

28.

The Foxborough barracks was and still is located on Route 1, approximately two miles from the stadium where the New England Patriots play. The enormous building was probably intimidating if one walked in with something to hide. Douglas arrived for his interview in the afternoon and made himself comfortable in the barracks kitchen. When Landry went out to meet him, Douglas was sitting peacefully, reading a newspaper.

Douglas had already been to the Malden police station for an interview. Borstel admitted to being intimidated by this gigantic professor who was obviously larger and more intelligent than most people he met on the job. Douglas told him Robin was a prostitute and he confessed to being an occasional client, but he knew nothing about her disappearance. When Borstel brought up the injury on his forehead, Douglas said he'd been attacked in Chinatown and hit with a lead pipe. This was the third explanation Douglas had given for the wound.

Landry immediately saw that Douglas was a large man. He was soft in appearance, but massive. Landry remembered the shirt found at the rest stop. It was just right for a man of Douglas's size. While Landry made coffee, he looked over at Douglas and noticed a long, fresh scar that started near his hairline.

Landry read him his rights and proceeded to question him for four hours.

Douglas spoke calmly, but gave more details than he'd given yet about his relationship with Robin.

According to Douglas, he'd placed an ad in a newspaper the previous year looking for a graphic design artist. Robin had answered it.

Landry took notes. What newspaper? Douglas couldn't remember.

Douglas told Landry that Robin revealed that she was a prostitute and asked Douglas if he was interested in being a client. He turned her down at first but eventually accepted the offer.

Douglas said that he and Robin sometimes went to movies or had lunch together. He admitted that he saw her often and that he liked to meet Robin at two or three in the morning so he could be her last client. Douglas even told the story of how Robin had been banned from Good Time Charlie's for grabbing a trick in the parking lot.

Douglas appeared to enjoy telling stories about the Combat Zone, as if he wanted Landry to know he was comfortable in such seedy surroundings, like an unpopular boy assuring his parents that he was a pal to all the cool kids.

He also explained that Robin was spending most of her nights in motels along Route 99. Her boyfriend was bringing other women home, Douglas said, and Robin wanted to be elsewhere on those nights.

Landry asked about the injury to his head. Douglas had already given DaRosa two explanations for the wound, and a third to Borstel. Now he offered Landry a fourth. He described being mugged by a couple of young hoodlums in Chinatown. They'd yanked his briefcase from his hands and ran away. As they tussled, the robbers hit Douglas with his own briefcase.

"What was in the briefcase?" Landry asked.

"Important papers," Douglas said.

"Did you report the theft?"

Douglas said yes.

Then Douglas talked about the night Robin disappeared.

Robin had called him that day to say she was fighting with her boyfriend. She wanted to deliver some slides to Douglas but wasn't sure how late she would be because of this fight with J. R.

She eventually arrived at 10:30 p.m. Douglas was alone in the house because his wife had gone shopping in New Hampshire and his children were out. The slides, he explained, had to do with his work at Tufts, something to do with cosmetics companies testing their products on the eyes of rabbits.

After presenting the slides to Douglas and even watching a few projected on a wall, Robin said she had to go to Charlestown to meet a client named "Joe." She was gone by midnight.

Landry gave Douglas some coffee and had him tell the story again. The trooper's plan was to keep Douglas talking so he might make a mistake or contradict what he'd already said. Douglas complied, but now he was making detours in the telling.

"He'd string you along," Landry recalled, "And try to get you off track."

Douglas added a new section to the story, recounting an event from before Robin's disappearance. He described going to see the new Dustin Hoffman comedy, *Tootsie*. He had parked his car on Marlborough Street near one of Robin's trick pads, but when he came out of the theater he saw that his car had been stolen.

The next afternoon, after a session with Robin at the Susse Chalet in Boston, Douglas claimed he was abducted by three black men and thrown into a white van. He said they punched him and yelled at him to stay away from Robin. After an hour or so of rough treatment, they pushed Douglas out of the van into an alley in Kenmore Square where, to his surprise, his stolen car was parked.

He didn't report the incident to police because he didn't want his family to know he'd been with a prostitute.

Landry needed a break. Douglas was an unusual man. He told his stories with utter confidence, even when they made no sense. Sometimes he seemed to make things up on the spot. It was also odd that sometimes he referred to Robin as "Nadine."

Landry made a quick call to Kivlan. The assistant DA said simply to keep Douglas talking. The plan was to get enough information to be granted a search warrant for Douglas's home.

When Landry returned for another round of questions, he asked Douglas to describe the events of February, when the Sharon police had been called to his home.

Douglas told a drawn-out tale of Robin trying to extort money from him. She had stolen some research papers out of his briefcase and was demanding he pay her for them. He called the Sharon police, he said. An officer came by and took them to the police station where he advised them to seek counseling.

Douglas described for Landry how his relationship with Robin had become difficult, and how his wife Nancy knew about it. He described the incident where Robin had driven Douglas to the hospital when he'd had chest pains, and Nancy and Robin had seen each other in the emergency room. But Douglas also claimed Robin eventually returned the papers, and they resolved their disagreement.

Landry kept probing. He asked if there had been some kind of fight between Douglas and Robin. At the suggestion that some violence had taken place, Landry detected a slight change in Douglas's body language and attitude. Douglas was breathing heavily and staring off into space, as if the four-hour interview had finally buckled him.

"He seemed nervous," Landry remembered. "I kept thinking, 'Why is this guy so nervous?'"

For a moment, Landry thought the professor might confess to everything. But nothing came.

Landry prodded a bit, telling Douglas it would help everyone if he just told what he knew.

Douglas was silent.

Then, as firmly as his squeaky voice would allow, Douglas said that he hadn't done anything to Robin. He also denied being in love with her.

"Not now or at any time," Douglas said.

They'd reached a stalemate, but Landry was satisfied that he'd done some damage.

"I'll be talking to your wife next," Landry said.

This was a nice little potshot to end the encounter, something for Douglas to think about on his way home.

Landry had something to think about, too.

"My first impression was almost empathy," Landry remembered in 2021. "He was a big fat guy, and he got involved with this beautiful woman who was far out of his league.

"I understood how he fell for her. Maybe he thought he could win her over, that she would start to respect him. So he insinuated himself into her life. He's taking her to shows, not realizing that he was a laughingstock. I'm sure people saw them together and just laughed; they knew what was going on. Most people wouldn't even try to win her over, but he had the fantasy going."

Landry continued: "He was a decent guy, I think, but he was seduced by the idea that he could impress her with how smart he was. And he was smart. A genius. But he wasn't a smart murderer."

29.

Landry picked up Nancy Douglas in Sharon and drove her to the barracks in Foxborough.

As he drove, Landry shared what he'd learned about her husband. He explained that Douglas had been unfaithful to her, spending time with a prostitute; and that he was a prime suspect in a woman's disappearance.

Nancy gently deflected the accusations. She didn't believe any of it, she said. Her husband had nothing to do with Robin disappearing.

During her interview in Foxborough, Nancy gave a measured recital of events from the night when Robin arrived to meet Douglas. Nancy claimed to have been out with her son Billy, not returning until 11:30 p.m. When she noticed Robin's car in the driveway, she decided not to pull in. She didn't want to be in the house while Robin was there. As she left the cul-de-sac, she picked up Pammy, who was coming home from babysitting. (The youngest child, Johnny, was staying at a friend's house.) Nancy drove around for forty-five minutes until she noticed Robin's car was gone. That meant Nancy and the two kids could go inside. There was nothing unusual going on, she said. Her husband was in bed asleep. She went to sleep on the living room couch.

Landry asked about the injury to her husband's head. Nancy said she hadn't noticed it but admitted she didn't pay much attention to her husband lately. They were not on good terms because of his relationship with Robin.

She'd given her story in the same dull tone that Douglas had used in his own interview, as if they'd rehearsed together. Like her husband, she sometimes referred to Robin as "Nadine."

At the interview's conclusion, Landry gave Nancy a ride back to Sharon. She asked to be dropped off at the top of the street rather than in front of her house; she didn't want the neighbors to see her getting out of a police car.

Later, the neighbors would see all sorts of police cars. The search warrant had been granted.

• • •

A five-car caravan arrived at 38 Sandy Ridge Circle carrying a team of investigators. Along with Landry was Lieutenant James Sharkey, a veteran of home searches who had been assigned to lead the raid on Douglas's home. There was also police chemist Ron Kaufman, and Corporal William Anderson, a photographer and fingerprint specialist. Assistant

DA Matthew Connolly was part of the team. He'd helped write the affidavit that led to the search, the gist being that the blood and items found at the rest stop may be a match to blood and items found in the Douglas house. Two road troopers were on hand to secure the area, as was John Kivlan, who would remain outside with Connelly.

It was 12:40 a.m. The house was dark. Landry pounded on the door and rang the bell.

Douglas answered. He was sleepy, rubbing his eyes. As Landry recalled, Douglas was wearing "rumpled old pajamas." He and his wife had been away in Plattsburgh for two days. Since it seemed they were going to be moving there soon, they were looking at the community and checking out real estate. Now a trooper was at his door, and several cars were parked along the street.

Landry offered Douglas a choice: He could tell what had happened to Robin Benedict, or his house would be searched.

Douglas said he had already told them all he knew. Landry showed him the search warrant.

"Why don't you come in," Douglas said.

Landry walked in and was shocked.

The Douglas home looked like that of a family that had hit rock bottom. There didn't appear to be a section of the house that wasn't piled high with trash or soiled laundry. The mess transcended ordinary sloppiness and leaned into a kind of madness, exemplified by one unforgettable image: an unwrapped stick of butter that had been left in the middle of the living room floor.

"I'd imagined Douglas would live in a tidy place," Landry recalled. "But this was just the opposite. Things were thrown everywhere. I remember an empty bucket of popcorn in the bathtub. You had to step over a TV set to get to the toilet."

Sharkey noticed a note stuck to the refrigerator. He assumed it had been written by one of the Douglas children. It read: "Won't somebody please clean up this house."

It was the kind of home where terminally depressed people might live, people too emotionally stunned to take out the garbage.

"I think the house reflected Nancy's frame of mind at the time," Landry said in 2021. "She'd given up. Her husband had spent every cent they had. I felt bad for her. She was frumpy, sort of a Margaret Thatcher–looking woman, and here was her husband having an affair with a beautiful young girl. The way the house looked was Nancy's way of saying, 'I just don't give a shit anymore.'"

Douglas seemed oblivious to the condition of his home. He guided the investigators in and stood by as they waded through the mess.

Nancy and the children could be heard stirring in another part of the house. Sharkey saw an opening. He approached Nancy and took her aside. He showed her the hammer that had been found at the rest stop; she claimed to have never seen it.

Sharkey then showed the hammer to Douglas, who also denied ever seeing it. Sharkey handed the hammer back to Kaufman, who gingerly placed it into the evidence bag.

Then Sharkey produced the blue shirt. Douglas said that it "might" have been his.

Nancy agreed that her husband had shirts just like it, and when Sharkey pointed out that a rip in the underarm of the shirt had been sewn. Nancy admitted that she occasionally mended her husband's shirts. When Sharkey asked what sort of thread she used, Nancy showed him a spool that matched the thread in the rest-stop shirt.

Satisfied, Sharkey told Nancy that she and the children were not needed, but he wanted to interview Douglas.

Sharkey brought Douglas to the kitchen. They sat at the table, brushing aside the stacks of dirty plates and silverware. It would be Douglas's first interview with a detective of Sharkey's caliber. Sharkey was orderly and friendly, a convivial Irish American lawman with many years of experience. To the veteran's surprise, the professor was cocky.

"Douglas was arrogant that night," Sharkey later explained to *New York* magazine. "He was looking down his nose at me."

Sensing Douglas felt superior to him, Sharkey played to the professor's vanity. He acted a little dumb as he took Douglas's statement, stopping to ask for the correct spelling on certain words. Sharkey felt if Douglas were cocky enough, he'd say something incriminating.

Meanwhile, Landry explored the house. Two weeks had passed since Robin's disappearance. Douglas would've had time to get rid of evidence or signs of a struggle. So rather than look for bloodstains or anything else so obvious, Landry was looking for areas that might be recently scrubbed, or even painted, anything that might be amiss.

With this in mind, Landry checked out what appeared to be the master bedroom. It was as cluttered as the rest of the house, but Landry spotted a Sanyo tape recorder and a pile of cassette tapes. He popped a tape into the machine and heard the unmistakable voice of Douglas making a call to the health club in Saugus, talking about "that whore from the Combat Zone." Other cassettes were found, including one with an unintelligible conversation between Douglas and Savi.

Nosing around the bedroom, Landry then turned up another collection of letters between Douglas and Robin, plus a stack of phone bills from Robin and J. R.'s Natick apartment. The bills appeared to be covered in Douglas's handwriting as if he'd made notes alongside the various phone numbers.

Landry's next target was the bedroom closet. On the floor was a Kodak carousel projector, the sort used by families to show their vacation slides. Beneath the projector was a Seagram's box. Landry moved the projector and looked inside the box. He found a pile of hardcore pornographic magazines, what Landry recalled as "the professor's secret stash." Most were publications about sadomasochism. Landry then found a large envelope bursting with clippings from newspapers, some from as far away as New York. It was all sexual material, some to do with private sex clubs and prostitutes, many with pictures of women advertising themselves as sex slaves. One of them, a scantily clad woman tied with ligatures, offered very descriptive services. The ad read: *Spank me, whip me, tie me up—I am your slave. Use me for your pleasures and fantasies. I am yours to command.*

Was Douglas planning a trip to New York to find a sex slave? And what sort of man kept such material in such proximity to his wife and children?

Landry found another large envelope that held the most notable find of the search: a pair of sheer pink women's underwear. Landry lifted the panties out and noticed they were wrapped around something small: a hunk of old chewing gum balled up inside a Trident wrapper.

This envelope also held two address books, including Robin's "black book" with 249 clients listed by nickname and coded phone number, as well as a stack of credit cards belonging to Robin. By now the other troopers had found a yellow plastic bag containing a woman's pocketbook and a flute.

The pocketbook reeked of the same perfume found on the tan jacket. The contents of the pocketbook included keys to a hotel room, condoms, cherry-flavored lip balm, and ticket stubs from an Olivia Newton-John concert.

On the closet floor Landry saw a Leica camera bag. He opened it to find keys to a safety deposit box, handwritten notes by Douglas about his situation at Tufts, including notes about Robin's involvement in the scandal, and a copy of the *Boston Herald*'s first article concerning the search for Robin: "DISTRAUGHT DAD HUNTS DAUGHTER."

Landry ran to the kitchen and interrupted Sharkey's interview with Douglas.

"Look at this!" he shouted, bringing Sharkey to the bedroom.

Douglas recognized the items as Robin's, but said he didn't understand why they were in his closets. The investigators eyed him for further reactions.

"Things don't look good," Douglas said.

Landry was particularly interested in the pocketbook since it smelled like Robin's perfume. Douglas admitted it was Robin's, even stating that she had been carrying his slides in it, but he didn't know how it had gotten into his house. As for the flute, a rather fancy Armstrong model, Douglas admitted it belonged to Robin but again couldn't explain why it was in his home.

Douglas said only that he, his wife, and children were often out of the house, and that Robin's boyfriend may have broken in and planted the items.

The search went on for hours. Troopers tore through closets, cupboards, and cabinets, and sifted through mounds of trash.

They found shirts that were the same size as the shirt found in the rest area, as well as kitchen bags that matched the one found by Plotegher and Jewell, the bottle collectors. They even found a beeper for Robin's answering machine.

All the items were bagged and tagged for evidence and handed over to Kaufman. For the sake of thoroughness, the troopers also collected Douglas's phone bills, an Amtrak train schedule, and his gasoline receipts.

Meanwhile, Sharkey continued to interview Douglas, asking how much money he had given to Robin during their time together, whether he had been in love with her, and whether she was shaking him down for money.

Kivlan had suggested he try to pin Douglas down on the exact nature of his relationship with Robin, but Sharkey was getting nowhere. Douglas claimed they were only friends and that no extortion had taken place.

It seemed unthinkable that Douglas was handling himself so well. His house was swarming with troopers and detectives, yet he stood before them like a forbidding mountain. Part of Douglas's success that night stemmed from his strong belief in his own intelligence. He had a long history of intimidating and bullying people. He was "The Man." He also had a seasoned crook's instinct for denying everything. He may have been outnumbered and caught by surprise, but he appeared no more troubled than if he were lecturing a bunch of undergraduates.

Sharkey was frustrated. He decided to change tactics. He started by calling Douglas a liar.

A woman was dead, Sharkey said, and her family deserved to give her a decent burial.

Douglas asked for a lawyer.

Sharkey went outside to confer with Kivlan.

Kivlan knew a defense attorney would create problems for them, so he had Sharkey ask Douglas for fingerprints and blood samples. When Sharkey approached him with this request, however, Douglas simply refused.

Then, ignoring the tumult in his house, Douglas disappeared to his bedroom and got into bed. He pulled the covers up, comfy and cozy.

The sight of the sleeping professor left Sharkey dumbfounded. He'd never seen a suspect curling up for a snooze while his house was being raided.

Unable to comprehend what he'd seen, Sharkey went outside again and informed the assistant DAs that the suspect was taking a nap.

Kivlan asked Connolly to interview Douglas. Connolly went into the house, saw the gigantic form under the covers, shook Douglas by the shoulder and woke him up. Then he led Douglas out of the bedroom and to a couch in his son's room. He asked if Douglas would give a blood sample, and again Douglas refused.

Reminding Douglas that a missing woman had last been seen at his house, Connolly then asked whether Douglas wanted to tell them where the body was located.

If Connolly had hoped to squeeze a last-second confession out of Douglas, he got nothing but a sleepy stare.

• • •

By 5 a.m., the crew was ready to leave Sharon.

Kaufman the chemist had felt strange being in Douglas's house looking for blood. For one thing, he recognized Douglas from the commuter rail. They were both suburbanites working odd hours, and Kaufman had seen Douglas many times on the last train out of South Station to Norfolk County. Now Kaufman was checking Douglas's home for evidence in a possible murder case. Of course, this was difficult in a house that was in a state of utter chaos. Still, the chemist filtered through the mess of scattered Christmas ornaments, cockroaches, and half-eaten food to find clues.

Having already done extensive lab work on the evidence from the rest stop, Kaufman had documented that the blood found on the hammer and clothing was Type A, the same as Robin's. Luminol tests were used in the house to detect blood spatter, but the conditions made them useless. The resulting glow on the floor and walls was almost comical. As Landry recalled, the luminescent splotches "were more likely from old food particles and dead bugs."

Kaufman had better luck when he examined a blue windbreaker found in Douglas's closet. There was a strong blood reaction in the right pocket. The investigators asked Douglas if the jacket was his. He sheepishly tried it on.

"It looks like mine," he said, "but I'm not going to say it was mine."

In the pocket of the windbreaker was a sliver of gray material, squashed flat, approximately one inch in diameter. Kaufman carefully removed it.

"It looked like a piece of snot," Landry said.

Later, it was identified as part of a brain.

30.

Monday, March 21. Landry started the day by visiting Nancy Douglas at the Norton nursing home where she worked. He confronted her with a bag of the items found in the house. She seemed surprised to see him but didn't change her story. As for the items, she said some were hers. She claimed the flute may have belonged to her daughter, Pammy.

Her statements countered what Douglas had said—he'd identified them all as having belonged to Robin.

Had Douglas not spoken to his wife at all since their house had been raided? Had he not told her that Robin's things had been found in the closet? Did they not spend one minute to get their stories straight? Or were they so estranged by this time that they couldn't speak to each other?

Landry pressed Nancy hard, telling her the story would be in the newspapers and that the family would be ruined. He reminded Nancy that Douglas had treated her poorly in recent months, ignoring her.

"Douglas even bought a Toyota Starlet to match Robin's," Landry remembered. "Here's a guy with a big family, and he buys a tiny car. What does that say to his wife?"

Landry felt Nancy would eventually turn against her husband, but he was wrong.

"I tried to get Nancy to roll over on him," Landry said in 2021. "But she wouldn't. I even said to her, 'Why are you sticking with him?' She just seemed sad."

Nancy's resolve became one of the stumbling blocks of the investigation. The veterans involved with the case would claim they'd never seen anyone like her. She was unbreakable. Lieutenant Sharkey spent time with Nancy as well but failed to learn anything from her. She apologized to Sharkey but refused to incriminate Douglas.

"You would have to be married to a man for twenty years to understand," she said.

• • •

After his fruitless interview with Nancy, Landry contacted the BayBank fraud department and inquired about Douglas's credit card use.

Landry also contacted Douglas, telling him that his children were scheduled to be interviewed. Of course, Landry added, Douglas could spare them the trauma if he would simply come out with the truth.

Douglas asked for time to think it over.

It had been Kivlan's idea to interview the children. Kivlan was known for piling up circumstantial evidence, and he sensed the children might reveal something that could help build the case against Douglas. Landry, however, wanted to keep chipping away at the professor and leave the children out of it. This point was the start of friction between the retiring trooper and the assistant district attorney, friction that would intensify as the investigation moved forward.

Satisfied that he'd bothered Douglas enough for the day, Landry then contacted J. R. and asked him to come look at the new evidence.

When J. R. arrived at the barracks, Landry was blunt. He felt Robin was dead, and Douglas had something to do with it. J. R. began to tremble. Then he sat down and cried.

He again revealed that he and Robin had planned to get married in a couple of years. With tears in his eyes, J. R. identified the purse, credit cards, and the rest of the items as having belonged to Robin.

"I knew nothing about pimps," Landry recalled. "As a state trooper, I didn't deal with them. J. R. supposedly had a few girls working for him. But he didn't seem like a pimp. He didn't dress like one, and he wasn't a wiseass, not like pimps you saw on television. For that matter, Robin wasn't like other prostitutes. She bought her own house, and fixed it up beautifully. That wasn't something prostitutes did.

"Whatever their relationship, whether or not he was her pimp, they had a life together. They were looking to the future."

• • •

Landry had learned that Douglas owned a quarter-acre lot in Narragansett, Rhode Island, approximately thirty miles south of Providence. Kivlan felt this was possibly where Douglas had buried Robin, so he and Landry drove out there to check it out. They arrived to find Narragansett and Warwick police combing the scrubby little patch, complete with searchlights and excavation equipment. Landry and Kivlan determined the location wasn't a likely place to bury a body; with homes on each side, a man of Douglas's size couldn't sneak in and dig a grave without being seen.

Finally submitting to Kivlan's desire to question the Douglas kids, Landry dropped by the Sharon Middle School and asked for thirteen-year-old Pamela Douglas. The school's principal told him that the girl had been advised to not speak to anyone.

Landry then visited 38 Sandy Ridge Circle where Douglas told him his new attorney had advised him to keep the children out of the case. Right then, Pammy appeared in the hallway and asked, "Why is everyone trying to get something on my father?"

Then on Thursday, Shirley Benedict called Landry and told him about a long-distance call Robin had charged on her recent phone bill. The date of the call was in February, when Robin was in Plattsburgh with Douglas. When Landry researched the number, it was from Charlestown. Douglas had mentioned that Robin had a client named "Joe" in Charlestown and that she had left his home on March 5 to go an all-night party at Joe's.

The client turned out to be Joe Murray, a thirty-seven-year-old drug dealer who counted among his associates a Boston underworld figure named James "Whitey" Bulger. Murray had his own Charlestown crew that helped him move cocaine on the street. Murray was known for dropping large sums of money on expensive cars, powerboats, and houses.

Landry contacted Murray and arranged to meet him at the Howard Johnson's restaurant on Quincy's Southeast Expressway. Sitting in Landry's cruiser, Murray said he had known Robin for a couple of years, that he had helped her out of a few jams. He'd been her friend and occasionally a client. He said that he had seen Robin with a man in a blue car in Charlestown several weeks prior to her disappearance. Douglas's Toyota was blue. Murray also claimed to have seen Robin with Douglas in her own car, sometime in late February.

But Murray denied being with her on the night in question. He also denied having hosted an all-night party.

"Where were you?" Landry asked.

"At home," Murray said, "with my wife, Suzanne."

"Do you mind if I call your wife and ask?"

Murray didn't care.

"I'll have to tell her about Robin," Landry said.

Murray said his wife could handle it. "She's a big girl," he said.

When Landry called Murray's wife, he was met by the same offhand attitude. Suzanne was obviously aware that her husband kept company with prostitutes.

"He's a big boy," she said. She also provided Joe with an alibi. He'd been home.

Months later, as Douglas's trial loomed, Murray denied having admitted anything to Landry. He realized he would have to testify in court and didn't want to be known as someone who had cooperated with an investigation. He was no snitch.

Murray had nothing to do with Robin's death, but he had other problems to come. He was a co-owner of the Valhalla, a small fishing boat used by Bulger to transport guns to Ireland. Murray would serve a prison term for drug smuggling and gunrunning, and then, in 1992, be shot and killed by the very wife who had vouched for him in 1983. It was self-defense, she said. He was coming at her with a knife.

But that grim night was in Murray's future. In late March of 1983, Murray was just another footnote in the case of Robin Benedict.

31.

There'd been a strange incident at Douglas's home just ten days before Robin's disappearance.

On Tuesday morning, February 23, Douglas spoke to Robin on the phone. She told him that she had been to the bank already, had gone into the safe deposit box Douglas had opened for them six months prior, and that she was on her way to Sharon. This made Douglas nervous. He immediately called the Sharon police and said someone had stolen important items out of his briefcase and was trying to extort him. (He claimed the theft had occurred on the night of his infamous chest pains, with Robin stealing papers from his briefcase and leaving her pink panties behind as a sign. In another statement he said she had stolen his entire briefcase and stuffed her panties into his coat pocket.)

Officer James Testa, who was slightly acquainted with the Douglas family through Pop Warner football events, took the complaint and drove out to Sandy Ridge Circle. It was still early in the morning; the children were leaving for school, and Douglas appeared tense. He informed Testa that an assistant named Robin Benedict had stolen some important slides and research papers. Now she was on her way to his house to exchange the items for something, but Douglas didn't tell Testa exactly what she wanted in return.

As Douglas had predicted, Robin showed up in her Toyota Starlet. Douglas went out to the driveway to meet her and the two began shouting at each other. Testa couldn't understand what they were yelling about, but rather than let the scene escalate, he brought them to the Sharon station to discuss the situation. Once she had calmed down, Robin claimed that she and Douglas had been having a long-term affair (she gave it as a year and a half, though it was much shorter) and that she was in Sharon to tell Nancy Douglas about it. Testa assumed this was just a suburban love triangle; he recommended everyone seek legal advice or marriage counseling.

Testa was questioned twice about the incident, once by Landry and later by Kivlan. In the first interview, he claimed to not understand what items were being swapped, but for Kivlan he provided more details. Robin had Douglas's briefcase, Testa said, but was demanding money as well as clothing and personal belongings that Douglas had in his possession. Testa claimed to have heard Robin say, "Give me what belongs to me, and I will give you back what belongs to you."

If the swap couldn't be made, Testa said, Robin was going to tell Nancy Douglas about the ongoing affair. This scenario sounds far-fetched if only because Nancy already knew about her husband and Robin.

Yet the incident is fascinating because it was one of the rare times the two were seen together outside of Boston. Robin knew where Douglas lived and was bold enough to go there alone. She was also brazen enough to show up when his family might still be there. This was the pushy Robin Benedict of legend, the one that had once screamed at Ray Costict and had strutted through the Combat Zone, stealing customers from the competition. It was also interesting that she described Douglas and herself as having an "affair." Obviously, she wouldn't tell a Sharon police officer that she was a prostitute, but her choice of words is thought-provoking.

The one detail Testa couldn't provide was the exact cause of the dispute. Kivlan guessed it might have been over cocaine or money. He felt it was something other than slides and clothing, but didn't know for certain.

Testa also recalled that when he asked Douglas if he wanted to press charges against her for the so-called extortion, the professor said he and Robin had cleared things up and that she had returned his slides to him. Testa hadn't seen any such exchange but was simply glad to get Douglas and his bickering "girlfriend" out of the station.

That same day, several hours after he'd been at the Sharon police station with her, Douglas filed a complaint with the Lynn police that his briefcase had been stolen, and he gave them Robin Benedict's name. Douglas had called the Lynn police on the advisement of Testa, since Robin had initially stolen his papers in Lynn while he was in the hospital. It was also learned that Robin had indeed visited the bank that morning where Douglas had invested in a safety deposit box for the two of them. No one ever figured out what had been in the box or what Robin had wanted from it.

As confusing as the Sharon altercation had been, Kivlan was glad to learn about it. It showed that Douglas and Robin had been fighting just a short time before she disappeared, and Testa had been a witness.

32.

At the end of the week, Landry received a call from Steve Boulton, Nancy Douglas's brother, from Pawtucket, Rhode Island.

He told Landry that he was concerned for his sister's well-being and feared she was on the verge of a mental breakdown. Landry was understanding and promised to keep Boulton informed of any new developments that might affect Nancy.

The next day, Saturday, March 26, Landry led another search of the Douglas home. This time he found a small amount of cocaine, more love letters, plus an Apple II computer and IBM typewriter that were the property of Tufts. Douglas had once reported the items as having been stolen out of his office, yet there they were in his home.

The big find of the search was an unmailed letter written by Nancy. The document was long and filled with angst, as Nancy described her "despair" and wondered why her husband hated her. She suspected Douglas was on drugs and wished he would seek help. Mostly, she blamed herself for the disintegration of their marriage, and even wrote about her own fantasy of suicide, suggesting that slitting her wrists would be "nice." It ended with a scream imprinted onto the page: "OH, GOD, PLEASE PLEASE PLEASE HELP ME. I can't take any more. PLEASE HELP. . . ."

Landry immediately called Boulton and told him that Nancy may need him.

"I think your sister may be on the verge of suicide," Landry said.

Landry wondered if Douglas, possibly on drugs and fearing his future, might even hurt Nancy or the children.

Douglas was certainly behaving oddly at this time, and with good reason. The department head at SUNY had learned about Douglas's problems at Tufts, as well as his association with a missing girl. Douglas was promptly informed that the offer from Plattsburgh had been withdrawn.

Then, at an executive board meeting of the Tissue Culture Association in Cherry Hill, New Jersey, Douglas was asked to explain why he had submitted Robin Benedict's name for membership, and why he had sought a $400 reimbursement, rather than the usual fifty dollars. He explained that he was under a lot of stress. According to Douglas, a resentful student was seeking revenge for a bad grade and was causing problems for him.

Stephen Boulton would recall a conversation with Douglas where the professor spoke frankly about contemplating suicide, which would be "the easiest way" to deal with the problems at Tufts. "He said he was going to do himself in," Boulton said.

On Monday, March 28, Landry visited the Bank of Boston with a search warrant. He'd brought one of the many sets of keys that had turned up in the search of Douglas's house. With a modicum of research, he learned they belonged to a safety deposit box at the bank, rented by Douglas the previous July. The account was held jointly with Robin Benedict, whom Douglas listed as his "wife." The box turned out to be empty, though the sign-in sheet revealed that Robin had last entered the vault on February 23, the same day the Sharon police were called to Douglas's house.

As Landry tried to guess what the vault box had to do with Robin's disappearance, he received another call from Boulton.

"I think I can identify the hammer," he said.

• • •

Landry raced down I-295 South to the Warwick, Rhode Island, police station, his foot mashing the gas pedal for the entire forty-mile trip. Trooper Brian Howe, newly assigned to the case by Kivlan, was with him. He was holding an evidence bag. Inside, like a valuable relic, was the bloody sledgehammer.

Boulton claimed Nancy had borrowed a hammer from their father several months earlier. She'd needed it for some sort of household project. However, she'd never returned it. His father, a meticulous man who kept a well-ordered workshop in his basement, had complained recently that Nancy hadn't returned the hammer. The comment stayed with Boulton.

Landry and Howe met with Boulton and his father at the Warwick station, then left together to see Boulton's father's workshop. Landry was gripped by what he saw, for along the basement wall was a series of hammers hanging neatly from hooks.

One hook was empty.

The hammer from the rest stop had always intrigued Landry because at the bottom of the handle was an eyehook. Now, as he looked over the workshop of Douglas's father-in-law, with less than two days before his retirement, he knew where the hammer came from.

33.

Landry's final days as a state trooper were spent talking to people at Tufts. As he and Howe interviewed Douglas's former colleagues, a new picture of the professor was emerging, one of a moody man who intimidated the staff.

They searched through Douglas's old office and found more pieces of correspondence between him and Robin. They also learned of a colleague named Stanley Spillman who some portrayed as a Douglas devotee. Spillman, it turned out, had left Tufts over a controversy about his credentials; he hadn't been in touch with Douglas for a while. The investigators focused briefly on Spillman, thinking that he may have known something about Robin's disappearance. This turned out to be a dead end.

By now Landry had spoken to Dr. George Katsas, the state's chief medical examiner, who had determined the tissue found in Douglas's jacket was likely part of a human brain. Katsas suggested it could also be from a monkey, but tests on Douglas's windbreaker showed distinctly human proteins. To be certain the tissue wasn't something Douglas had inadvertently brought home from his lab work, Landry asked Douglas's former supervisor, Karen Hitchcock, if Douglas had ever worked with human brain tissue at the school. The answer was no, which was damning for Douglas.

Landry was supposed to turn in his gear on Thursday, March 31. Despite the impressive work he'd done, he was ordered to pass his findings along to Sharkey and Howe, who would take over the investigation.

Kivlan asked Landry to write up a report on his investigation and to send any evidence from Foxborough to the Dedham office. Annoyed with the swiftness of his being replaced, Landry lost his temper. A shouting match on the phone with Kivlan guaranteed Landry's time on the case had ended.

"Kivlan was stiff," Landry recalled. "He had no patience. It was his way or no way."

Landry had hoped to stay involved with the case after his retirement as a private investigator for the DA, but this seemed unlikely. Kivlan felt Landry had become too close to the case and that Landry's impending divorce and retirement was playing on him emotionally. Though troopers often assisted the DA's office, Lieutenant Sharkey had not wanted troopers on the case to begin with, claiming they were generally inexperienced with major investigations such as this one.

Kivlan was especially concerned when Landry suggested the case was a state police matter and that he might file his reports through the Boston headquarters instead of the DA's office. Kivlan feared Landry's approach could raise questions about the handling of evidence and even bring up a jurisdictional dispute. If Douglas had a smart lawyer, questions about the chain of custody from Douglas's home to the courthouse could result in some evidence being suppressed. Kivlan chose to remove Landry from the investigation entirely.

Nearly forty years later, Landry still speaks of the period with a tinge of anger in his voice.

"I didn't really care that much," Landry said. "I knew Douglas had done it. I don't want to knock anybody's balls off, but this was an easy case to build. It was premeditated murder. I just wouldn't be around to see him arrested."

One of the problems in the case was that it involved so many different counties. J. R. had reported Robin as a missing person in Malden, which was Middlesex County. Douglas lived in Sharon, which was Norfolk County. The Combat Zone and the Tufts Medical School were in Suffolk County. The hammer and bloody clothes were found in Mansfield, which was Bristol County. It was a logistical mess for Landry, though his captain told him to stick with it until the DA took it away.

Landry was also physically exhausted. The peculiar demands of the case had forced him to stay up long hours to find people in the Combat

Zone, all of which was unusual for a road trooper. He'd worked non-stop for more than two weeks, but Kivlan's lack of appreciation left him feeling sour.

"Kivlan wanted my report as soon as possible so they could go to a grand jury," Landry recalled. "I had an office set up in the Foxborough barracks. There were rooms of evidence. Rooms! It would take eight hours per day, for a few days, to log everything. You have to pick up each piece and log it in. Kivlan wanted me to write the report at his office, which was ridiculous. We went around and around on that. He kept badgering me and then threatened to take *me* before a grand jury. They thought I was trying to extort them or something. I was absolutely friggin' steamed.

"Anyway, I typed up a fifty-two-page report, and someone from Kivlan's office would come by each day to pick up sections of it. That turned me off. I'd done everything Kivlan had asked, and then he treated me that way."

Landry looks back at his role in the investigation with pride. Yet there was one thing he might've done differently.

"There was one big gaffe," he said in 2021. "When we were searching the bedroom, Douglas was sprawled across the bed. He was just lying there, watching us, not saying anything. That turned out to be the bed where he killed her."

Lying on the bed may have been Douglas's way of hiding evidence. There may well have been something incriminating under the mattress. This could also explain why he had been so quick to lay down and take a nap while the investigators were still there.

"At the time, we didn't even think about the bed," Landry said. "We should've looked under it, or just examined it. But we didn't suspect that he'd killed her in the house."

34.

In April, a report on Douglas's credit card usage revealed his steps on the night Robin disappeared.

At 11:40 p.m., Douglas called the Americall answering service from a phone booth near a Bradlees department store in Foxborough. This was the call where he'd pretended to be Robin, leaving a message for J. R. that she was going to Charlestown.

Fourteen minutes later, just before midnight, Douglas made two calls to his home from a phone booth in North Attleboro.

At 2:12 a.m., Douglas called home a third time, this time from Atlantic Avenue near South Station in Boston.

At 5:29 a.m., he called home from a gas station in Pawtucket, Rhode Island.

At 6:51 a.m., Douglas called home from a Bonanza Bus terminal in Providence.

Obviously, Douglas wasn't home sleeping. He'd lied. His wife had lied.

The scenario imagined by Landry was that Douglas had killed Robin, then called the answering service pretending to be her so it would seem she was still alive and on her way to a party in Charlestown.

He then used Robin's car to get rid of the body, the hammer, and the bloody clothing. The phone booth in North Attleboro fit this scenario, as it was just across the highway from the Mansfield rest stop.

Then he drove to Rhode Island, abandoned the car, and took the bus back to Sharon. His calls home were to inform Nancy of his whereabouts and, he would say later, to ask if anyone had come to the house looking for him.

Trooper Howe actually drove the route dictated by the phone calls and Douglas's tolls and found Douglas could've traveled the distance with ease, even by driving under the speed limit.

Yet nothing pointed directly to Douglas murdering Robin. The investigation so far had revealed only that Douglas was a strange man fixated on prostitutes, a man whose home life was in shambles, a man with a bit of brain tissue in his coat pocket.

• • •

Douglas made many phone calls to the Benedicts in the next few weeks. Sometimes he would say he was going on a work-related trip and was leaving a phone number for the Benedicts to call in case they needed him. The insinuation was *Call if you hear anything about Robin. . . .*

During a couple of these calls he said disparaging things about J. R. In one, he told about having seen Robin with a black eye, hinting that J. R. had hit her.

In April, the Benedicts received a Western Union telegram purportedly from Robin. It read: "Happy Easter. I'm working in Las Vegas and things are well. Please don't tell J. R. where I am. Love to everyone. Love Robin."

John and Shirley felt the telegram was a fake. For one thing, it was signed "Robin," and she still signed her notes to them with her childhood nickname, "Bin-Bin."

Kivlan contacted Western Union and tracked down the operator who had taken the message. She recalled that the person had sounded like a woman but couldn't be sure.

Douglas later admitted to having sent the telegram.

• • •

More activity: Troopers went through Douglas's trash looking for clues but found nothing. Then, based on one of Douglas's phone calls being made near the Boston waterfront, investigators wondered if Robin's car was dumped in the Fort Point Channel, perhaps with her body in it; professional divers were sent down into the murky water to explore. They found plenty of rusted out vehicles but no silver Starlet. Since Douglas had also made calls from Providence, the divers were also sent out to Providence Harbor. Again, they found nothing.

Meanwhile, Howe and two other troopers took turns sitting in an unmarked car near Sandy Ridge Circle to keep an eye on the suspect. The hope was that Douglas might reveal something about the case, just in his coming and going. There was a theory that he may have buried Robin somewhere and might be tempted to visit the location. What they saw, however, was a typical suburban existence, with Douglas and his wife running errands, bringing their children to sports events or the shopping mall. As many who saw Douglas at this time would say, he seemed amazingly unfazed by all that was going on. He simply plodded along in his usual manner.

There were a few instances of Douglas leaving his house at midnight to take a long, aimless drive. Kivlan suspected Douglas was doing this to fluster the surveillance team. The assistant DA knew by now that he was dealing with a diabolical man. Even Savi, who had worked in the Combat Zone for years, told Howe in an interview that Douglas was an unusual man, one who knew all sorts of ways to con banks, and had involved her in scamming Tufts. Though she was one of the Zone's tougher women, Savi admitted to being somewhat afraid of Douglas.

Kivlan had been studying a second collection of Douglas's handwritten papers. He was particularly intrigued by Douglas's meticulous notes about Robin's phone calls and messages, as if Douglas were trying to map out her every move and connection. Most interesting were some pages that appeared to be Douglas's own timeline of March 5, as if preparing a statement in case he had to go to court. It was consistent with the versions he'd given to Landry and Borstel, though some of the details were off. Douglas also wrote that Robin loved him, and that she had said as much to the Sharon police.

Was this comment nothing more than an idiot's blather? Or was it the gibbering of a confused and increasingly tormented soul, one whose grip on reality had loosened long ago?

35.

As investigators were going through his garbage and examining his phone records, Douglas still had to deal with Tufts. The auditors had determined that Douglas had embezzled more than $8,000 of federal money, leading to murmurs that he might face prosecution by the U.S. attorney. He'd hired a lawyer, Harvey W. Freishtat, to advise him in career matters. Douglas's hope was that Tufts would be restricted in what they could say about him should he seek employment elsewhere. He seemed less concerned about the embezzling charges and his link to a missing woman than his reputation as a scientist. He wanted it known that his lab work was still strong.

With cooperation from Douglas's psychiatrist, Freishtat prepared a defense for Douglas and then arranged for him to appear before a Tufts tribunal that consisted of Manos, Hitchcock, and others from the university. What transpired at the hearing, however, had less to do with stolen funds than with Douglas's weight problem.

Douglas's theory was that his excessive dieting of the previous year had somehow altered his behavior. He believed his inflated expense vouchers were merely part of a year's worth of manic episodes brought on by starvation. In support of his argument, Douglas enlisted the aid of several diet and nutrition specialists. Most of his research, however, came from a series of articles written by Dr. Myron L. Glucksman, a Yale professor who had studied the effects of starvation diets on obese patients. According to Glucksman, an obese person subjected to extreme fasting could experience anything from hallucinations to sexual deviancy.

Armed with such esoteric information, much of it from medical journals of a dozen years earlier, and accompanied by an entourage that included his psychiatrist and attorney, Douglas appeared before his accusers with confidence.

In his reedy voice, Douglas referred to problems with a "girl," and how she had instigated his dieting, and how his starving had resulted in ketosis. Douglas explained that ketosis could cause paranoia and even hyper-sexuality.

He refused to discuss his expenses. He refused to sign anything. All he talked about was how drastic weight loss had hampered his thinking.

The panel took little interest in Douglas's presentation and dismissed him.

Douglas responded by writing a lengthy letter to Tufts president Jean Mayer, who happened to be a nutritionist. In it he argued that the board had completely ignored his research on ketosis. He accused the school of "insensitivity."

His appeals were ignored, as were several angry and pleading phone calls to Karen Hitchcock.

Realizing he'd lost his battle, Douglas signed a letter of resignation on May 27.

He was no longer a Tufts professor.

36.

Douglas's name first appeared in the *Boston Globe* on June 24. The *Herald* had covered the missing girl story sporadically since March, but now the paper with the largest circulation in New England was on it.

The brief article appeared on page eighteen with no byline. It discussed how Douglas had been forced to resign from Tufts under accusations of misappropriating funds. There was also mention that Douglas's home had been searched in connection with the disappearance of Robin Benedict, described in the article as a twenty-one-year-old graphic artist. The case was being investigated as a homicide and would be put before a grand jury. The *Globe*'s first article concerning what would be Boston's biggest crime story in years was crammed next to a story about a disbanded chicken farm in the Berkshires.

Four days later, a more detailed article appeared. Written by Mike Frisby, it established Douglas in the minds of *Globe* readers as a suspicious character.

"At that time, the *Globe* was considered the paper of the suburbs," Frisby recalled in 2021. "It was the 'establishment' newspaper, something for Harvard graduates. The *Herald* was considered a city paper, read by average Joes. There was a sense of frustration that we weren't considered a city newspaper."

In the Douglas–Benedict case, the *Globe* saw a chance to challenge the *Herald* on its own turf.

"When the story first came out, Douglas wasn't even a murder suspect. He was just someone who knew this missing girl. So initially, this was just a dark little murder story. We didn't know it would grow into something bigger. As it grew, there was a push to stay on top of it, because it was gritty, and it could help give the *Globe* some of that grittiness, and help make us a city newspaper."

Frisby continued: "I had a background as a crime reporter. I had spent time covering crime in Dayton and Cleveland, so when I came to the *Globe,* I seemed to be the right reporter for this type of story. We knew the *Herald* would be all over it, and we knew the *Herald* had good people.

"It turned into a newspaper battle. Newspaper battles are fun."

Throughout July the *Globe* heaped on the coverage, matching the *Herald* page for page.

There were stories about the Malden home Robin had purchased and redecorated, and stories of Robin's parents offering a $5,000 reward to anyone with information about their missing daughter. There were articles about the Douglas children being subpoenaed to appear before a grand jury and their refusal to testify.

Then, just as the Boston papers were running out of material, a couple of New York police officers found an abandoned car near Penn Station. It was a silver Toyota Starlet. The interior was speckled with blood. Anyone who came near it noticed the unmistakable odor of rotten flesh.

37.

Officers Christine Miler and Cornelius Dever had been patrolling New York City's Sector F at 9 p.m. on July 9 when they noticed a 1982 Toyota Starlet in a tow-away zone on West 29th Street. The car had no plates, no inspection sticker, and was unlocked. A check under the hood revealed the battery was missing. Dever found the car's vehicle identification number on the engine block and reported it over the police radio. They learned that the car had been reported as stolen and its owner was a missing woman from Massachusetts.

When Kivlan heard Robin's Toyota had been found, he immediately assigned trooper Bobby Murphy the task of bringing the car back to Massachusetts. Murphy left at midnight in a borrowed flatbed truck and arrived in New York at five in the morning. Satisfied that the car matched the description of Robin's, he loaded the vehicle aboard the truck, covered it with a tarp and, after some unproductive investigating of his own, returned to Foxborough.

Kivlan looked at the car the next day. He noticed the driver's seat had been adjusted to make room for someone much larger than Robin.

Determined to find a witness who may have seen Douglas with the car in New York, Kivlan sent Brian Howe into Manhattan to investigate Sector F parking garages. Howe checked more than fifty garages but found nothing. Not satisfied, Kivlan sent another trooper, Rick Zebrasky, to Manhattan for a follow-up search.

Zebrasky and a pair of New York detectives visited ten garages and eventually learned that the car had initially been left in Meyer's parking garage on West 31st. It sat unattended for several days before employees pushed it onto the street. Checking the garage's books, Zebrasky found out that the car had been left there on March 6, the day after Robin's disappearance, and the same day Douglas had bought his Amtrak tickets to Washington. Zebrasky showed Douglas's photo to people at Meyer's, but no one recognized him.

Boston newspapers treated the car as if Robin herself had been found. Readers were offered almost daily updates on the Toyota, how it had been trucked back to Boston, how it was undergoing testing for clues, and how the interior reeked of death. Dried blood was found near the inner wheel well and near the hatchback area, as well as the base of the driver's seat and near the handle of the passenger door. The biggest news of all was when the Boston forensics lab identified a substance found in the car as more brain tissue.

The car being in New York tied in with Douglas's travel schedule on the weekend of Robin's disappearance. It was now surmised that he'd taken her car to New York and dumped it, hoping it would be stripped for parts or stolen. From there, he bought a train ticket to Washington, rather than leaving from Boston as he'd claimed. Amtrak employees at Penn Station had been shown Douglas's picture and verified that he'd purchased a ticket to Washington from New York. Lieutenant Sharkey sorted through boxes of ticket stubs at Amtrak headquarters until he found the very ticket sold to Douglas, proving that the professor had lied about his travels.

Kivlan loaned Douglas's love letters to a handwriting expert. He hoped to verify that Douglas's signature was on his Amtrak ticket, which would prove to a jury that Douglas had left for Washington from Penn Station, not Massachusetts. Douglas had been asked to supply recent samples, but it appeared he was deliberately disguising his handwriting. Still, an FBI analyst noted similarities between Douglas's samples and the signatures provided by Amtrak. In a case full of ironies here was another: Douglas's handwritten declarations of his love for Robin were being used to help prove he had something to do with her disappearance.

38.

The Benedicts reacted with mixed emotions to the car being found. John Benedict told the media that he was pleased to hear the news, but it wasn't Robin.

"There is still pain and agony," he said. "It has been difficult. I have to deal with questions from the other children and we have to accept that she may never be back."

By now the Benedicts had brought in their own attorney, Anthony R. DiFruscia. A trial lawyer and victim's rights advocate since 1967, DiFruscia had represented the Benedicts in the past with issues involving the White Eagles. Smart and genial with a background in politics—he had served three terms in the Massachusetts House of Representatives and had mounted an unsuccessful bid to become the Democratic nominee for lieutenant governor—DiFruscia was the right man to help the Benedicts understand the web of police work and investigations.

Looking back forty years later, DiFruscia insists the Robin Benedict case was "just another job." But at the time, the growing media attention alarmed him. Right away he accused the investigators of "playing to the media" and voiced his concern that the press would not offer balanced reporting.

He was right to be uneasy. The names of Robin Benedict and William Douglas were already familiar to Bostonians, and information about the case would become standard morning reading. Even *Boston* magazine, a glossy publication usually reserved for local politics and homemaking tips, offered a lengthy feature called "Fallen Angel" that focused on Robin's disappearance.

How one felt about the case may have depended on which papers you read. *Herald* readers may have considered it a major story. Readers of the *Boston Phoenix*, however, may have never heard about it; the hip liberal weekly barely mentioned it. Lawrence journalist Russell M. Glitman felt the story was becoming a Boston event, with less impact on Douglas's town of Sharon or Robin's Methuen/Lawrence connection. "It wasn't about those communities," he recalled. "My editor in Lawrence wanted us to take ownership, but most people viewed it as a story about the big, bad city."

The story was also being covered in New York papers. Since Robin's car had been found there, speculation grew that her body was hidden somewhere in Manhattan. Associated Press reports on the case were being read all around the country, from Florida to Washington to North Carolina to New Jersey and Delaware.

"It became such a big deal," said Kelley Bartlett, Robin's friend from the White Eagles. "Being from Methuen, I felt like I was at the center of it. I would always hear from people who said, 'I just saw Robin in Methuen two days before she disappeared.' She never cut ties to Methuen. She did her work far away, probably so she wouldn't risk being seen by an old neighbor, but people still saw her in Methuen all the time. Once the information came out, it all seemed surreal and crazy, crazy, crazy. I couldn't get my head around it. And every time I saw a picture of [Douglas], I wanted to vomit."

The *Herald* had already dubbed it "The Missing Beauty" case, and though the Benedicts had obliged the *Herald* with several childhood pictures of Robin and plenty of cooperation, the tabloid was ramping up the sleaze factor each week. At one point the paper vowed to pull back on the more prurient aspects of Robin's past, but the promise didn't stick, not when Robin's so-called "secret life" was such good copy.

The television coverage was just as relentless. Local TV news reporters were tripping over themselves to cover the case. The early winner of the Douglas–Benedict television sweepstakes was WHDH Channel 7, where reporter Mike Lawrence broke the story about Robin and Douglas having a relationship. It was also on Channel 7 where Delahunt bluntly said that he thought Robin was dead.

Boston's ABC affiliate, WCVB-TV, featured the case as part of its evening newsmagazine show, *Chronicle*. The missing prostitute and her bloody car were odd choices for a program that usually focused on stories about quaint New England neighborhoods, but one of the show's reporters, Ron Gollobin, had already spent many hours with Paul Landry, outlining plans for a possible book. They'd hit a snag when Landry revealed his dislike of Delahunt and Kivlan; Gollobin, during his years as a crime reporter, had grown friendly with the Norfolk DA's office. Still, when *Chronicle* decided to cover the Douglas–Benedict story, Gollobin had extensive notes to pull from.

Airing on Channel 5 in mid-July, the *Chronicle* episode was John Kivlan's worst nightmare. Key parts of the case were becoming public knowledge. The show covered everything from Douglas's early morning phone calls to what the troopers turned up while searching his home. There was even footage of Landry talking casually about the case, which must have spiked Kivlan's blood pressure. Worse was the focus on Douglas's children and whether they would be called to testify.

Thomas C. Troy, a local attorney with a taste for the spotlight, was questioned about the children being forced to take the stand. *Chronicle* couldn't have picked a better player, for Troy roared on cue. "This is not Russia," Troy said, his lips practically dripping with the indignity of it all.

"There was quite the frenzy over this story," Gollobin recalled, "partially because Robin was such a beautiful girl and she chose the street life." The fact that Robin's father was a photographer for Raytheon and took dozens of high-quality photos of Robin "was good for us TV types. I did a couple of shows on the case for *Chronicle*—big ratings!"

Though Landry had appeared on *Chronicle*, he felt it was his due since he'd been so close to the case. But as the story became a major Boston news event, he noticed many unqualified people were appearing on the nightly news to share their thoughts.

"We had a lot of news programs, and every detective in Boston had to go on and discuss the case," Landry recalled. "They were on TV talking like heroes, like they had tried to save Robin. You could see them try to ingratiate themselves to the Benedict family. The case was making stars out of people who'd been nowhere near the investigation."

As the case grew into a news phenomenon, Delahunt expressed his fears that crucial information would be leaked to the press. Of course, this didn't stop Delahunt from getting his own face in the news. When Robin's Toyota made its return to Boston, the *Globe* featured a large photo of Delahunt peering into the side window; an obviously posed shot making it appear the Norfolk DA was conducting his own search for clues. He may have been concerned about media coverage, but there was the dapper Delahunt posing alongside the bloodstained deathmobile.

Kivlan agreed that the media coverage was an issue. "The investigators were definitely caught up in it," he said in 2022. "They became pretty good at whispering to whatever reporter was around, if they wanted to be in that particular newspaper. It was just one of those cases.

"It had everything the media wanted."

• • •

The early 1980s was a peculiar time in America. The lingering effect of a 1960s hangover had lasted through the 1970s, climaxing with Ronald Reagan winning the presidency. A lunatic had murdered John Lennon in New York, and a similar lunatic had tried to kill Reagan. There were still communist bookstores in Harvard Square near Boston, and small groups of young people were still living out the hippie lifestyle of getting high and scavenging for food. They were in the minority, though, as America tried to police itself and move forward. Pot-smoking hippies were replaced in the culture by coke-snorting investment bankers.

We tend to mythologize the 1980s, remembering the decade as rather simple and silly—the age of MTV, Hulk Hogan, and Madonna. But in many ways, the decade was awful, fraught with scary political upheavals around the planet, a hideous new street drug called "crack," and AIDS, a new and deadly disease that could be transmitted through sex. Hollywood presented fresh new stars like Molly Ringwald and the "Brat Pack," but their lighthearted films competed with lurid stuff like Brian DePalma's *Body Double*, where a woman was penetrated and killed with a giant drill. Ken Russell's *Crimes of Passion* featured Anthony Perkins as a demented street preacher planning to kill a prostitute. His weapon of choice was a sharpened metallic vibrator he had nicknamed "Superman."

Perkins and his malignant sex toy could've existed only in that period of cinema history, when Hollywood was releasing a flood of movies depicting the brutalization of women. Women's groups protested these movies, sometimes storming theaters and throwing garbage at the screen. This apparent Armageddon against women wasn't restricted to the cinema. Protesters declared a simple weekend of television would show hundreds of scenes where women were being beaten, stabbed, raped, or murdered. A simple network cop drama of the period generally had at least one scene where a woman was abused in some way, shoved or slapped.

It certainly appeared that America's entertainment industry, which included the daily news, was fattening itself on the abuse and killing of women.

The story of William Douglas and Robin Benedict was a perfect fit.

39.

And where was Douglas as the investigation deepened and the media took aim?

He was back in the Combat Zone looking for prostitutes.

"He was such a weak person," Landry recalled. "He was so nervous, on one hand, almost frightened. On the other hand, here's the number one suspect in the murder of a prostitute, and he's in the Combat Zone. I thought that was ballsy."

Lieutenant Sharkey saw Douglas in the Zone during those heated weeks of the investigation. From an unmarked car, Sharkey observed Douglas skulking around his old haunts, meeting prostitutes and then accompanying them to their trick pads. Sometimes Douglas went with them to cheap hotels; other times he simply slid his obese body into a parked car for a quick session. Sharkey claimed Douglas would finish with one prostitute and then return an hour later with another one. Months later, Sharkey questioned Douglas about these Combat Zone visits. He asked how many prostitutes Douglas saw while he was being investigated.

"I can't give you specific numbers," Douglas said. He estimated between five and ten, but denied that he found women at Good Time Charlie's. As for what they did in those parked cars and cheap hotels, Douglas insisted, "it's not sex."

Trooper Howe interviewed a tall, red-haired prostitute named Julie about her own dealings with Douglas. According to Julie, Douglas had paid twice for her services, the first dating back to the time Robin had been banned from Good Time Charlie's in January, and then again shortly after Robin went missing in March.

Julie brought Douglas to a Back Bay hotel for what she described as oral sex, with no touching. Her rates were even higher than Robin's, $100 for a mere fifteen minutes. She recalled Douglas as different from her typical customer. He was polite.

When Julie learned about the investigation, she decided to avoid Douglas. But a few weeks after the second date, as Julie recalled for Howe, Douglas called Good Time Charlie's looking for her. It turned out he was outside in the parking lot, calling from a pay phone.

She was suspicious of Douglas now. She asked him to come inside Charlie's so she wouldn't be alone with him, but he insisted she come outside. Douglas must've seemed ominous out there in the shadows. He had become the bogeyman of LaGrange Street.

Julie grew so uncomfortable that she called Billy Dwyer, who was apparently a friend of hers; by the time Dwyer arrived at Charlie's, Douglas was gone.

The incident bothered Julie. For a while she was convinced Douglas was watching her, maybe even following her home.

Kivlan doubted the prosecution could use Julie's story. It made Douglas sound like a creep, but it didn't prove he killed anybody. And since Douglas was seeking the attention of another prostitute back in January when Robin was still alive, it actually diminished the idea that he was obsessed with Robin. He just seemed to be fixated on prostitutes of any size or type.

But Douglas's return to the Zone had less to do with him being an insatiable sex fiend and more to do with his disintegrating mental state. His life was a disaster, and it was only through risky sex that he could distract himself from the hell he was about to face.

40.

Douglas was so broke and desperate that he applied for a night clerk's job at the YWCA in Boston. The position turned out to be at the Berkeley Residence, a hotel for women in Boston's South End.

It may have seemed like a long drop in status for the disgraced professor, but he needed money. In August he admitted that he had falsified vouchers that tallied more than $7,000 worth of checks for Robin. A company in Hartford that had reimbursed Tufts for their losses had recently placed a lien on Douglas's house. With his legal bills mounting—as well as the ongoing prostitute fees—Douglas had taken a part-time job at Scott Laboratories in Rhode Island. It must've been embarrassing for him when his work was deemed unreliable and he was dismissed. Being the subject of an investigation was destroying his ability to focus; a simple reception job was about all he could handle.

The job was low pressure, so Douglas killed time by reading books, scribbling notes to himself on a yellow legal pad, and answering phone calls at the service desk. He helped wherever he was needed, whether it was folding towels or hauling ice buckets from the kitchen. He said nothing about being a professor. If anyone asked about his past, he'd say that he was a freelance writer.

Eventually, the hotel's manager saw a picture of Douglas in the *Herald* and learned that her new night clerk was the subject of some horrific accusations. Douglas was promptly suspended.

Once the folks at the hotel realized that a suspected killer had been in their midst, they recalled Douglas's attempt to purchase a second-hand car from one of the residents, a middle-aged woman named Betty Sanborn.

Douglas hounded Sanborn for weeks about her car, a clunking Gran Torino she had nicknamed "Bette Lou." Sanborn was unsure of Douglas, saying later that he gave off "wicked bad vibes."

Douglas kept changing his story about why he wanted the car; sometimes it was for himself, sometimes he was buying it for someone else. They haggled over the price but failed to reach an agreement. Eventually, in early July, Sanborn sold the car to someone else, only to learn it had broken down on a Boston side street. Shortly after, Sanborn found twenty-eight dollars in her mailbox and a note from Douglas saying that was his best offer. Then, to her surprise, Douglas tracked down the stalled Gran Torino and, despite it having neither plates nor registration, somehow got it started and drove it away.

Sanborn contacted Douglas, saying that his twenty-eight dollars was not enough; he agreed to pay her more money, but only if she supplied the plates and registration.

The following day Douglas came to the hotel in a fury. He yelled at Sanborn, slamming his fists on a table, shouting that he wanted the plates immediately and that he had tried to sell the car but no one wanted it. This was a different Douglas than Sanborn had ever seen at the hotel. He'd always seemed strange, but never this angry.

Sanborn gave Douglas a moment to calm down, but their issues over the car went on for days. She was forced to report Douglas to the police, which angered him. He finally agreed to return the car, but not before telling her it was "a piece of junk."

There was another incident at the hotel where a resident was watching a television in the lobby. To her surprise, Douglas's face appeared on a local news broadcast. The guest couldn't make out exactly what was being said, something about bloody clothing. But she was sure the man on the television news was the same man working at the front desk. She said something to the effect of, "Hey Bill, you're on television."

He barely looked up from what he was doing.

"It had to be another Bill Douglas," he said.

The next day was when Douglas's picture was seen in the *Herald,* which led to his dismissal.

Lieutenant Sharkey learned about the police report Sanborn had filed and was soon interviewing her about Douglas. After hearing her story, Sharkey decided to give the Gran Torino a round of lab testing. Sharkey's theory was that Douglas had wanted the car to haul Robin's body from one hiding place to another, but when the tests turned up negative, he put the car out of his mind. Later, Douglas would tell Sharkey that he'd been interested in Sanborn's car simply because he had wanted "a second car, until I realized it was really a rat trap."

As for the Berkeley Residence, a legend was born. Now, any memory of Douglas was fraught with sinister meaning. For instance, Douglas was once seen with an overly stuffed suitcase that bulged at the sides. He claimed it was full of tin cans to be recycled, but now the residents wondered if it was bulging with Robin Benedict's torso. They were convinced that he had hidden parts of Robin around the hotel.

A group of women calling themselves the "Agatha Christie Crimestoppers Club" spent weeks searching the hotel for clues that might incriminate Douglas. Their heads full of true-crime stories and old movies, the ACCC determined that Douglas's temperamental outbursts proved his homicidal nature. Was he not a doppelgänger for Raymond Burr in *Rear Window*, going about his daily business while his wife was buried in the front garden?

Inspired by having a real mystery within their walls, as well as the reward posted by the Benedicts, they combed every inch of the hotel. But what exactly were they looking for? Did they expect to find Robin's skull tucked away in a medicine cabinet? Or maybe, hidden among the many towels Douglas had folded, a severed finger? Sharkey tried to discourage the amateur sleuths, but nothing could dampen their enthusiasm.

The women developed a wild theory that Robin had once lived at the Berkeley. They came to this conclusion because a picture of Robin in the *Herald* greatly resembled a former resident named Regina. This Regina character supposedly lived at the hotel during the summer of 1982. She was described as a lively woman who, though much younger than the other residents, was friendly and always willing to stop and talk in the lobby. She tended to wear slinky clothing and allegedly worked in the Combat Zone as a dancer. She claimed to have a boyfriend in Providence and joked about finding an older man to take care of her.

It was only a mild stretch to link "Regina" with "Robin," both working in the Zone, both names beginning with "R." Regina even claimed to be an artist, though she never showed anyone her work. The women theorized that Douglas had taken a job at the hotel because he was looking for information about Regina/Robin.

One of the residents who owned a cassette recorder happened to have taped a conversation with Regina. This, the women were certain, would blow the case wide open.

Armed with their tape and their belief that Robin Benedict had been among them, the women visited WHDH and demanded to speak to someone from the news department. Mike Lawrence, the young reporter who had broken a few stories on the case, greeted them and listened to their tale of intrigue. He was polite but had no intention of playing the recording over the air.

This was the ACCC's last shot. One of them was soon convinced she was being followed and set up for her own murder, having learned too much about Douglas. As for the mysterious Regina, she was never heard from again.

• • •

Douglas followed his stint at the hotel by taking a part-time job as a telemarketer, which was short-lived. Other odd jobs came and went, some lasting only a few days.

Douglas's ventures into Boston to work always ended the same way: he'd take the commuter rail back home, where Nancy picked him up at the Route 128 station in Westwood, about eight miles north of Sharon. That particular station was perhaps the bleakest on the South Shore line in those days, a lonely wasteland next to an industrial park. Douglas and Nancy must have cut quite a pair, two forlorn figures in a dreary suburban train station.

Sometimes Douglas would have a bag full of empty bottles. He'd become so desperate for money that he'd started to rummage through dumpsters and trash cans, looking for empties to deposit. The irony was brutal. After all, it had been a couple of bottle scroungers who had found the bloody items that led detectives to his house. As Lieutenant Sharkey would later tell *New York* magazine, "It was the bottle law that put Douglas behind bars."

• • •

The Douglas clan spent some time in the Dedham courthouse in August, though the appearances rarely lasted more than a few minutes. On one occasion Douglas spent an hour at the DA's office to have a secret meeting with Delahunt, but nothing was revealed to the public. Delahunt told the media, "We continue to be optimistic that the disappearance of Robin Benedict will be resolved."

In September, the Benedicts petitioned a probate court to declare Robin legally dead. Delahunt had presumed the case to be a murder investigation, and the family wished to probate Robin's estate, including her home and car.

On October 13, Douglas appeared in Suffolk Superior Court and pleaded innocent to ten indictments charging him with thirty counts of larceny and thirty-one counts of filing false reports.

Entering the court carrying a small, shabby umbrella, dressed in a blue windbreaker and running pants, Douglas looked timid and unkempt. He spoke in his usual meek voice and was then released on $10,000 bail, the case continued to November 2 for a pretrial conference. He left the courtroom through the back door with his attorney. A crush of reporters followed and tried to surround him, but Douglas made no comment.

This had been the local media's first real look at Douglas. Journalists had to be disappointed. He hardly resembled a man facing charges that carried a total of 450 years in prison.

But if Douglas was not the prince of darkness everyone had hoped to see, the media still had other angles. In fact, the Benedicts had taken a step guaranteed to assure the case's tabloid pedigree: They'd hired a professional psychic.

41.

Marie Stephenson looked like a fifty-seven-year-old country grandmother, but she'd come to some national acclaim as a psychic and spiritual healer.

Stephenson shunned publicity, content to use her mental powers to assist her neighbors in Tucson, Arizona. She did most of her work out of her home, a trailer decked out in multicolored lights. In 1981 the Iowa police praised her for helping them find a missing boy in a cornfield. The case made the reclusive Stephenson into a minor celebrity, albeit a reluctant one. She was even featured on the cheesiest of ABC programs, *That's Incredible*.

Her method was to recite the Lord's Prayer in order to "open her channels," and receive information from "the Divine Creator" or "the Universal Mind." Once she had reached the proper "vibratory levels," she'd use a pen and paper and go into a fit of automatic writing, her hand flailing across the page. Somewhere in her scribbling would be the answers to questions about anything from missing pets to missing people.

When the Benedicts contacted Stephenson, she was already on her way to Massachusetts for another case. She agreed to meet the family at a Howard Johnson's restaurant. Stephenson impressed the Benedicts, especially when she referred to Robin as a "call girl" rather than a common street whore. The Benedicts agreed to supply Stephenson with some of Robin's favorite belongings, including a necklace, hairbrush, and bathrobe. Paul Landry provided a map of Mansfield and a photo of the hammer.

The psychic industry enjoyed phenomenal growth during the 1980s. ABC-TV executives hired a psychic to guide them in their decision-making, and even the Reagan White House consulted with an astrologer. This reached an apex in 1991 with the advent of the "Psychic Friends Network," where teams of psychics could bilk clients to the tune of $3.99 per minute, attracting them with late-night infomercials that advertised a convenient 1-900 number to call.

As far as psychics helping to solve crimes, that had been going on for years. Indeed, the Chicago Police Department had been working with a local clairvoyant named Irene Hughes since the 1960s. The most famed psychic detective in the world, Peter Hurkos of the Netherlands, was often called to America to aid in major investigations, including the Boston Strangler and the Manson Family murders. Hurkos loved the publicity but was no help in catching a killer. While Stephenson was using her special powers to locate Robin, an entire team of psychics on the other side of the country was assisting the Seattle police in the hunt for the Green River Killer.

With the items in her possession, Stephenson returned to Tucson. Back in her trailer, she attempted to solve Robin's disappearance. While wearing Robin's bathrobe, she ran her fingers over the map of Mansfield. Then she went into her automatic writing phase; her notes were intriguing. She described Robin as a "con artist" with an ego "out of whack." She wrote that Robin had "bullied" Douglas, "demeaning him," while Douglas was a man "yearning to be flamboyant, but couldn't hold onto that image of himself." The combination of Robin's bullying and Douglas's lost image, she declared, "led to turmoil." Stephenson was unclear as to who threatened who, but in her mind's eye she saw a flurry of images: a man wearing glasses and a soft, unstylish hat; a trunk bound by a leather strap; a reservoir; and a blast furnace. She suggested Robin's body was somewhere near Douglas's home. Overall, her description of events was intriguing. But Stephenson wasn't the only psychic involved in the search for Robin's body.

Edith Locke was a self-proclaimed "criminal astrologer" from Nevada who was known to insinuate herself into investigations. If Stephenson was maternal and earthy, Locke was right out of a carnival spook show, favoring pink peasant blouses and a loud persona. Troubled by Robin's disappearance, Locke reached out to the Benedicts and told them that the body was within a fifteen-mile radius of Douglas's home, possibly in the Sharon dump.

The resulting search party, organized in part by Landry as a favor to Robin's parents, involved more than twenty people and a camera crew from Boston's Channel 4 news, all converging on Sandy Ridge Circle on a Sunday morning, no doubt putting a scare into the Douglas household. The search, which included a trek to nearby Lake Massapoag, turned up nothing.

Locke was persistent. Among her psychic conclusions was that Robin's death was sudden, not planned. She also drew up Robin's star chart and concluded that Douglas had helped fulfill her destiny, for it had been her "time to die."

When the search failed, Locke blamed Landry. The psychic claimed the retired trooper was too cynical and that his attitude affected the search in a negative way.

"Shirley Benedict strongly believed in her," Landry recalled. "I thought she was very vague in her predictions, but I was willing to check out things she felt, and locations she thought were relevant. The family was willing to do anything to find Robin."

Meanwhile, the Benedicts were advised to stop associating with psychics. If they were to be portrayed as a clean-cut, normal family, they weren't served well by Locke and her expedition through Sharon, nor her later assertion that Robin had been frozen and stored somewhere in Tufts. (The Benedicts went so far as to report Locke's "frozen" theory to the Boston Central Secret Service Bureau. The baffled detectives purportedly promised to look into it.)

Kivlan felt the family was presenting itself as a bunch of desperate wackos, especially when DiFruscia boldly demanded to know why Kivlan hadn't ordered an investigation of local incinerators, which left the assistant DA exasperated.

The notion that Douglas had placed Robin in a Tufts incinerator stayed with Shirley Benedict for many years. Douglas had already been banned from Tufts by the time of her daughter's disappearance and couldn't have smuggled a dead body past security, but Shirley never gave up on the idea.

It was a time of high-flying theories coming from all corners, including one where Douglas chopped Robin into pieces and left parts of her all over the state, while some investigators pondered whether Douglas had been framed. Meanwhile, divers explored ponds in the Methuen area, on the chance that Robin's corpse might be down in the sludge.

42.

Kivlan had a theory about Douglas and Robin and the trip to Plattsburgh.

As Kivlan saw it, Douglas still believed Robin was going to fall in love with him, maybe run off with him to live in Plattsburgh. Kivlan had come to view the professor as foolish and unrealistic, a believer of fantasies. But Kivlan also felt Plattsburgh was where Douglas realized his fantasy was crumbling. Maybe something happened that caused the reality of their arrangement to finally be illuminated to the point where even Douglas could see it. Whatever happened, Kivlan believed the chain reaction that led to Robin's death began in Plattsburgh.

J. R. had told Kivlan that Douglas was going to reveal Robin's role in the embezzling scam, and she had threatened to expose Douglas by talking to the *Globe*. Kivlan thought this had merit, but there were still parts of the story that made no sense.

From what J. R. had reported, Douglas had lured Robin up to Plattsburgh by promising her an "expensive gift." J. R. had also told detectives that Douglas had promised Robin a trip to St. Thomas. When J. R. had first contacted detectives to tell them Robin was missing, he was thinking she had skipped off to the Virgin Islands and might be waiting there for Douglas. If Douglas was flat broke, how was he paying for these so-called gifts and trips? And if there'd been friction between them, why would Robin consider going to an island paradise with Douglas?

J. R. was no longer a suspect, but he was shifty, changing his story slightly from one telling to the next. J. R.'s statement that Robin had gone to Sharon to tell Douglas she didn't want to see him anymore also seemed unlikely. She could've easily done that over the phone, or written a note to him. On the night of her disappearance, Douglas had to be offering something she couldn't resist, what Kivlan deemed "the big pay day."

True, Robin had distanced herself from Douglas, and she suspected that he had caused her to be fired from the Saugus health club, yet she was still doing business with him.

Just two weeks before her disappearance, Robin had rented out another trick pad in Boston. On the lease agreement she'd listed Douglas as her employer. As he'd always done, Douglas vouched for her. Despite their situation growing volatile, they were still using the ruse of Robin being his assistant. And Robin wouldn't have agreed to go to Sandy Ridge Circle on March 5 if she sensed danger.

Fortunately, an FBI lab in Washington had verified that the bloodstains in Robin's car matched the Type A blood found on Douglas's jacket. It also shared traits with blood samples from the Benedict family. The small amount of tissue found in the Toyota also turned out to be white matter from deep inside a human brain; only gunshots or the most violent blows to the head could've produced it.

There was no way to prove the brain tissue was Robin's, though Kivlan was feeling confident. The circumstantial evidence was adding up.

43.

On Friday, October 28, after a week of testimonies, a seventeen-member grand jury watched as Nancy Douglas took the stand. Kivlan asked several pointed questions, but Nancy offered him nothing in return but a spiteful expression. When it became obvious that Kivlan couldn't crack her concrete shell, she was dismissed.

Dr. George Katsas was next, answering Kivlan's questions about brains and how the tissue found in Robin's car could only be from a dead person.

At the end of the morning, the grand jury returned an indictment charging William Douglas with first-degree murder. That afternoon, Douglas was arrested near a Burger King in Cambridge and indicted for the murder of Robin Benedict.

While in the Sharon police headquarters, Douglas made two phone calls.

First, he contacted his current boss at a car rental service, letting him know that he wouldn't be able to finish working that day.

Then he called Nancy to let her know he'd been arrested and would be spending the weekend in the county house of correction.

"I'm not kidding," Douglas said to his wife. "Really, I'm not kidding."

An Associated Press photographer snapped a photo of Howe and Sharkey escorting Douglas to the courthouse jail. They look like weekend hunters who just caught a big one. The professor looks sweaty and disheveled, like any criminal who had been on the run for a long time.

• • •

The clothing officer couldn't find pants big enough to fit Douglas, so he was allowed to wear his own for his first night in jail.

Nancy had called the jail and informed officials that her husband was in declining mental health. In deference to her, Douglas was taken to a wing for those under "administrative protective custody" and placed under suicide watch.

Lieutenant Sharkey, who had developed some sympathy for Douglas, asked the deputy on duty to fetch him a sandwich and a glass of warm milk. He introduced the new prisoner as "Billy Douglas" and described him as "a good guy."

Sharkey was an old-fashioned Catholic who viewed the Combat Zone as a devilish place. He saw Douglas as a man who had lashed out after being abused by a conniving hooker. In that regard, Sharkey was one of many who viewed Douglas as a poor, defeated soul.

"When I got into this case I thought I knew everything," Sharkey told *New York* magazine after the investigation concluded. "But it's a new world out there in the Combat Zone. I've seen girls there who frighten even me."

• • •

At his arraignment on October 31, Douglas pleaded innocent.

He arrived at Norfolk Superior Court wearing a tan jacket, a light shirt, and brown pants and tried to put up a calm façade. He didn't believe he could be indicted without a body but seemed shaken as Kivlan read aloud the evidence against him. The *Globe* noted that as Kivlan narrated an ugly tale of obsession, Douglas "sat with his head down, twirling his thumbs."

The arraignment was on Halloween day, a time of masks and disguises. For William Douglas and Robin Benedict, the masks were about to come off. What the public would see, however, wasn't necessarily the truth. It was as if the masks they'd worn concealed yet another pair of masks, guises that were even more enigmatic.

The next day, November 1, was Douglas's forty-second birthday. He spent it in the Dedham jail, hidden away from the County of Presidents.

44.

Photos of William Douglas and Robin Benedict began appearing in newspapers regularly. Their pictures were usually side by side, his jowly face juxtaposed next to her lovely, smiling visage. They were the crime couple of the moment, sometimes getting a full page in the *Globe*'s Sunday edition.

By now the story being imprinted on the public's mind was that Douglas had been obsessed with Robin, and that she had wanted to end their relationship. The general coverage involved the ongoing debate among legal experts as to how the case should be approached. Was Robin really dead? Was a tiny piece of brain tissue and a few bloodstains enough to convict a man of murder? Could a man be convicted of murder when there was no body? Would his children testify against him? And could state pathologist George Katsas be of use with no body to examine?

Katsas was a familiar name to people who followed morbid court cases. As Suffolk County's medical examiner, he had helped investigators with everything from ice-pick murders to shotgun blasts. He'd examined some of Boston's most notorious murder victims, including a pair of women supposedly killed by the Boston Strangler. He'd performed more than 4,000 autopsies, and in 1970 his testimony helped authorities lock up Antone C. Costa, a necrophile who had killed and dismembered two women on Cape Cod. Just weeks before he was called in for the Benedict case, Katsas was examining the corpse of a five-year-old South Boston girl who had been raped and strangled by a sixteen-year-old neighbor boy.

A short, balding man in his sixties with a thick Greek accent, Katsas had the steely, matter-of-fact attitude of one who regularly dealt with the most depressing and ghoulish of crimes. He loved his work, was known for his strong opinions, and often chided the Commonwealth for not investing in more-modern forensics equipment. But Katsas was accustomed to working on bodies. Even in the Costa case, he had severed limbs and skulls laid out before him. Now, without Robin's body, he couldn't tell how hard the victim had been struck, or how many times, or from what angle. After examining the tissue, he determined that it was from deep in the brain and also contained a small skull fragment. He stated that the victim, whoever it may have been, "positively is dead."

It wasn't much to go on. Criminal lawyers across the city played devil's advocate. Among them was George Balliro, who pointed to President Reagan's press secretary James Brady. Shot in the head during an attempt on the president's life, Brady survived. "Brain tissue went everywhere," Balliro said, "but he is still alive."

Douglas's new attorney, Daniel J. O'Connell III, was a seventy-five-year-old who had served in the navy during World War II and had a background in Boston politics. O'Connell approached the case with a kind of serene patience. He agreed that Robin might still be living.

"I haven't determined whether there is sufficient evidence to prove that a person is deceased," O'Connell said. "It's certainly an issue, but I won't take a position on it until I have to. The key questions are whether or not she's dead and whether or not Professor Douglas had anything to do with it."

The prosecution was inspired by a recent Oklahoma case where a man named Gary Lee Rawlings was convicted of murdering his ex-wife. Her body was never found, but the belief was that it had been dumped from the air into the Gulf of Mexico. Rawlings was convicted based on blood found in his car and in a plane he'd rented prior to her disappearance. Scientists identified the blood as having genetic traits matching the victim's. Delahunt and Kivlan believed the same verdict could be reached in the Douglas case.

America's most celebrated trial lawyer, F. Lee Bailey, was consulted at his Boston office for his take on the prosecution. Having been involved with some of the most infamous murder cases of the century, Bailey knew a conviction without a body or witnesses was difficult, but he felt the circumstantial evidence against Douglas was "not to be ignored. There are plenty of hammers out there, but not many of them have brain matter on them."

The talk of new technology being used to link the brain tissue to Robin gave the case some novelty. The love letters from an obsessed professor gave the case a sense of the absurd. The hammer, with speckles of blood and a long strand of hair stuck to it, gave the case a dose of Edgar Allan Poe morbidity.

But when Kivlan announced to a grand jury on October 31 that Robin had been a prostitute, and that Douglas had spent thousands of dollars on her, the case's coverage took an outrageous turn.

Robin was no longer a mere graphic artist from Malden. Now she was a Combat Zone prostitute. With that new detail, there was a new story to tell. While people sipped their morning coffee or rode the subway and commuter rail to work, they lapped up the details of the prostitute and the weird professor. By the end of the year they knew all about Robin's pink panties and her fee of $100 per hour. What sort of sex-witch was she to make such a respected man as Douglas embezzle money, they wondered.

Though the *Herald* had identified Robin as a prostitute from the start, the *Globe* and other newspapers usually referred to her as a graphic artist or as Douglas's "lover." J. R. was referred to as Robin's "friend" or "roommate," not a pimp. After Kivlan's announcement, however, the pretenses and niceties were dropped. For the rest of the investigation's coverage, she was a prostitute and only sporadically referred to as a graphic artist. Some newspapers tried to play on the double-life angle, suggesting she was a graphic artist by day and a prostitute by night. This wasn't accurate, but it fit the theme of secret lives that made the case so intriguing.

The Benedict family objected to the revelation—some members even went public and claimed it wasn't true—complaining that the media was putting too much emphasis on this aspect of Robin's life. Her brother Rob would say many years later that the press's use of the word "prostitute" was overdone and unnecessary. "Don't treat her like trash just because she went down the wrong path," he said.

Shelly Murphy of the *Herald* once explained that the decision to declare Robin a prostitute wasn't taken lightly. As she told the Investigation Discovery channel, "I felt bad for the family, but the editor said, 'You know this is relevant.'"

Once the word was out, there was no going back. Robin's father acquiesced, telling the media, "There must be some truth about it."

Robin's mother told the *Globe* in 1999 that once Robin was identified as a prostitute, the news coverage seemed to favor Douglas, as if he'd been a decent man lured into a world of wickedness.

"The papers never portrayed [Robin] as a person," Shirley said. "It was always just 'the prostitute and the professor.' They would never say 'Robin Benedict,' they'd say 'Robin Benedict, the prostitute.' Without saying 'the girl' or 'the lady.' I'm sure they're not going to say 'lady,' but they always made so much of him, like how she took him down the dark road. But she tried to get rid of him, and he just wouldn't give up."

The Benedicts' anger at the media never subsided.

"I can see the family feeling that way," said *Globe* writer Mike Frisby. "But there were two angles to the story. How did such a revered professor fall for this prostitute? And how did this girl from a good family *become* a prostitute?

"I think we always emphasized that she came from a good family, and there was a reason for doing that. Had Robin Benedict been just a regular prostitute, and not a girl from a good family, would there have been such a strong investigation? By our mentioning that she was a prostitute, we kept her on the front pages every day and probably helped keep the investigation going."

Yet Shirley Benedict's point was accurate: The revelation brought out sympathy for Douglas, especially among his old collaborators at the university. Bryan Toole, chair of Douglas's department at Tufts, told a reporter from out of state that once the shock had worn off, the feeling at Tufts for Douglas was one of pity. "People see that he got himself into an incredible trap he couldn't get out of," Toole said.

Scientists from around the country offered similar thoughts on their fallen colleague.

"I'm very surprised to learn about his troubles," said Dr. Ethel Thurston, director of the American Fund for Alternatives to Animal Research. She explained that Douglas had impressed antivivisection groups with his pioneering research. He'd been on the verge of discovering an alternative for animal testing by cosmetics companies, a new method that would reportedly save half a million rabbits per year. Douglas's work was considered light-years ahead of other scientists in the field, and he was in line to receive Federal Drug Administration approval. "He is," Thurston said, "a well-known and very good scientist."

The media coverage remained in this vein for a while. Robin Benedict was a prostitute. William Douglas was a genius trying to save bunnies.

45.

Douglas also earned sympathy because of his children.

The *Globe* and *Herald* kicked off several reports on Douglas with items about Billy, Johnny, and Pammy. Three times the children had been subpoenaed to testify before a grand jury, and each time they refused. Having children testify against their father was a major issue, and many readers wrote in to condemn the idea. Most felt Douglas's children had suffered enough and should be left out of the investigation. "One can only hope that the children will withstand this emotional wringer and emerge without serious psychological damage," wrote a concerned couple from Sharon to the *Globe*.

Journalist Linda Wolfe made a point of driving by Douglas's home before the trial, making note of a child's rusty bicycle left upturned on the front lawn. After waxing poetically about the bike, she added, "Until then, I'd thought of the story as a tragedy for Douglas. I'd forgotten that a father's tragedy is never his alone."

Though the Douglas defense team argued that the children shouldn't be forced to testify, five justices of the Massachusetts Supreme Judicial Court had determined in August that there was no such thing as family privilege to prevent a person's offspring from testifying against them. Yet the Douglas kids were as stubborn as their mother. When they'd reluctantly appeared before a grand jury in April and again in August, they said nothing, offering only stone-faced stares.

Legal red tape had kept the children somewhat protected since the investigation began, but DiFruscia, the Benedicts' lawyer, developed a plan. He filed a motion with the Massachusetts Supreme Court to have a guardian represent the Douglas children, rather than putting them under the pressure of a legal interview. DiFruscia wrote that the Douglas children were likely "laboring under great emotional turmoil and distress because of the conflict they face: on the one hand wanting to protect their parents, and on the other hand wanting to unburden themselves of any knowledge they may have."

DiFruscia may have sounded like he had good intentions, but his ultimate plan was to separate the children from their parents. Without Nancy hovering over them daily, Billy, Johnny, and Pammy might loosen up and talk. DiFruscia consulted psychiatrists who suggested the kids might've been traumatized if they'd witnessed a murder. Getting those children away from their parents, the experts claimed, would be helpful in preventing further "abuse." The Benedicts and DiFruscia prepared a statement saying the Douglas children would likely be relieved if they could be removed from the Sharon house and placed under the care of a guardian.

A psychiatrist, Dr. Sheldon Ziegelbaum, spent two one-hour sessions with the Douglas children and also interviewed Nancy Douglas. In an affidavit to be used in a possible appeal, he noted that the children had been victims of extreme public scrutiny and even threatening phone calls. In his estimation they were suffering from, among other things, "severe anxiety disorder."

Indeed, the children seemed increasingly upset whenever anyone approached them. Reporters were belligerent, allegedly tracking the house on Sandy Ridge Circle and acting as if they had no intention of leaving until someone spoke to them. Some reporters stood by with stopwatches to time the children as they came in and out of the Dedham courthouse. It is possible that the Douglas children were more disturbed by the local journalists than the investigators.

On slow news days, the press tried to make characters out of the kids, describing them as an unruly trio of none-too-bright brats, alternately crying or stuffing their mouths with pizza during courtroom recesses. But when the *Globe* ran a photograph of Billy, Johnny, and Pammy during one of their trips to the courthouse, the children looked like typical New England teens of the day.

Most likely, the Douglas family wanted to conceal the exact whereabouts of the children on the night of Robin's disappearance. When Douglas was first interviewed, he said only that the kids were away at "basketball or babysitting." Yet Nancy's statement taken by Paul Landry was more detailed, and more puzzling.

She said she had been shopping in Manchester, New Hampshire, all afternoon. She came home in the evening to find a note from Douglas saying that Robin was coming by. Since she didn't want to be around to see Robin, she left the house, this time with the oldest son, Billy. She took him to McDonald's for dinner and inadvertently ran into Pammy. According to her statement, she returned to the house after midnight with two of the three children in tow. The prosecution believed the children had been in a perfect position to see something. If they didn't witness an actual murder, they may have seen their father in the process of covering his tracks.

Behind the scenes, DA Delahunt and Judge Donahue considered various options. If the children remained in contempt of court and refused to testify, they could be placed in a juvenile facility or a foster home, in hopes that they'd ultimately break down and willingly speak about their father.

The judge and Delahunt decided to wait before taking such a drastic and unpopular step, but on November 7 it was ruled by the Supreme Court that minors could not refuse to testify. The Douglas kids would have to appear in court and tell what they knew. Though Douglas's attorneys would file more than one appeal, the ruling was impossible to overcome.

More controversy came when Douglas was ordered held without bail in the Norfolk County jailhouse. Kivlan had won on this count, arguing that Douglas had committed a "particularly brutal murder" and then "callously disposed [of the body] at a location still not known."

Kivlan added that Douglas might flee, commit suicide, or possibly cause harm to his wife and children, describing the atmosphere at Douglas's home as "volatile and explosive."

O'Connell, Douglas's lawyer, called the ruling "outrageous" and filed a petition, arguing that Douglas had been nothing but cooperative. He'd had plenty of opportunities to flee since the investigation had started, and had notified the DA's office that he would surrender if an indictment were issued. "Yet," O'Connell said, "he was arrested. There was no need. It just fueled public interest."

O'Connell portrayed Douglas as having already been judged guilty by the public and the press. "I don't think he can be tried fairly anywhere in the state. I've never seen the media try and convict someone like they have in this case."

Douglas had struggled from one job to the next, O'Connell said, "because untrue and unfounded things have caused employers to terminate him." If Douglas's home life was volatile, he continued, it was because the press was bombarding the Douglas family with phone calls. "He has been under intense pressure."

O'Connell proposed that a respected professor with no criminal record was deserving of bail, possibly as low as $2,500 cash.

Massachusetts Supreme Court Justice Francis P. O'Connor sided with the prosecution. Douglas would remain locked up until the trial.

• • •

Dedham. County jail. Row Seven. Murderers Row.

This was where the immigrant anarchists, Nicola Sacco and Bartolomeo Vanzetti, sat and waited before their execution in 1927.

This was where William Douglas would spend the months prior to his trial in 1984. He shared a cell with a twenty-two-year-old man who had killed his girlfriend by running her over with his car.

Douglas spent most of his days watching a television fastened to the wall of his cell. When not staring at the television, he filled an accordion file with notes about his case. He took his meals in his cell and only came out rarely. Sometimes he heard taunts from other inmates.

Nancy came to visit twice a week, usually wearing her white nurse's uniform. The meetings with her husband were highly formal, with a sense of quiet drama. Douglas usually ended them with a declaration of love for his long-suffering wife.

The other men on Row Seven, the killers, rapists, and disembowelers, were curious about the professor, but learned nothing. Other than occasional games of chess with another inmate, Douglas kept to himself.

46.

If there were still places in America that hadn't heard of William Douglas and Robin Benedict, that changed on Sunday, November 6, when the story of Douglas's arrest was picked up by the United Press and syndicated across the country.

The case was blowing up on a national level. There were half-page spreads with such gaudy headlines as "PROF. HOOKED ON HOOKER, BUT DID HE MURDER HER?" and "PROSECUTORS BASE THEIR MURDER CASE ON BITS OF BRAIN." Douglas was called "Professor Love" and "The Mad Professor." The texts conveyed the grisly matter of the case, and the accompanying photographs—the obese, pasty-faced suspect, the attractive victim—effectively captured the tabloid feel that had already taken hold in Boston. Whether a small-town rag or a big-city publication, covering the Douglas case turned your paper into a tabloid for the day.

Two weeks later the case received coverage through another syndicated outlet, the Times News Service, which, despite being launched through the austere *New York Times*, was as garish as any newswire. The author, Dudley Clendinen, aimed his story at a pulp audience, describing the "eminent professor" with the "sexual obsession," the "yellowish neon glare" of the Combat Zone, and Good Time Charlie's, where, "Women in thin dresses loiter along the walls." As if the case's mingling of adult entertainment and violent murder weren't enough, the *Times* article added a reference to an old Boston case from 1850 where a Harvard professor, John W. White, was convicted of murdering a colleague over an unpaid debt and "incinerating his body in a university furnace." The linking point of the Douglas and White cases was "the lack of a body."

Clendinen's story resulted in the inevitable "*New York Times* effect," which meant that any story picked up by the *Times* was deemed worthwhile. In late November, the *Detroit Free Press* featured Douglas and Benedict on page one. By late December, reporters from Philadelphia, Miami, and other cities invaded Boston. Their destination was the Combat Zone, many finding their way to LaGrange Street and the bleak recesses of Good Time Charlie's.

One journalist, Joe Starita, was stunned. Nothing in his past had prepared him for Boston's raunchiest neighborhood.

"I'd come out of Miami, and Times Square in New York, so it's not as if I was coming to Boston from Disneyland," Starita recalled. "But I was taken aback by the tawdriness of the Combat Zone, and the density of the peep shows and the strip clubs, all crammed together. You couldn't help thinking this was a place where a lot of shit could happen.

"There were too many people, too much traffic, too many naked bodies, too much neon; it felt combustible, like it could blow at any minute."

Starita and others filled their stories with observations about the pink track lighting and the music that blasted from wall speakers but learned very little from Charlie's prostitutes and barflies. Most denied knowing Robin personally, though some remembered her as a stylish dresser. Barmaids claimed to not know her and moved along.

Gradually, more drops of information came out, namely that Robin was unpopular at Good Time Charlie's. Regardless of whether reporters had set out to portray Robin in a negative manner, the details being recorded were unpleasant. A prostitute who gave her name as "Cindy Jackson," suggested that Robin's personality was such that someone other than Douglas could've murdered her. "Last year here, a pimp killed two of his girls," said Jackson. "Prostitutes get killed all the time. It's no big thing."

Reporters took these morsels and strung them together, keeping the story in the news like a kind of morbid national item. On December 27, The *Philadelphia Inquirer* put Douglas and Robin on the front page in a lengthy feature complete with pictures.

The story took on elements of a medieval fable, with the Zone representing a sort of unknown wilderness, its lawless men and loose women acting as a mirror for society's squalid nature, a receptacle for our worst traits.

"It was like something out of the Bible, or ancient Greece," said Starita. "It's about that person who takes a wrong turn that leads to something dreadful. It's the kind of story that goes back centuries. It goes beyond journalism in a lot of ways. It's about obsession. It's like Herman Melville, only instead of a whale, it's a guy trying to land the hooker. There is a classical arc, like a haunting Shakespearean tragedy. There's *Pygmalion* in its DNA, with the professor and the street girl. There's a bit of Charles Manson in its DNA, too."

For that matter, there was also a bit of Elizabeth Short, the young woman whose body was sliced in half and left in a vacant Los Angeles lot back in the 1940s. Nicknamed "The Black Dahlia" by the press, Short's photo appeared in LA newspapers day after day, with male readers developing macabre crushes on her. For a brief time, Robin had threatened to become Boston's version of the Dahlia, smiling out from newspaper pages. Robin had the same doomed mystique of all murdered women who stare at us from beyond the grave. Think of Sharon Tate. Think of Kitty Genovese.

There were other similarities between Elizabeth Short and Robin Benedict. Though Short had been killed in LA she was actually from Massachusetts. They were roughly the same age and, like Robin, Short was from a conventional background but had yearned for a ritzier life. The newspapers of her day eventually depicted Short as a femme fatale, not a prostitute but a party girl with dozens of male associates. Though she remained mysterious and fascinating, there was decreased sympathy for Short as each layer of her troubled past was revealed. The same would happen to Robin.

The difference, of course, was that Short's killer was never found. Robin's was in a county jail, awaiting trial.

Another difference was that no one doubted Short was dead.

Some were claiming Robin was still alive.

47.

O'Connell was out. Richard Clayman was in.

Douglas's new attorney was a sharp young man who had handled many high-profile cases, including prosecuting the men who assaulted Theodore Landsmark, a black businessman attacked by white protesters in Boston during the 1976 antibusing riots. The attack was immortalized in an iconic photo of a protester striking Landsmark with a flagpole. A local fellow who always introduced himself as "Richie from Chelsea," Clayman was known for being emotional and theatrical in court. "My mannerisms are what they are," he once said. "I am what I am."

In a pretrial conference, Clayman declared Robin had been seen the day after her alleged disappearance. Clayman said a lawyer from out of state had given him the news, but added, "We are investigating this ourselves."

If the Benedicts were inspired by this information, they didn't show it. The family had decided to sue Tufts University for $1 million under the ridiculous premise that the school had been negligent in Robin's death. This was in response to Tufts having filed a suit against Robin for the money Douglas had given her, which saw Malden District Court place an attachment on Robin's home.

• • •

Meanwhile, Douglas made himself useful in jail by volunteering for menial jobs. He even assisted deputies with tax advice and insurance forms. When Deputy Sheriff Bob Campbell stopped by his cell to ask how he was doing, Douglas would smile and say everything was fine, like a restaurant customer assuring a waiter that the service was just dandy.

Douglas was adapting to his new environment. He was fitting in with the other prisoners and quickly learned the jailhouse lingo. He even mocked the prisoners who hadn't committed major crimes. When younger hoods tried to intimidate him, he ignored the taunts. It appeared Douglas could fit in anywhere, a university, a seedy bar, a jail; he was a 300-pound chameleon.

Yet Douglas had some concerns. He was still worried that his children might be forced to testify. For a while it had appeared the strong public reaction against the kids testifying was in his favor, what with the American Civil Liberties Union and other organizations expressing concern. The children's court-appointed legal guardian, Stephen Keefe, had approached the Supreme Court to grant them the same privilege that a husband or wife would have if they were asked to testify against a spouse. His argument that the children could suffer psychologically by having to testify seemed perfectly sound. The Supreme Court, however, felt no concern about the Douglas children's emotional welfare. Keefe's point was rejected.

Douglas also struggled in his search for legal help.

Since he was first questioned as a suspect, Douglas had been through several lawyers. There were always problems, anything from a conflict of interest to Douglas's inability to pay their fees, to his simply not liking them. Clayman, who seemed ready to defend Douglas, wouldn't last long.

A new name in the mix was Thomas C. Troy, a noted criminal defense lawyer who loved attention and knew how to get it. He was the man on television who had yelled "This is not Russia!" when asked about Douglas's children being forced to testify.

Not that it needed any, but the case was about to get a new splash of color.

48.

Tom Troy was a minor legend in Boston legal circles. He was a former marine, an amateur boxer, and a police officer. After being injured on the job, he studied law at the Portia School in downtown Boston. Upon passing the Massachusetts bar in 1967, Troy rented a helicopter to escort him over the city and land on the lawn of the District Court of Dorchester. It was a highly dramatic image; he was telling Boston that a new legal force had arrived, descending from the sky like a god.

Thickly built with a large head and a mane of shaggy hair, Troy was the classic bulldog defense attorney, the sort of two-fisted loudmouth of old-time courtroom dramas. In 1983, *Boston* magazine declared Troy one of "The Toughest SOBs in Town," a moniker he wore proudly. He was only fifty-four at the time of the Douglas case, but decades of excessive drinking, smoking, and eating had given him heart problems and full-blown diabetes, to go with a bad back from a car accident twenty years earlier. Still, he was a battler. "If somebody throws down the gauntlet," he once said, "pick it up and beat the shit out of them."

What separated Troy from most attorneys was his apparent disregard for the profession. "Trial attorneys are salesmen," he once told the *Globe*. "They sell to groups known as juries."

Though many were put off by his bombastic style, Troy had his share of admirers.

"He was a colorful guy," Kivlan recalled. "An old-school criminal lawyer who loved the press. There were still a few like him around in those days, but they don't exist anymore. I'd be lying if I said I didn't like him. He was funny. But you had to keep your guard up around him. He was capable of anything."

Early in Troy's career he was hired to represent the purported Boston Strangler, Albert DeSalvo. Troy gained his first major bout of publicity when he tried to ban *The Boston Strangler*, a biographical film by Twentieth Century-Fox, from playing in Boston theaters. Troy failed but got his name and image in the newspapers, right next to the hatchet-faced DeSalvo.

Troy often reached for the wackiest new legal concepts. In 1969 he claimed that new tests revealed DeSalvo lacked an extra Y chromosome that some scientists linked with violent criminal tendencies in the male. DeSalvo, Troy said, was just a "normal, red-blooded American boy," and "not the type" to kill women. (Though his involvement in the other killings has been disputed, a posthumous DNA test linked DeSalvo to at least one of the Strangler victims.)

Troy could be buffoonish in court. He was known to recite poetry or sing a little song for the jurors. But he was also a vicious cross-examiner and had used his blustery personality to become a successful attorney. He was also a millionaire many times over. He wore expensive suits and diamond-studded watches, and buzzed around the city in a shiny black Jaguar. When the *Boston Phoenix* once asked about his wealth, Troy winked and said, "Not bad for a shit bum, huh?"

At different times he considered running for Suffolk district attorney or applying for a judgeship, but Troy knew what he was: a trial attorney who got into law because a lawyer acquaintance once told him he was a good bullshitter. Now his life's mission was to keep dirtbags out of prison, to save the unsavory. "I happen to be good at it," Troy said. "But then I'd be good at selling cars—new or used."

By his own estimate, Troy was undefeated in over fifty criminal cases. Most felt this was an extreme exaggeration and that much of his career was built on garbage cases and plea-bargains. In his favor, however, along with his theatrical bent, was a long-standing friendship with Delahunt. No criminal defense lawyer ever suffered by being pals with a DA.

Just sixteen months earlier, the *Globe* asked Troy how he wanted to end his career. "I'd like to get a von Bülow type case and go out in a blaze of glory," he said, referring to the Rhode Island millionaire recently imprisoned for trying to kill his wife. In Douglas, Troy may have seen his own Claus von Bülow.

There are two versions of how Troy came to defend Douglas. The first stemmed from Douglas's inability to pay Clayman's fee. Clayman allegedly reached out to Troy for advice. Attracted by the chance to publicize himself, Troy lobbied the court and was appointed Douglas's lawyer. The other version is that Nancy Douglas had contacted Troy's office about defending her husband. After some backroom legerdemain, Troy effectively muscled his way in and sent Clayman packing.

Regardless of how it happened, Troy was now part of what promised to be the trial of the decade.

As expected, Troy came out with guns blazing. To the media, Troy referred to Robin as a "blackmailin' whore," and Kivlan, he said, was a "piece of cake."

Troy also insisted Robin was alive. If she was really dead, Troy asked, where was her autopsy report?

At a pretrial hearing, Troy lost his temper and began grandstanding.

"Dead, dead," Troy shouted. "You keep saying she's dead. I hope she walks in here in the middle of this."

Later, Troy said Robin's exact whereabouts would be revealed during the course of the trial. He even announced plans to call Robin as a witness for the defense.

Among Troy's first motions was for the trial be moved to another location. The man who loved publicity felt the case had attracted too much of it. And of course, by saying as much, he attracted more publicity to himself.

In all, Troy presented more than seventy motions during his pretrial hearing.

Fighting to have evidence suppressed, he argued there was no probable cause for the search of Douglas's home and that the search warrants were insufficient. Therefore, anything found in Douglas's home shouldn't be presented in court.

Troy also wanted to ban reporters from the trial, fearing the widespread media coverage had already ruined any chance of finding impartial jurors. In this, he had a point. People had been reading for weeks about the professor, the prostitute, the bloody hammer, the skull fragments and bits of brain, plus the constant assertions from Kivlan that Robin was dead. Even if Douglas had killed her, he did it only once; the media was beating her to death every morning.

To impress upon Judge Donahue that Douglas was already a victim of too much negative press, Troy subpoenaed all reports from Boston's major newspapers, plus the *Lawrence Eagle-Tribune*, as well as Boston's three major television stations and eight radio stations.

• • •

Judge Donahue dismissed Troy's motion to ban the press.

He also dismissed Troy's motion to have the evidence found in Douglas's home banned. He did, however, grant Troy permission to test all of the physical evidence and listen to the tapes found in Douglas's home.

Donahue's nod to the growing media circus was to place gag orders on the attorneys and investigators.

"The whole case is Mickey Mouse," Troy told the Associated Press. "That's all I can say to you because of the gag order."

At one point, Troy claimed that Joe Murray of Charlestown might have killed Robin. Murray had created some small controversy by refusing to appear before a grand jury in late February and was purportedly out of the country. Aside from Murray's initial interviews with Landry, he'd been less than cooperative, refusing to speak to prosecutors.

Kivlan, the stickler for protocol, was losing patience with Troy's tantrums, assuring the judge that Murray had been investigated but not indicted.

"There isn't a shred of evidence that Murray did anything at all," Kivlan said.

"I have a perfect right to show that someone else committed the crime or participated in it," Troy countered.

Troy was like a feisty baseball manager, kicking up dust and arguing with umpires, even though his team had no chance of winning.

"Troy was a good lawyer, but his whole defense was that Robin was going to walk in at any minute," recalled Landry. "We don't know what he really had planned."

49.

With the one-year anniversary of Robin's disappearance approaching, the desperation around Douglas's legal team was palpable. Still, Troy presented a cool front. Simultaneously with preparing the Douglas defense, Troy was planning a new venture as a boxing promoter, organizing an eight-fight show for March in Waltham. The public saw Troy as so sure of himself that he could dabble in a sports promotion while preparing for a major murder trial.

Deep down, however, Troy was leery of his client. From his first encounter with Douglas, Troy felt he had met his match as a bullshit artist. Troy was chiefly irritated by Douglas's new insistence that the Massachusetts State Police had framed him.

Troy wanted Douglas to plead insanity, but Douglas refused. Then Troy suggested Douglas pass the blame for Robin's murder onto his wife, Nancy. Douglas refused again.

Only one idea appealed to both Douglas and Troy. It had to do with Douglas's starvation diet. Douglas maintained that a lack of nutrients had caused his odd behavior of the previous year. This was just the sort of concept Troy liked to spring on a jury, scientific gaga that might cast doubt in their minds.

Five years earlier, when Dan White was on trial for the shooting deaths of San Francisco Mayor George Moscone and Board of Supervisors member Harvey Milk, the public learned of the infamous "Twinkie Defense." It was proposed that eating too much junk food the night before the shootings had diminished White's mind, since he ordinarily followed a healthy diet. The argument resulted in White receiving a rather mild manslaughter sentence that saw him released from prison after a mere five years. Granted, a California jury might be more easily swayed by such an argument, whereas an old-fashioned Norfolk County jury might be more cynical, but there was talk that Douglas's defense was considering his old "psychonutritional" theory.

The defense may have included a study done at the University of Minnesota during the years after World War II. Thirty-six male subjects underwent a so-called "starvation experiment," and the results included anything from auditory hallucinations to disruptions in heart rhythms. In some cases, the brain actually shrank. But it was the effects of starvation on the obese that Troy might've cited, particularly the theory of Dr. Glucksman that the obese dieter might cling to a maternal figure, going to extremes to control her.

In the coming weeks, Troy revealed that Douglas had been so weakened by dieting that he hadn't been in his right mind for much of the investigation, and had actually misunderstood his Miranda rights, waving his right to remain silent. Though Douglas's dieting had taken place many months before the investigation, Troy's plan was to present Douglas as being sapped by weight loss and easily confused by the interrogations of experienced cops. Troy thought he could make the diet defense work if he added Douglas's cocaine use, but he had his doubts.

Troy had dealt with rapists, drug dealers, and other venal characters. But he'd never met anyone like Douglas. The professor would be flighty one moment, and then stubborn as a mule the next. A full murder confession wasn't forthcoming.

At one point, Troy was so impatient with Douglas that he handed over the interviewing duties to a new associate from his firm, William J. Doyle. A third-generation lawyer, Doyle fared no better with Douglas, who kept altering his story about how he first met Robin.

Doyle found Douglas's daily changing of the story unfathomable. In one version, Douglas claimed he had been attacked by a prostitute in a parking lot, taken to a trick pad where he was given some drugged apple juice, stripped nude, and posed on a bed while she took photos in order to blackmail him. It was a story Douglas had conjured up months earlier on one of his mysterious tape recordings, a scenario that may have originated in one of his pornographic books. To Doyle, it seemed Douglas was confusing fact and fiction.

In his conversations with Troy and Doyle, Douglas denied he was obsessed with Robin. Gradually, though, he came as close as he ever did to revealing the inner workings of the relationship.

Douglas compared his feelings for Robin to an addiction. Just being near her, he said, charged him with adrenaline, made him want to be alive. Whether he loved her, Douglas couldn't say. But she'd made him feel like a different man.

50.

March 1984. Suffolk Superior Court, Boston. For several days a grand jury listened to presentations from both sides. Douglas sat with his defense team, crouching down as if to stay hidden. Occasionally he glanced around the room or peeked out from his shell to better hear the testimony.

Paul Landry talked about the initial interview he'd conducted with Douglas nearly a year earlier. Lieutenant Sharkey was asked to describe the search of Douglas's house. Jurors heard about pink panties and beepers. They heard about Douglas being kidnapped by Robin's friends and thrown into an alley.

Meanwhile, followers of local trials were eager to see how Troy fared against Kivlan. Kivlan was a no-nonsense type, staunch as a Sunday school teacher. For Troy, the courtroom was a vaudeville stage where he'd grown rich defending rapists and crooked judges. Fireworks were inevitable. But Troy was not so fiery during these initial hearings. Instead, he took a few easy warm-up shots, mostly about irregularities in the search warrants, something about the state troopers withholding information about one of Robin's phone messages, and the involvement of Joe Murray. The Douglas team also debated with Kivlan whether Douglas fully understood his rights at the time of his interviews. "He is a baby in the arms of an experienced police officer," the defense said of Douglas.

It was mostly bluster and bluff, cheap rabbit punches from the old boxer.

Troy allegedly had a number of schemes in mind. Among the most ludicrous was his plan to hire a woman who resembled Robin and have her walk in during a pretrial hearing, her face concealed by a veil. (Billy Dwyer claimed this actually happened, though other sources say it never got beyond the idea stage.) Another of Troy's ideas was that Robin had staged her own death and framed Douglas, just so she could escape to Las Vegas or the Caribbean.

• • •

The trial was set for April in the Norfolk County courthouse. As expected, jury selection was difficult. Judge Donahue asked each citizen if they'd be affected by what they had heard in the media, if they would be affected by the fact that Douglas had cheated on his wife or that Robin was a prostitute. To the judge's frustration, most answered yes.

At one point, Troy accused Kivlan of "challenging" young jury panelists. Troy wanted a young jury, because he felt young people were not trusting of the government and "want things proved," which played into his belief that without a body there was no real case against Douglas. Kivlan countered by saying the young people being interviewed seemed timid or immature.

Douglas seemed at ease during the jury selection. As the Associated Press observed, "He appeared relaxed in court, conferring with attorneys and studying the list of juror's names and addresses." But as the jury hearing went on, Douglas grew agitated. He fiddled with a pen, stopping now and then to scribble notes on a yellow legal pad. Journalist Linda Wolfe asked Doyle about the defendant's incessant note-taking. Doyle revealed that Douglas wrote the same words over and over again: "There must be a way."

After an arduous process, a thirteen-member panel of men and women were selected, ages ranging from twenty to sixty-four. There was a receptionist from Brookline, a pharmacy student, an employee of the state Correction Department in Norfolk, two engineers, a mail handler, a custodian, a machinist, a salesman, a car wash manager, a business executive, a sheet metal worker, and a homemaker.

In public, Troy put on a brave face, downplaying the scientific studies on the blood samples, adding that they could match "four hundred thousand other people." Troy's main concern was that jury members could see the difference between Douglas and a truly hardened criminal type. As Troy had once done with Albert DeSalvo, he was presenting Douglas as a man unlikely to kill.

In private, Troy worried. The press was leaning into the story harder each day, with more information leaking out about Douglas. Practically everyone in Massachusetts knew about the evidence found in Douglas's windbreaker, which had initially been described as a tiny piece of tissue but now was depicted tabloid-style as "a chunk of human brain." None of the media coverage benefited Troy's angle that Robin was possibly alive and that Douglas was just a respectable fellow, not a killer.

During the week of jury selection, Troy encouraged Douglas to avoid the possibility of life in prison by pleading guilty. Troy knew Kivlan planned to bury Douglas under a landslide of circumstantial evidence.

Troy admitted later that he knew Douglas's case was hopeless. Yet his pessimism didn't stop him from making grand statements. During the week of jury selection, Troy claimed to have a list of twenty witnesses, including a Florida attorney and his wife, who allegedly saw Robin days after she'd disappeared.

51.

It wasn't the only murder case going on in New England.

Val Mayfield, an eighteen-year-old Dorchester man, was on trial for the rape and murder of Mary Ann Hanley, his eleven-year-old neighbor.

Twenty-six-year-old Lorenzo Perdomo of Jamaica Plain was soon to go on trial for killing his fifteen-year-old girlfriend with a shotgun blast to the stomach.

Leonard Paradiso, a forty-one-year-old fish peddler from Revere, would soon be on trial for the murder of twenty-year-old Marie Ianuzzi, whose nearly naked body was found on some rocks near a marsh in Saugus.

A Randolph man, twenty-seven-year-old David Willoughby, was on trial in Maine for the kidnapping and murder of twenty-one-year-old Paula Roberts.

In Concord, New Hampshire, a Vietnam veteran, Gary Place, was hoping a new concept called "posttraumatic stress disorder" would help him avoid the death penalty after strangling his fiancée. His lawyer claimed the smell of Vietnamese cooking from a nearby restaurant rendered him temporarily insane.

There were others. None received the coverage that accompanied the tale of *amour fou* between the slain prostitute and the obsessed professor.

One of the reasons the case attracted attention was that it contained everything that exists in the dark side of humanity: greed, violence, lust, lies, and infidelity. Douglas was the sort of disgraced figure we knew from Russian literature or film noir. The most obvious comparison was to Professor Rath in *The Blue Angel*, the 1930 Joseph von Sternberg film. Based on a Heinrich Mann novel, the movie still played occasionally on PBS and at local art houses like the Brattle Theater in Cambridge, and one could see the Douglas–Benedict story in it. Rath (Emil Jannings) becomes obsessed with sultry cabaret performer Lola Lola (Marlene Dietrich, who also sang what became her signature tune, "Falling in Love Again"). She brings Rath to his ruin. He loses his teaching position and then, out of frustration, attempts to kill her. There's even a scene where Rath's students play a trick on him involving the singer's panties, recalling the moment when Robin's panties were found in Douglas's closet—but Rath had a kind of sad dignity that was lacking in Douglas. And Benedict, in the end, wasn't as smart as Lola Lola.

If Douglas harkened back to classic novels and films, he was also in line with a provocative nonfiction book published the month of his arrest. Written by a Minnesota social worker and PhD named Patrick Carnes, *The Sexual Addiction* suggested our modern culture had peddled sex so relentlessly that it had created a generation of people leading shameful, secret lives. Some mocked the book as a throwback to 1950s fear mongering, but it was revolutionary in depicting sex addiction as being on par with gambling and even drug addiction. Reviews of the book invariably appeared in the same newspapers covering the case. With flawless timing, here was an author suggesting obsessive sex could ruin lives, and here was Douglas, who seemed to bear this out.

There'd also been a growing interest in the crimes of the middle and upper classes. There'd been an explosion of books related to the new phenomenon of serial killers, with publishers churning out quickie biographies of Ted Bundy, Ed Kemper, and their ilk. But serial killers appealed to a small portion of consumers, those outliers who weren't ashamed to be seen reading such explicit material. By Douglas's time there was a shift, and the new fascination was for the crimes of the wealthy.

These stories of suburban slaughter, with their quirky details and improbable twists, combined to create a sort of American mythology, where members of posh communities did unspeakable things; this, more than killer clowns and a crawl space full of dead teenagers, was what the public now craved, neatly crafted narratives that signaled the cracks in polite society. Ann Rule began her career writing about serial killers under the pseudonym "Andy Stack," but by the late 1980s she was writing under her own name about affluent suburbanites and their wicked, wicked ways, people just like Douglas.

In the next few years there was a surge of television programs—*A Current Affair, America's Most Wanted, The Reporters*—all focusing on the most salacious tabloid cases of the time, usually to do with suburbanites behaving badly. Stories about serial killers were all more or less the same. But these suburban killings were like unique little puzzles, something for the Miss Marples of the world and the busybodies over at the Berkeley Residence.

It was fitting that just months before the Douglas case broke, News Corp. chair Rupert Murdoch bought the *Herald* from the Hearst Corp. Under Murdoch's ownership, the *Herald* evolved into the kind of aggressive tabloid that was perfect for hammer murders and the dying days of the Combat Zone. In previous incarnations, the *Herald* had won Pulitzer Prizes for both photography and journalism, but under Murdoch's banner, though still employing fine journalists, the *Herald* won no more Pulitzers. There was, however, between 1982 and 1984, a major increase in circulation for the *Herald*, partly because of a promotional game called Wingo, and at least partly because of its often-nasty subject matter.

Shelly Murphy, who began her career at the *Herald* and later went on to the *Globe*, felt there was no real difference between the city's two newspapers, and that the *Herald*'s tacky reputation was undeserved. "Sure, they had some crazy headlines at the *Herald*," she recalled, "but the reporters always worked hard to get at the truth." Still, it is difficult to forget that 1980s tabloids such as the *Herald* were built on lowbrow content. John Brady, former editor of the *Boston Globe Magazine*, said in 2021 that the Douglas case had "tabloid appeal" and was better suited to the *Herald*. The *Globe* "bent its standards to report it."

As enthusiastic as the *Globe* was in covering the case, it struggled to match the *Herald*'s style. The *Globe* usually put stories about Douglas in its Metro/Region section, while the *Herald* featured them on the first few pages. The *Herald*, with its occasional lapses in taste and punchy headlines ("PROF IN SIX-MONTH BINGE OF TRAVEL AND SEX," "PROF'S SHOCKING CONFESSION: I GAVE ROBIN CASH") existed for characters like Douglas and Robin.

It helped that the main players in the case were so visually striking. Newspapers almost always showed their pictures side by side, highlighting the contrast between the fine-featured beauty and the mountainous brute suspected of killing her.

Yet something was changing in the reports. Though Robin had received most of the early coverage, Douglas had emerged as the star of the tale. There was an increasing fascination with what the United Press referred to as his "Jekyll and Hyde existence," though the idea that Douglas went from being a humble professor by day to a sex-starved predator at night was hardly accurate. Douglas was no more a split personality than any other customer on LaGrange Street. But Jekyll and Hyde was an easy concept to understand, and it certainly helped sell newspapers.

Of course, tabloid journalists couldn't have asked for better than a bloody weapon in a garbage bin, or a horny scientist. Plus, colorful new details surfaced on an almost weekly basis. For instance, once the press learned that Robin had been a member of the Jehovah's Witness church, she became "a former Jehovah's Witness turned prostitute," which had a nice tabloid zing to it. The story also provided entry into the Combat Zone, a place most New Englanders had heard about but never visited.

Despite being covered from Mexico to Canada, one had to wonder if the story deserved such massive coverage. Joe Starita, the New York bureau chief of the *Miami Herald*, recalled being asked to go to Boston to cover the case. With so many New Englanders retiring to Florida, the Miami paper often sought stories that would appeal to the so-called "snowbird" readership. Aside from the demographics, there was a compelling reason to visit Boston. Starita recalled in 2022, "This was not a typical murder case."

"Looking through a lens of journalism, there are three levels by which we judge a story. Let's say a drunk guy shot Robin Benedict and left her to die in an alley. That's still under the heading of 'dog bites man.' Even hookers would tell you it's not a big deal. It might be an item for the city section. The second level is when there is a more spectacular murder, and she's missing for seven months, and then we learn that she was decapitated by her pimp. That might get front page in a local paper, but it is still 'dog bites man.'

"But now we have a case that starts in a roadside trash bin, leading all the way to a bloodstained coat in a suburban closet, with an intense investigation, and the suspect is an overweight professor from a wealthy suburb whose jacket pocket contained part of her brain. This is Alfred Hitchcock meets *Columbo*. It is no longer 'dog bites man,' but now it has become 'man bites dog.' That gets you the front page not only in Boston, but in LA, in Chicago, in Kansas. And if your editor says go to Boston and cover it, you do it."

And how often was Starita asked to leave his New York office for a news story?

"It had to be something out of the ordinary," he said. "Like the space shuttle."

Novelist and critic Florence King used one of her columns to explain the widespread allure of the case. "To qualify as a legendary case, 'nice people' must be involved," King wrote. "The murderer must combine extreme violence with extreme respectability, like Lizzie Borden, or else he must be a sound family man who leads a double life." According to King, the flaw that would prevent this from becoming an all-time Hall of Fame crime story was "the lack of anyone to like or even pity."

Likeable characters or not—and it's telling that King found no reason to pity Robin Benedict or her family—the Douglas case was gaining momentum for a few vital reasons. One was that it was given an easy name to remember: The professor and the prostitute. Media professionals know that a handy label will stick in the public's memory, like a brand name. There was also in the 1983–84 period an increased fascination with prostitutes in the pop culture. Television critic Bill Hayden noted in a 1984 column that there hadn't been a recent week where some "pro, semi-pro, or amateur lady of the evening didn't wiggle onto primetime television."

Finally, the fact that Robin's body was missing provided New Englanders with the most tantalizing of mysteries. Each day, readers expected Douglas would break under pressure and lead the authorities to some unholy location, perhaps a shallow grave near his home or a lonely wooded area near the Mansfield rest stop, where Robin's corpse would be revealed, decaying and cobwebby; that was the only way this story could end, wasn't it? Television news viewers wanted the moment where a blanketed body would be hoisted out of the weeds and carted away from the death site, concerned cops looking on, probing around in the tall grass for more evidence.

That was how these stories ended. Then there would be the inevitable details about how the corpse had been affected by the New England weather, or chewed on by animals.

But it wasn't going to happen quite that way.

52.

The Norfolk County Courthouse stood somberly on High Street in Dedham, like a decorated old soldier at parade rest.

It was April 27, 1984, a Friday. The weather was beautiful, sixty degrees and sunny, more appropriate for a graduation or a wedding than a murder trial.

The courtroom was packed. People jostled for seats; reporters tried to estimate how long the trial would last.

Yet the judge and the jury were nowhere to be seen. Douglas, Troy, and Kivlan were also missing.

The Benedict family arrived and took their seats. J. R. was with them.

The murmuring in the courtroom took on the sound of musicians warming up in the pit before the opening notes of a musical. Spectators grew restless. Still, there were no signs of the key figures.

Finally, a door at the side of the courtroom flew open. Judge Donahue marched out to take his place at the bench.

Douglas came out next, slow and ponderous. He looked freshly scrubbed, in a baggy, tan-colored suit and striped tie, his hair neatly combed. With Troy at his side, he moved toward the defendant's area. As he ambled along, Douglas looked a bit like a circus bear being led to the ring.

Just a few moments passed when Kivlan appeared and began speaking.

Douglas wanted to change his plea to guilty, Kivlan said.

Kivlan spoke to the judge in a monologue of legalese that meant, in short, that Douglas would confess to the lesser crime of manslaughter, not murder.

The courtroom erupted in shouts of astonishment and the beginning of a hand-clapping ovation, stopping only when Donahue asked for silence and spoke to Douglas directly.

He asked if Douglas understood that he could still receive a long sentence, as much as twenty years.

"Yes," Douglas said.

Then the judge asked if Douglas fully understood the meaning of "manslaughter," that it entailed reckless behavior committed, perhaps, through fear or passion.

"Yes," Douglas said.

"And did you kill Robin Benedict?"

"Yes, sir," Douglas said.

Kivlan spent forty-five minutes summarizing the pile of evidence he had planned to present to the jury, including a description of Robin becoming a prostitute, "despite the good close family background she had, the attractiveness she had," and how Douglas grew obsessed with her, to where he embezzled from Tufts in order to pay her for her time.

"He was literally throwing money at her," Kivlan said.

Kivlan then described Douglas's constant harassment of Robin, her disappearance, the hammer, and the blood evidence.

Donahue asked if Douglas agreed with Kivlan's description of events.

"Respectfully," Douglas said, "I don't agree with every detail of what Assistant District Attorney Kivlan stated, but I do in fact agree with it substantially."

Kivlan had more to say, but Douglas interrupted and asked if he could speak. He wanted to address the Benedicts.

"I know Mr. and Mrs. Benedict and they're fine people," Douglas said. "They've raised a wonderful family unit."

From the spectator section someone shouted "Fuck you!"

This was J. R., on his feet like he was ready to pounce. Robin's mother was weeping.

Douglas went on, his falsetto voice filling the courtroom like a mist.

"I want to say I'm sorry to the Benedict family because I have caused that family a great deal of pain and anguish and grief and sorrow and wonder about Robin Benedict."

J. R. yelled again, "Shut up!"

Though Douglas's wife and children were not in the courtroom, Douglas addressed them, too.

"I'd also like to apologize to my family," he said, "to my wife and three children because I've caused them a great deal of suffering also."

Douglas was once again the bad boy promising to be good.

It had always worked in the past.

53.

Why did Douglas confess?

Some felt that his ego and status had kept him alienated from ordinary men and women, and that he feared facing a jury of regular folks.

He may have also believed that a confession would spare his wife and children from having to testify. He may have wanted to protect them from the pressure. Either that or he was worried about what they might say.

Another possibility is that Douglas had a history of intimidating people, whether it was his sickly mother, his staff at the medical school, or older women at the YWCA hotel. Having seen John Kivlan operate before the grand jury, Douglas knew he couldn't bully Johnny America.

Apparently, Troy and Doyle had visited Douglas at the Dedham jail during the week of jury selection. Troy explained that Kivlan was going to squash him.

It was decided that Douglas would offer a basic story that would pass for manslaughter.

The story was not easy to come by. Troy would later say that the details had to be carefully teased out, that Douglas was suppressing memories and couldn't recall exactly what happened. Still, Douglas and his attorneys eventually sculpted a confession of sorts.

On the subject of defense attorneys working with clients to create something that sounded like a confession but blurred certain facts, Anthony DiFruscia admitted that such things happen. "It shouldn't," he said. "They should just be confident in telling the truth. But Troy was good at stretching the truth."

When they finally agreed on the story to be presented, Troy contacted Delahunt. Over drinks at the Bostonian Hotel, Troy talked about a plea bargain for his client. Troy pointed out that the Commonwealth would look bad if Robin's body remained missing. He offered a caveat: Douglas would help find the body in exchange for a manslaughter charge. If the case went to trial and Douglas was found guilty of murder, he didn't have to say anything about the body. But if he could plead guilty to the lesser charge of manslaughter, he'd take investigators to the body that, as Troy told Delahunt, was "out of state."

Delahunt liked what he heard. A plea bargain would eliminate a costly trial and would prevent the Douglas children from being put on the stand. Of most importance, it would produce Robin's body.

Forty-five minutes and two beers later, Delahunt suggested Troy contact the prosecution with his offer of a manslaughter plea.

Kivlan was reluctant. He wanted to nail Douglas. Yet he knew Troy's offer had merit. Even if Kivlan successfully put Douglas away for murder, there'd be an appeal and, most likely, a reversal. A confession to manslaughter would get Douglas as much as twenty years, while a murder conviction followed by a successful appeal might have him in and out of prison in only a few years. Besides, Delahunt's office was encouraging Kivlan to take the plea deal.

There was also the issue of Kivlan's witnesses. He doubted a jury in Norfolk County would respond well to a parade of Boston prostitutes. Kivlan had considered using J. R. and Savi as witnesses, but J. R. seemed entirely untrustworthy. Kivlan also feared the jury would be less sympathetic to the Benedicts knowing they'd befriended her daughter's pimp. Between J. R. and the psychics, the Benedicts appeared to lack common sense. As for Savi, Kivlan felt she might embarrass the prosecution. Savi had, Kivlan would say later, "a head of mush."

Kivlan had other concerns. One of the key witnesses, Nancy's father, had backed off from identifying the hammer. Now he claimed the hammer from the rest stop wasn't exactly like the one from his workbench. It was older, he said, more weathered. Kivlan suspected Nancy had worked on her father, convincing him that the police were unfairly hounding Douglas.

Ultimately, the assistant DA understood that a murder trial with no body could end up as a farce with no conviction.

Kivlan relented. Manslaughter it would be.

"I kind of expected it," said DiFruscia in 2021, recalling the infamous moment of Douglas's confession. "Because of Troy. He was a braggart. And the way he kept saying that Robin was going to show up at any minute, I mean, come on! I thought it was very possible that he and Douglas would come up with something."

It must've pained Troy to come up with a plea bargain. By not going to trial, he was toppling what stood to be Boston's tabloid event of the year. He'd have been in his glory, with cheap Combat Zone characters flouncing across the stately Dedham courtroom, and cross-examinations about everything from brain spatter to starvation diets. Troy would've commandeered the whole circus like a ringmaster. To pass on what would've been a climax to his career meant he didn't think he could win. And it pained Kivlan a bit too, since he felt he could lock Douglas up for murder. Yet he wasn't sure.

It appeared neither side felt certain of victory.

Kivlan spoke to the Benedicts, telling them what he'd learned from Troy, that Robin's body had been put in a dumpster in Rhode Island, and

Douglas would help find it if he could plead guilty to manslaughter. He explained that if the Benedicts preferred Douglas be tried for murder, the state would prosecute him to the fullest. But if that happened, he didn't have to help find the body. Without a body, Kivlan added, there was a still a chance Douglas could go free.

Wanting to find their daughter's body and give her a proper funeral, John and Shirley Benedict gave Kivlan permission to negotiate for the plea bargain.

There was still a bit of bargaining, but, in the end, it was agreed Douglas would plead guilty to manslaughter, a crime committed in the heat of the moment, not premeditated murder.

Troy made sure that Douglas understood to behave himself, because Delahunt could easily make his life miserable. There were still variables to consider, not just the length of his sentence but also whether Douglas would end up in the state's maximum-security prison in Walpole or a less dangerous spot. Plainly put, Douglas needed to prove that he deserved leniency.

• • •

To the media members gathered in front of the courthouse, Delahunt crowed with satisfaction.

"I don't know of any other case in this country in the history of criminal jurisprudence where an individual has pleaded guilty where a body has never been discovered," Delahunt said.

Troy, too, had to be somewhat satisfied. Exhausted from weeks of negotiating, he went home shortly after Douglas's plea for a much-deserved rest.

• • •

After his guilty plea, Douglas was taken back to his jail cell where he changed out of his suit and tie and into his blue prison clothes. Then he was escorted to Delahunt's office nearby. Awaiting him was Doyle, Howe, Sharkey, and a court reporter. Douglas sat down at a table, and was fitted with a microphone.

Then, once everyone was ready, he explained what had happened to Robin Benedict.

54.

The story we know is the story he told.

She'd begged to join him in Plattsburgh. That's what he said.

He was going there to meet his new colleagues and to take part in a seminar. She pleaded to go with him. She needed the money. She and her boyfriend were having troubles.

Douglas felt it would be wrong to go to Plattsburgh with anyone but his wife and children.

"Teaching at my alma mater, you know, that's precious to someone," he told his interrogators.

When he told Robin this was a bad idea, she threatened to just show up and "raise hell." Douglas described himself as "shocked and dismayed" by her behavior.

Seeing that she wouldn't be denied, Douglas made arrangements for her.

She arrived in Plattsburgh on the agreed-upon date. He picked her up at the airport. They spent Thursday together. He taught a class Friday morning, and they returned home that afternoon.

Before the trip was underway, Robin wanted to stop somewhere and buy some sexy lingerie. They decided on the Grandway Shopping Center where, coincidentally, Douglas had worked as a teen bagging groceries. This shopping center, he explained, was where Robin bought the pink panties that had been found in his home.

The confession grew more bizarre during the next few hours. Douglas told a strange tale of Robin stopping in Charlestown to buy cocaine and then growing paranoid that they were being followed, possibly by one of J. R.'s friends.

As Douglas told it, a distraught Robin stopped at a Red Roof Inn. After booking her room, she changed her mind and took Douglas on a haphazard trip over the backroads of Natick and Framingham before settling on a second hotel on Route 9. Still certain someone was following them in a van, Robin demanded they leave and find another place to stay.

Douglas described Robin driving in darkness until they were near the Natick library. She parked and instructed Douglas to bury the bag of cocaine in a snowbank. He did as she ordered. Then they checked into a third hotel. Still paranoid, Robin demanded Douglas go back outside and retrieve the cocaine bag. Like an obedient servant, Douglas went back to the snowbank and fumbled around for the bag he'd buried. He couldn't find it. He couldn't even remember the exact location.

When he returned to the hotel and told her, she accused him of stealing it. Together, they returned to the snowbank and searched but gave up. Robin assumed someone else had found the cocaine and taken it.

The peculiar episode came to an end when Douglas dropped Robin off at the Revere Showcase Cinema. From there, she took a taxi home to Malden.

He met Robin again two days later at a Saugus restaurant called The Ship. To his surprise, she demanded $5,000 from him. This was far more than their original agreement. She was asking for $1,000 for her services, plus $2,000 for the extra time they'd spent together, including the time on the road, and another $2,000 worth of "interest."

They were arguing in the parking lot when Douglas felt pains in his chest. Robin took him to Lynn Union Hospital where he was examined; nothing was wrong. But as he lay on a hospital bed, he claimed Robin began demanding the $5,000. To emphasize her point, she tortured him by digging her fingernails into his ears.

When Nancy arrived at the hospital, Robin introduced herself as "Chris." Then, according to Douglas, Robin prepared to leave. In a parting gesture, she took her pink panties and discreetly slipped them into the pocket of his jacket.

The story continued with Robin threatening to do harm to Douglas and he, in turn, borrowing money from his father-in-law to pay her off. He informed the interrogators that he feared Robin would hurt him. He was worried that she might show up with some "associates" and attack him physically. He explained that Robin had a violent past and often made people pay for bothering her. He even interrupted his confession to tell about Robin seeking violent revenge on a cab driver who had taunted her.

He moved on to the part of the story where he called the Sharon police out of fear that Robin was going to extort him. There was talk of Robin going to the bank where Douglas had opened a safety deposit box in both their names, perhaps looking for money that he claimed to keep there.

"At that time," Douglas said, "there was no money in the box. If there had been money . . . I would have certainly given her the $5,000 to get her off my back."

He talked about slides she had from an old project he'd worked on, and that she was going to hold them until he paid her the full $5,000, and how they'd met in the parking lot of a White Hen Pantry in Boston where he offered her $2,000, only to be told she wanted the entire sum or nothing.

Eventually, Douglas got to the night of Saturday, March 5, 1983. According to Douglas, Robin arrived at his house alone. He claimed Robin had the hammer with her; she'd borrowed it from him, he said, to do some work around her Malden home. He said she had kept it concealed underneath the coat draped over her arm.

He brought her to his bedroom where he kept his money hidden. When he told her he only had $2,000 and not $5,000, she struck him in the head with the hammer. Douglas said the blow was hard enough to knock him onto the bed.

Douglas then described a wild scene of Robin attacking him, pummeling him with the hammer. According to his confession, she hit him several times. As she hit him, he described himself as "yelling and screaming," begging her to stop. "I'm surprised the neighbors didn't hear," he said.

When asked for the exact number of times she hit him, Douglas remembered counting the bruises on his body and estimating that she'd hit him six times.

Douglas finally wrestled the hammer away from her, but even without her weapon, she was like a wildcat, scratching and kicking and biting. Douglas claimed that a bite on his leg was inflamed for a week.

To stop her attack, he had no choice but to strike her in the head with the hammer. She reacted with "a surprised look on her face," Douglas said.

"And there's no excuse for what I did," he added. "I just hit her two or three times, and I must have hit her awfully hard."

He couldn't remember exactly where he'd hit her, finally saying it had been "the front of the head," near the temple. She fell on the bed, he said, and didn't move.

"There was damage," Douglas said. "The skull was cracked and I could see the internal part of the brain."

He checked her pulse and felt nothing.

"I was scared to death," he said.

First, he dealt with his own head wound. To stop his bleeding, he claimed to have covered his head with a wool stocking cap.

He described his panic at having realized what he'd done, and how he couldn't risk his children seeing the carnage. His first thought was that he had to remove Robin's body. He went to a hall closet and found a brown shopping bag.

"And so I went back into the bedroom and I took the bag and I put the hammer and her jacket and my shirt in the bag because my shirt was covered with blood also. After that, the blood started seeping through the bag; so I ran into the kitchen and I got a garbage bag and I took the contents of the brown bag and dumped them in the garbage bag and I remember keeping the brown bag for a couple of reasons; number one, there was blood in it and I didn't want the children to see that; and secondly, when I got back into the bedroom, I took some towels from our bathroom adjacent to that area, ran the water and wiped up what little blood was around. I know there was some blood on the radiator that runs behind our bed. There was a little blood on the floor but not very much. Most of it was on the bed and on the comforter and on the blankets on the bed."

He described using a blue comforter and two blankets to create a kind of cocoon for Robin's body. The comforter, he added, "was part of a king-size sleeping bag where you have two of them and they zip together to form a king-size sleeping bag and we often had one of those on our bed sort of as a cover up on the top because the kids would often watch TV in there. . . ."

He managed to get the body out of the bedroom, drag it through the kitchen and out the back door, and across the redwood deck of his home, where he reckoned his family's Christmas tree had been laying. The forensic team had found pine needles in the trunk of Robin's car, which originally made investigators think Douglas had killed Robin in a wooded area, but he explained to Sharkey and Howe that his deck had been covered in pine needles.

Douglas hoisted the bundle into the trunk of Robin's Toyota. Then he got in the driver's seat and started the engine. He described driving for a bit and then "just pulling over and sort of catching my breath and wondering what the hell to do now with this body in the car." He would also describe himself in a later statement as "literally shaking and screaming and, you know, just out of control. Just clearly out of control" and wishing Robin would come back to life.

He explained the phone calls he made that night. The first, to Robin's answering service at 10 p.m., was just to "tease" her. The second, also to the answering service, was to buy some time. The first two calls to his wife were to ask if anyone had come by, if everything was ok, and to have her lock the doors. He was concerned that some of Robin's friends might arrive looking for her. He didn't tell Nancy that anything was wrong, only that he had a "problem."

He pulled into a rest stop on I-95. He wanted to put the body in a dumpster, but there were too many trucks and cars going by, headlights shining on him.

Douglas drove on to another rest area. This was where he dropped the hammer and clothing into the garbage can. The thump, he said, made "an eerie sound."

From there he drove around until he reached Boston's South Station where he called Nancy again. Once more, he told her that he had a "problem."

Howe scoffed and said Nancy must've been getting tired of this so-called problem.

"I did have a problem," Douglas said.

Douglas said he then drove to Brookline, a well-heeled community that borders several Boston neighborhoods. He stopped at a dumpster and opened the Starlet's trunk, only to hear a horrible sound coming from the corpse. It was a wheeze, as if Robin were struggling to speak. Douglas was a man of science who understood it was only "residual air in the lungs being expelled," but the sound worried him. Then he saw lights flickering in a nearby house, as if a sleeping home had suddenly come awake. Frightened by the ghastly noise coming from the body and the flickering lights, Douglas hurried back inside the car and drove away.

After more aimless driving, Douglas found himself in Pawtucket, Rhode Island. He stopped at a Howard Johnson's restaurant for coffee. Then he called home once more. He grew paranoid, he said, when he saw two police officers eating ice-cream cones. He was certain they were watching him.

Douglas drove for eleven minutes until he reached the east side of Providence, stopping at the University Heights Shopping Center. He wasn't far from the apartment complex where he and his family had lived when he attended Brown University. He wanted to leave Robin's body in an area that had once been his own backyard.

He backed the Toyota up to a dumpster. Furtively, he lifted the body, what he referred to as "the material," and threw it in. Then he covered it with garbage bags.

As Douglas did his dirty work, he noticed something in the distance. It was a man in a window of a nearby apartment complex. Douglas feared the man had been watching the whole time. He told Sharkey and Howe they could potentially find the man and use him to confirm the story.

Finally rid of Robin's body, Douglas drove south on I-95, unloading more items in various locations. He threw his bloody coat and some bloody blankets into dumpsters at the Garden City Shopping Center and tossed Robin's purse out at a hospital in Providence, keeping her credit cards and red address book. He claimed to have no idea why he wanted the credit cards but kept the address book out of "curiosity and fascination."

He drove to a bus terminal in Providence and left Robin's Toyota in the parking garage.

He took a bus to Foxborough, where Nancy picked him up.

On the ride home Douglas admitted to his wife that he had killed Robin and put her body in a dumpster. He described Nancy as "just livid that I could do something like that."

He added that he had "promised my wife that I would never tell anyone that she knew. . . ."

Douglas had trouble remembering what happened when he and Nancy arrived home. He recalled trying to remove his bloody stocking cap and then leaving a message for J. R., telling the answering service that Robin had left Charlestown for Longfellow Place in the West End.

Then he went into his bedroom and closed the door.

55.

There was more to the confession: the disposal of Robin's car in New York; strolling around Penn Station for approximately three hours; tossing away the license plates at an airport in Washington.

It had taken four hours. Everyone in the room was exhausted. As the session ended, Howe said there would be problems if Douglas were lying. Douglas promised he had told the truth, but at different times Howe told

Douglas to his face that he sounded "ridiculous," while Sharkey accused him of "having a little problem again with the truth."

Indeed, Douglas stumbled in recalling the events, unable to remember specific dates or times. At one point, Douglas seemed so confused that a recess was called so he could collect his thoughts.

The hokum about Robin forcing herself into the Plattsburgh trip was in direct counterpoint to Douglas's letters. In his letters to her, he had begged Robin to come to Plattsburgh. Her erratic drive home seemed contrived by Douglas and his attorneys to enforce the idea that there was tension between them. Robin buying the pink panties while on the road was purportedly a detail concocted earlier by Douglas's lawyers, who wanted to illustrate how the panties ended up in Douglas's closet. The anecdote about Robin digging her nails into him as he recovered in the Lynn hospital bed also sounded like nonsense. The confession seemed designed to make Robin sound as treacherous as possible.

Douglas was selective about what he could and couldn't remember. For instance, he couldn't remember how he had gotten his wife and children out of the house on the night Robin was killed.

"I don't think I told her to leave," he said of Nancy. "I don't tell my wife things to do. I probably discussed it with her, and she decided she didn't want to be there."

Douglas's depiction of Nancy was inconsistent. Sometimes she was a headstrong woman who berated him, and at others she was somewhat subservient. At one point in his confession Douglas claimed he simply told his wife to ask her father for some money to pay off Robin, and she did so immediately. Sharkey thought it was odd that Douglas would simply ask Nancy for money and she'd get it.

Sharkey asked, "Do you always speak to your wife this way?"

Douglas assured Sharkey that it was unusual for him.

"Before I met Robin Benedict," Douglas said, "things like this never happened."

Sharkey and Howe did catch Douglas in some lies. He admitted that he had lied about being abducted by black men and thrown in a van. He also revealed that Robin hadn't, as he'd once reported, stolen grant reviews from his briefcase on the night of his chest pains. In fact, he disclosed that he hadn't even written the alleged grant reviews.

Sharkey and Howe were especially dismissive of Douglas's claim that Robin showed up at his house with the hammer. Sharkey thought the idea of tiny Robin Benedict arriving alone to confront a 300-pound man, even with a hammer, sounded "crazy." Surely, she would've brought someone with her if she planned to intimidate Douglas. (Troy and Doyle hadn't wanted Douglas to say Robin brought the hammer, but Douglas allegedly insisted on keeping this detail.)

The interrogators also doubted she had somehow kept something as large as a sledgehammer hidden under her jacket. Later on, Sharkey went on record saying he believed Robin arrived with the hammer, though this was in line with Sharkey's ongoing sympathy for Douglas, and possibly the old detective's way of toeing the company line, the company being the Norfolk County DA's office.

Meanwhile, Howe doubted Robin could've lifted the hammer and struck Douglas with any accuracy.

"Didn't you see the blow coming?" Howe asked.

"Yes," Douglas said, "And I couldn't stop it."

Howe must've given him a look of disbelief, because Douglas sheepishly added, "I guess I don't have very good reflexes."

The details of the supposed fight were also ludicrous. Douglas tried to describe their positions around the bed, but could never decide if they were wrestling, or if he had stood over her while delivering the death blow. As journalist Teresa Carpenter noted after reading the confession, the description of the bedroom battle sounded "fabricated by someone who had never been in an actual fight."

The timeline was questionable, too. If Robin left the West End at 9:45 p.m., as her other customer alleged, she would've arrived at Douglas's house at 10:30 p.m. or so, possibly later if Saturday night traffic was heavy. Douglas claimed he left his house with Robin's body no later than 11:30 p.m., possibly earlier, meaning he had tussled with Robin, killed her, cleaned up the mess, tended to his own wound, wrapped up the body, and brought it out of the house and into the Starlet in less than an hour. The investigators never questioned this detail, but it is not likely that Douglas alone could've done so much in such a short time.

As for the killing, Douglas couldn't remember the exact number of blows he struck, nor the exact spot on Robin's head where the hammer landed. He finally said he hit her on the left temple. "Definitely not in the front and not in the back," Douglas said.

At one point, Sharkey stopped the story and asked how the bit of brain tissue ended up in the pocket of Douglas's own coat. Douglas backed up and told the story again, now adding that he may have put the hammer in his coat pocket, then decided it wouldn't fit so he grabbed a second coat with bigger pockets, before deciding to put the hammer in the kitchen bag.

"When you find her body," Douglas said, "you'll find (it) completely clothed. There was no sex that evening, and there was no monkey business with the body."

Why would Douglas say such a thing? No one had asked if he had violated the corpse. If the body was recovered and investigators determined there had, in fact, been "monkey business," was he trying to remove himself from such accusations? Or was he addressing the ongoing speculation that he had dismembered the body?

More peculiar wording came from Douglas when he described leaving his home at 11:30 p.m.

"I drove," he said. "And as we got to the top of the street . . ."

It is odd that he chose to say "*I* drove."

Who else would drive? Robin? With her brains leaking out like noodles?

And then, "*We* got to the top of the street. . . ."

We? This is odd on many levels. Was he still thinking of himself and Robin as a couple, as a "we?"

Or was someone else in the car with him?

Sharkey and Howe didn't pick up on these word choices. Perhaps they were tired after a long afternoon of Douglas's often nonsensical confession. Or perhaps, now that they had a confession on record, they were in a hurry. One can only wonder what direction this interview might have taken if only Sharkey or Howe had said, "What do you mean, 'We?' Who else was with you?"

Sharkey and Howe also should've inquired about Pawtucket cops eating ice-cream cones at the early hour described by Douglas. It had been cold that morning, temperatures recorded at below freezing. Granted, Sharkey and Howe couldn't instantly know what the weather had been like more than a year later as Douglas was confessing, but, as New Englanders, they both knew that early March wasn't ice-cream weather. Were they so perplexed by other details from Douglas's confession that they simply couldn't stop to review the ice-cream cops?

Since then, many are still bewildered by Douglas's description of events.

"Douglas was a very smart guy," recalled Mike Frisby in 2021. "Here he is confessing to the crime, giving details, and the police were still confounded."

The confession seemed calculated to make Douglas sound like a fool. There was even a moment where Douglas talked about being in New York trying to abandon Robin's Toyota. When he stopped near Madison Square Garden to buy a Coca-Cola from a vending machine, he accidentally locked the keys in the car with the motor running. He had to go to a nearby gas station, consult a phonebook, and call a local locksmith for help. Or so he said.

Was Douglas really such a bumbler? Or did Troy think the judge would show leniency if Douglas posed as a dunce?

Also peculiar was Douglas's statement that a man had been watching from a nearby window as he put Robin's body in the dumpster. It was as if Douglas were creating a witness to prove the events had happened as he'd described. (The ice-cream cops and the locksmith were probably mentioned for the same reason.)

The entire confession felt manufactured. Here was a man who had stalked a woman and caused her endless torment, yet he claimed to have killed her to protect himself. Interviewed in 2016, Robert Benedict still felt his sister's killer had created a ridiculous ruse. "Self defense? That doesn't make sense to me. It was all lies."

Speaking about it in 2022, Kivlan was resigned to the machinations of the legal system, where a 300-pound man could kill a woman with a hammer and present himself as a victim.

"Troy was very experienced," Kivlan recalled. "The plan was to spin it the best they could. That was Troy's job, to put Douglas in the best light possible."

Paul Landry, who spent many hours interviewing Douglas in 1983, never accepted the confession.

"I don't believe a word of it," Landry said in 2021. "It was self-serving. It was him saying, 'She hit me first!' He was trying to get people to think, 'Poor Bill.'"

56.

Douglas finally appeared on the *Boston Globe*'s front page.

The headline: "DOUGLAS CONFESSES TO KILLING BENEDICT."

The front page also featured President Reagan in Peking eating with chopsticks; Claus von Bülow being freed from prison on a technicality; and a report on the funeral of David Kennedy, a member of New England's most famous family, who had recently died in a Miami hotel room of a drug overdose. It was a busy news day. But on April 28, 1984, William Douglas towered above them all. The *Globe* featured a picture of him being escorted from court, clutching a worn briefcase in his cuffed hands.

The *Philadelphia Inquirer* put Douglas on the front page, too: "FORMER TUFTS ANATOMY PROFESSOR ADMITS HAMMER-SLAYING OF LOVER." The *Boston Herald* offered a surprisingly subdued banner: "PROF: 'I'M SORRY I KILLED ROBIN.'"

Douglas made the front page in other cities, but regardless of the page he was on, there wasn't a newspaper in the country that didn't mention the case and the surprise confession.

As Saturday-morning readers poured over the morbid news, Douglas was taking investigators to a shopping mall in Rhode Island.

He wanted to show them a dumpster.

• • •

They'd arrived in Providence in the early afternoon—Douglas, Howe, Sharkey, and Doyle—hitting the University Heights alley where Douglas claimed he had tossed Robin's body. But . . .

There was no dumpster.

Douglas started muttering, pacing around.

He'd drawn a childlike map of the mall's layout during the previous day's interrogation. Now he seemed confused and upset. Where had it been? Was it behind a Radio Shack? Or a supermarket?

Howe remembered Douglas saying that a man had been watching him from a nearby window. He asked Douglas to point out where the man had been standing. Douglas scanned the townhouses over the bluff but couldn't identify the exact window.

Later that day, Howe asked the Rhode Island State Police to contact the businesses in the mall and find out what sort of dumpsters they may have been licensing back in March of the previous year. He learned that, indeed, Radio Shack had leased a small blue dumpster that possibly fit Douglas's description. A trucking company in Attleboro, Massachusetts, had supplied it.

Howe also learned that the contents of the bin would've been dumped in an Attleboro landfill on the Massachusetts–Rhode Island line. A landfill manager informed Howe that any refuse from fourteen months earlier would be beneath thirty-five feet of additional debris. As for finding anything dumped out that long ago—the trooper didn't specify what was being sought—Howe was told the chances were slim.

Still, Delahunt told the media that the State Department of Public Works was "standing by" to begin digging as soon as the exact location was established.

Meanwhile, the plea bargain gave the top legal minds in Boston something to discuss. The general consensus among local attorneys was that Douglas had done Kivlan a favor; the plea bargain was appropriate since the prosecution had no guarantee of a conviction, and it would result in the body being found.

"I've known John Kivlan for a while, and he doesn't give away anything," said Earle C. Cooley, a criminal lawyer from the prominent Boston law firm Hale & Dorr. Cooley told the *Globe* that if Kivlan thought he had a chance to prove Douglas guilty of murder, "he would never have bargained this down to manslaughter."

Most felt Kivlan would've failed if the case had gone to trial, and Douglas would not only have gone free, but the body would never be located. "I think the possibility that the body would never be found if they didn't accept the plea weighed heavily," DiFruscia said.

Now the issue was whether the body would be found at all. Landfill managers were coming forward, eager to be part of New England's big crime story. They were pessimistic.

"In one year, we take in 700,000 tons of rubbish," said James Doorley, manager of Central Landfill in Johnston, Rhode Island. He told the *Globe* that police often visited the site searching for murder victims.

"They get there, they look around, they get disgusted, and then they leave."

57.

On Thursday, May 3, New England readers were socked between the eyes with a blast-off *Globe* headline reading "HOW ROBIN BENEDICT WAS KILLED." President Reagan had met with Pope John Paul II to discuss world peace, but the *Globe*'s top story was still William Douglas. Clearly, the *Globe* was trying to out-tabloid the *Herald*.

Troy's lust for publicity continued by giving Douglas's confession to the *Globe*, which had kept the case on page one for consecutive days. The *Globe*'s presentation, however, destroyed whatever was left of Robin's persona.

The *Globe* did a thorough hatchet job on Robin. Anyone reading the story would believe she was a cunning young woman who had used her beauty to manipulate a weak and stupid man. Readers learned about Robin the cokehead, the woman who had encouraged Douglas to embezzle and then, out of greed, "struck him on the forehead with a hammer." Nothing was written about Douglas stalking Robin or how he had harassed her. It certainly appeared that the *Globe* was cooperating with Troy and helping to smear Robin.

By now the *Globe* had turned the story over to Jerry Taylor, a journalist known for his strong social conscience. Taylor died in 2007, so we'll never know why his conscience had no room for the twenty-one-year-old woman with the shattered head.

Taylor also handled a front-page story a few days later where Nancy Douglas spoke about her struggling to survive on her meager pay from her nursing home job. The story was promoted as another *Globe* exclusive, with the paper acknowledging that it was working with Douglas's attorneys. Though the *Herald* had given the case more coverage, the *Globe* had the greater circulation; it was essential that Troy feed the *Globe* as much as possible to make Douglas look sympathetic prior to sentencing. And in Nancy, he had another pitiful figure geared to earn sympathy.

"I know Bill must be punished for what he did," Nancy said. "I only hope Judge Donahue doesn't forget how much we have been punished and will be punished. I just hope everyone could remember they have a heart, and see it in their heart to have some forgiveness."

Nancy went on to describe the hardships the family had endured, and the difficulty of the investigation and court procedures. She added that her children had been deeply troubled by the case, especially thirteen-year-old Johnny, who "seemed to take it personally." Mostly, she spoke about Douglas, describing him as a wonderful husband and father, an almost saintly figure, a man who was driven too hard at Tufts but was too kind and selfless to say no.

"He was doing work on infantile diseases," she said. "Babies are so helpless and he was just trying to help babies."

Nancy even seemed to forgive Douglas for the time he'd spent at Good Time Charlie's. "His job was so hard," she said, "he needed change when he got out of work and the Combat Zone was right there."

The Benedicts were disgusted. They were angry that the *Globe* had depicted Robin so negatively while promoting the sorrows of Nancy Douglas. The Benedicts were also mad at Troy. They didn't believe Douglas's flimsy confession, and they regretted the plea bargain. They felt Troy had invented the whole story about Douglas putting Robin's body in a dumpster. Ultimately, they felt duped by the legal process, especially when Delahunt told the press that the chances of finding Robin's body were "very bleak."

For the Benedict family, it appeared neither the journalistic profession nor the American legal system was particularly interested in the truth, and that both seemed like branches of show business.

58.

Douglas had asked to be hypnotized.

The L. W. Fontaine Company confirmed that one of their dumpsters was next to the Radio Shack site back in March of 1983, but it didn't match Douglas's description. Howe and Sharkey were losing patience with Douglas and his dumpster story. That's when Douglas volunteered to be hypnotized.

To no one's surprise, Troy loved the idea. It was just the sort of thing to get him a bit more publicity. Plus, he had his very own hypnotist waiting in the wings.

The hypnotist's name was Dr. Marshall Knox Jr. A former minister and family counselor, Knox had known Troy for years and was familiar with the pitfalls of the Combat Zone. He purportedly had wept when he heard the Douglas story, feeling great sympathy for the fallen professor.

The session took place in the guard's room at the Dedham jail. Knox started by taking Douglas back to the time he met Robin, and retracing their entire relationship.

Douglas gave Knox the same basic story he'd been giving for a while. He denied that he had ever loved Robin but said he was infatuated with her, crediting Troy with the word "infatuation." He said sex was "a minimal part of the relationship," and that he and Robin would sometimes spend a whole day playing tennis or canoeing. (Douglas was surprisingly nimble in his memories.) He also said Robin found him more "interesting" than other clients, letting him stay with her much longer than the agreed-upon time.

In between tennis games and discussions of his lab work, Robin suggested Douglas start embezzling from Tufts. It was Robin, Douglas said to Knox, who "came up with this scheme. . . ."

Douglas maintained that Robin had forced her way to Plattsburgh. He also recalled the hectic all-night ride through Natick where she grew paranoid. Douglas threw in a new item about Robin rubbing so much cocaine on her tongue that she would need to go to Mass General to receive special treatment on what he described as cocaine burns.

When they reached the point where he killed her, Douglas couldn't remember exactly what happened. With some prodding from Knox, he claimed Robin bit him on the leg. The pain made him raise the hammer and hit her.

Knox asked how Douglas felt as he brought the weapon down.

Douglas couldn't remember.

"Would it help," Douglas said, "if I told you I was high on coke?"

• • •

While in a trance, Douglas eventually returned to the point where he was at the dumpster. Speaking in a babyish voice, he talked about a dumpster full of green garbage bags and the urgency he felt at having to dispose of the body.

"I remember the head," Douglas said. "The hair with matted blood... I covered it back up. I didn't want to look at it. . . ."

He described his struggle to heave Robin's body into the dumpster, and how he put two garbage bags on top of it.

Troy encouraged Knox to go over the story again to focus on any identifying numbers or words on the dumpster.

Douglas blurted a series of numbers, lots of sevens and threes and zeroes.

Then, cryptically, Douglas began whispering.

"It's not me by the dumpster," he said.

Journalist Teresa Carpenter, who had access to the tape recording of the hypnosis session, claimed to hear Douglas say three times, "It's not me by the dumpster."

But no one, not Knox, Troy, nor Doyle, asked what Douglas was talking about.

• • •

While under hypnosis, Douglas revealed that he hadn't discarded Robin's body in the Radio Shack dumpster at all, but instead used a dumpster behind the Rhode Island Blood Center, only four doors down.

It was then established that the dumpster in question had been emptied in Central Landfill, a disposal site in Johnston, Rhode Island, that until 1982 had been used primarily for dumping liquid industrial waste. It would eventually be deemed one of the worst polluters in New England. This allegedly was Robin Benedict's final resting place; with several tons of trash on top her.

But there were doubts. Even as the investigation placed the corpse in Johnston, there were still diving expeditions in ponds anywhere from Sharon to Methuen and all points between, and self-styled crime solvers routinely checked out wooded areas for signs of a body, a newly dug grave, or a struggle. And as always happens in such cases, there was the scourge of anonymous tipsters and crackpots.

"I would receive phone calls at odd hours," Mike Frisby remembered. "It would be two or three in the morning, and someone would have called the *Globe* with a tip about a body turning up in a dump somewhere. I'd get in my car and drive all over New England in total darkness until I found the place. There would already be reporters there from competing newspapers, because everyone wanted to be the one to find Robin Benedict.

"Not a single one of those tips turned out to be useful, but I had to get out there and check, just in case."

As Howe researched the likelihood of finding Robin's body, it was estimated that such an endeavor might cost the commonwealth as much as $150,000.

The word being used by everyone associated with the task was "foolhardy."

59.

May 7, 1984. Monday.

It was another packed courtroom on the day of sentencing.

Though there would be no trial, Troy and Kivlan put on a performance that hinted at what might have been.

Kivlan argued for a maximum sentence and depicted Douglas as a fiend.

"If it weren't for one of the most exhaustive police investigations in the history of the Commonwealth," said Kivlan with a bit of exaggeration, "he would have gotten away with it."

While Kivlan spoke, Douglas squirmed and appeared to gulp for breath.

"Manslaughter it may be," Kivlan said. "But it's about as close as you can get to murder.

"There's no question there was passion. There's no question there was provocation. But there's also no question that this man picked up a two-and-a-half-pound sledgehammer and struck her two or three times over the head with such force as to crush the skull and dislodge brain tissue.

"He placed her body in a dumpster like a piece of trash. Then he exploited it for nearly a year.

"He lied. He fabricated evidence. He hid behind his own children. The worst of all was attempting to cause the false hope that she may be alive. At Easter 1983 he caused a telegram to be sent to her parents allegedly from Robin saying she was alive and well and working in Las Vegas.

"No matter that Robin was a prostitute, she had a family she was devoted to and a family that was devoted to her."

Seeking a five- to fifteen-year sentence, Troy countered Kivlan with his own grandiose effort. He portrayed Douglas as a respected man, an internationally recognized scholar, brought down by Boston's seedy district of prostitutes and X-rated movies. Surely, Troy argued, Douglas's standing in the world of science had to count for something. He'd been no match for Robin's world of "sex, dope, and intrigue" and deserved a lighter sentence.

"Yes, I say this gentle, sensitive, educated man left the Alice in Wonderland world of academia and entered the world of sin and sex in Boston's Combat Zone. Yes, it was there that Samson met his Delilah." Troy went on to describe Douglas as "a prisoner of sex. She was a clock that ticked away at $100 an hour, $1,000 a day.

"The world of sex, violence, and larceny—the world of pimps and prostitutes—reached out and consumed him . . . he broke from the meek world he knew. He entered the world of the Combat Zone. He killed."

A supreme showman, Troy brought his argument to an unusual climax. Those familiar with Troy wondered if he had a poem or song in mind. Instead, he produced a page from his briefcase and proceeded to read it aloud. It was one of Douglas's letters to Robin.

Troy had chosen the most embarrassing one, the sniveling paragraphs written after Robin had told Douglas she no longer wanted to see him. It made the professor sound pitiful, especially with his talk of inventing a time machine so he could go back and repair their damaged relationship. The *Globe*'s Jerry Taylor observed that as Troy read, Douglas's "eyes were downcast and appeared to redden."

Was Douglas getting emotional at hearing how foolish he'd sounded? Maybe he was simply realizing that he was about to be sent away for a long time.

"Judge," Troy said, "this was a childlike infatuation that cost him his job, his family, and yes, Robin Benedict's life. . . . Robin Benedict is dead, but for all intents and purposes, so is Bill Douglas. Just a few days ago, Bill Douglas told this court, told the world, he had killed Robin Benedict. In effect, this courtroom became his confessional, your honor. He has repented . . . I have heard his words, 'I hope the good Lord will forgive me.'"

Troy asked Donahue to consider Douglas's reputation as a scientist and give him a light sentence. It was important that Douglas get out soon so he could contribute to society once again. Troy coyly pointed to the members of the press, imploring the judge to ignore the case's immense publicity and the pressure to hit Douglas with the maximum punishment.

Donahue sided with the prosecution. He sentenced Douglas to the maximum of eighteen to twenty years. He would be eligible for parole after twelve years, which included time already served.

As a clerk read the sentence, Douglas grimaced.

• • •

Throughout the sentencing, Robin's mother Shirley sat calmly, her eyes closed, resting her head on the shoulder of her husband John. There was little joy in seeing her daughter's killer sent to prison, not when Robin's body was still missing.

"What we needed, we can't have," Shirley said later from her lawyer's office. "We needed her, even just to put her in the grave. That's what we really wanted. Now that's impossible. She was very, very special to us."

John Benedict added, "One thing never changed. She was still our daughter, regardless of what she might have done or not done."

Meanwhile, Troy planned to appeal. The attorney who had been feeding the *Globe* with exclusives now blamed the news media for turning the case into a "Roman holiday." He declared the undue attention had increased Douglas's sentence by seven years.

• • •

One moment captured the absolute strangeness of the case. It was when medical examiner George Katsas took Shirley Benedict aside after the sentencing and explained that there was no point in searching for Robin's body. By now, he said, it would be nothing but fragments, shards of teeth. It certainly wouldn't be the Robin anyone remembered, and finding the mangled remains would not provide any relief. Shirley seemed to understand, though her disappointment was still etched in her face.

Katsas then produced some tiny boxes, offering them to Shirley as something that might be buried in lieu of a body.

They were the bits of Robin's brain.

60.

A Combat Zone prostitute named "Jackie" spoke to the *Globe* the next day.

"I'm not going to mourn her," she said.

The paper had sent a reporter into the neighborhood to collect reactions to the sentence. Though many at Good Time Charlie's and nearby establishments felt Douglas should've been given a life sentence—some thought Massachusetts should bring back the death penalty just for him—the story led with Jackie's quote that Robin Benedict's death was of no concern to her.

"Why should I care?" she said. "She was making a thousand dollars a day. I'm struggling to make a hundred."

The article included a healthy portion of Douglas's confession, with an emphasis on the trip to Plattsburgh and the wild ride home, points that were doubted later but at the time provided good copy.

Douglas came off as the gentlest of murderers. He denied he was a "sex maniac" and was depicted as a man who wanted nothing from Robin but to go for walks or to the movies. ("We must have seen *Rocky Horror Show* three or four times.") The struggle over the hammer was recounted, with Douglas insisting Robin brought it with her "to use it on me if I didn't give her the five thousand."

The *Globe* also focused hard on the sleazy milieu of Charlie's, "the gyrating dancer clad in a G-string and jewelry on an elevated stage," intent on continuing the negative portrait of Robin. It was as if the *Globe*'s determination to match the *Herald* for sensationalism could be achieved only by trashing the dead woman. Robin was no longer the Combat Zone's fallen angel. She was Tom Troy's "blackmailin' whore."

Increasingly, the public viewed Robin not as an unfortunate victim but as someone who had played a role in her own destruction.

"They were both crooks," is how one Bostonian later remembered the case. "One killed the other."

• • •

Meanwhile, Kivlan turned over transcripts of Douglas's confession to various authorities interested in Robin's Charlestown cocaine connections, and he also addressed the fact that there would be no search for the body.

He backpedaled on the original announcement that Douglas would help investigators locate the corpse. Now he claimed that Douglas had only promised to "tell what happened," and that there had been no guarantee that the body would be found. This was news to the Benedicts, who had only agreed to accept a manslaughter charge under the condition that Douglas would help locate the body.

On May 11 there was an official announcement that the search was called off. Delahunt told the media, "Due to our inability to precisely locate a reasonable portion of Central Landfill in which the body is buried, any attempt at excavation would be unreasonable and prohibitively expensive."

That evening, the Benedict family held a eulogy for Robin at the family's church in Methuen. A large framed color photograph of Robin stood before an altar flanked by two white floral hearts edged in red. More than two hundred people attended to pay their respects.

"If only this can help someone else," Shirley Benedict said, "then it can be all right."

• • •

By now, the case was off the *Globe*'s front page. The eulogy story was deep on page nineteen, next to a photo of a harbor seal at the New England Aquarium and a story about U.S. Senate candidate James M. Shannon. Shannon was apologizing for referring to Chinese citizens as "short communists."

The media blitz was tapering off. Stories were brief, with no follow-ups.

• • •

The summer after Douglas was sentenced, Robin's Toyota Starlet was returned to her family in Methuen. When Robin's younger sister attempted to clean the car, she was horrified to realize the trunk was still saturated with blood. She screamed when she saw how bad it was, and was reminded again of how badly her sister had bled. The family kept the car for a while, but eventually sold it. Hopefully, the buyer had a taste for the morbid.

"When it got warm," Shirley said, "you could still smell the blood in it."

61.

"It's a woman's book."

Troy was explaining that Douglas fascinated women, and that a book on the case would be a smash with female readers.

He was talking to the *Globe* by telephone. He'd spent the weekend at a couple of political events and claimed "at least one hundred women came up to talk about the case. . . .They wanted to know what Douglas was like."

Troy admitted there was no deal at the moment, though he was fielding inquiries from various authors and publishers. Troy acted as if he were sitting on a potential money-spinner, especially if publishers were willing to pay Douglas or his family members to take part.

Since he was still Douglas's attorney, Troy stood to benefit from a book deal. Troy probably imagined himself writing the foreword. Ever since Vincent Bugliosi scored with *Helter Skelter*, every attorney in America thought he was one case away from a best-selling book.

But Troy knew Douglas was the key.

"Everybody wants to talk to him," Troy said. "No one has. It won't be much of a book without Douglas. And the book is no good without Nancy Douglas, either. The only one that'll make any money is the authorized version, but I'm not sure it'll happen."

Douglas was reluctant to speak to writers. His silence likely had to do with a state law that prohibited anyone to profit from a crime in which they'd taken part, should it be turned into a book or movie. This was the so-called "Son of Sam law," established when "Son of Sam" killer David Berkowitz achieved massive notoriety after shooting and killing several people in New York; the Supreme Court denied Berkowitz the opportunity to benefit financially from his story. Most states followed New York's precedent. In Massachusetts, Douglas's wife could make money on projects about her husband, but Nancy was unlikely to collaborate with publishers or film producers.

Books had become an ongoing source of discussion. At one point after Douglas was first incarcerated, John Benedict wanted a personal meeting with his daughter's killer. Troy blocked it, claiming the Benedicts had their own book deal and were merely trying to get information from Douglas to sell to a publisher. Meanwhile, Pulitzer Prize winner Teresa Carpenter of *The Village Voice* was writing about the case, yet she, too, was denied an interview with Douglas.

Troy's interest in these projects may have had to do with him seeking payment. Douglas had been flat broke when Troy agreed to defend him, but Troy's shady clients had often paid in ways other than money. He once defended a drug dealer who couldn't afford Troy's fee but paid him instead by signing over a seventy-six-foot yacht. Another of his clients had signed over some prime real estate. With Douglas, Troy was probably planning to benefit from books and movies.

The front-runner to write about Douglas was Harry Stein, a regular contributor to *Esquire*. His backlog included a biography of the eccentric 1960s entertainer Tiny Tim. Stein, who had purportedly visited Douglas in prison, felt the Douglas story was typical of "middle-aged men who've led straight lives and feel they're missing out on all the goodies."

In July, Troy announced that Douglas had signed a contract with Stein for either a book or a movie, the proceeds to be shared by Troy, Nancy, and the three Douglas children.

"No title has been picked for the book," Troy said. "If we go with a book, it could be out within six to eight months. It we go with a movie, it could be out sooner." Troy added that Robert Redford should play him in the movie. "He's not good enough but he'll try hard," Troy said.

Stein never wrote a book about Douglas. Redford never played Troy in a movie.

In August of 1984, Douglas pleaded guilty to embezzling from Tufts. He was given a three- to five-year sentence to be served concurrently with his manslaughter sentence.

Later that summer, the Benedicts filed a wrongful death lawsuit against Douglas for $29.5 million. Tufts, meanwhile, filed a damage claim against the Robin Benedict estate for the $13,600 she had received for her phony "consultant" services. The later suit would be settled out of court.

By then, as Troy told the *Globe*, Douglas had resumed his scientific research and was "writing papers in his cell at Walpole State Prison."

• • •

Derek Walcott, who would one day win the Nobel Prize for literature, oversaw a class of aspiring playwrights at Boston University. He occasionally mentored productions in a cramped "black box" theater on Commonwealth Avenue, an unassuming space next to a gas station and a convenience store. Known as Boston Playwrights' Theater, the little group mounted a production in May of 1985 called "Natives on the Green."

It was about a professor who murdered a prostitute.

The production was amateurish, made up of local actors working on a miniscule budget. The Benedicts attended on opening night. The rumor was that the family would sue Boston University if the play seemed too close to Robin's story or portrayed her in a negative manner. Just about one year after her daughter's eulogy, Shirley Benedict sat grimly through the performance. She was unimpressed but saw nothing that would require a lawsuit. "It really wasn't much of a play," she said.

The *Globe* hated it, too, accusing the playwright of exploiting a tragedy, with no reason to write the play "other than to give the audience a titillating glimpse of life in the lower depths."

The *Herald* praised it as one of the best plays of the year.

Regardless of the production's quality, it was further proof of the case's impact on the city. Like villagers performing a ritual, actors were re-creating the story just blocks away from Robin's last trick pad.

62.

The tabloid culture was booming. Television networks offered constant movies of the week based on recent crimes. Some were of high quality. Heartthrob Mark Harmon was cast as Ted Bundy for a 1986 NBC two-part drama, *The Deliberate Stranger*, while Karl Malden had already starred in *Fatal Vision*, a TV adaptation of Joe McGinniss's best-selling book about an army doctor accused of murdering his family. Tommy Lee Jones had been starring as Gary Gilmore in *The Executioner's Song*, also for NBC, in 1982. When the major cases thinned out, there were always new ones on the way. There was no shortage of suburban housewives murdering their husbands or small-town cheerleaders killing their rivals. As Teresa Carpenter wrote in *The Village Voice*, this bonanza of material added up to "a form of exorcism." Though some didn't care to hear about violent crime, a large section of the public, Carpenter asserted, "prefer to see the demons flushed out into the open."

NBC needed only three months to shoot a feature depicting the Douglas–Benedict case. *The High Price of Passion* aired on November 30, 1986, as the network's *Sunday Night Movie*, a plum spot on the TV schedule.

In a strange bit of casting, Richard Crenna was hired to play Douglas. Crenna was a handsome actor who had been in some well-known movies that decade, including *The Flamingo Kid, Body Heat*, and Sylvester Stallone's Rambo movies. Though the costume department fitted Crenna with dowdy sweaters and large glasses, he never quite matched the cartoonish figure of the professor. Crenna also had a strong, commanding voice, nothing like Douglas's babyish whine.

As for olive-skinned, dark-haired Robin, she was portrayed by fair-skinned, sandy-haired Karen Young. An unknown at the time, she'd later have a recurring role on *The Sopranos*. She portrayed Robin as a bubbly type, a toothpaste commercial on stiletto heels.

The movie was shot in Toronto rather than Boston and bore only a surface resemblance to the actual case. The venue where Douglas and Robin first meet looks nothing like a Combat Zone bar but is instead an enormous, disco ballroom, with a clientele of well-dressed, middle-aged white men. Robin's trick pad is not a bleak, lifeless studio but a nicely turned-out apartment, with candlelit ambience. Robin is also shown wearing the sort of traditional prostitute garb we know from movies—short skirt, fishnet stockings—which goes against the dress code maintained at Good Time Charlie's, and Robin's own style, which was known to be tasteful. She also approaches Douglas as soon as she sees him, unlike the real-life scenario where she avoided him for several days because he was grossly overweight.

The High Price of Passion shows Robin in a more sympathetic light than the newspapers had ever shown her. In this movie, she's less a moneygrubbing prostitute and more of an insecure young woman. At the movie's end, she tells Douglas to forget the money he owed her because she was giving up prostitution. Douglas/Crenna killed her anyway. The movie left viewers to think Douglas killed Robin because he couldn't stand being apart from her.

As played by Crenna, Douglas is not the socially clumsy oaf obsessed by prostitutes. He's just a lonely middle-aged man who happens to wander into the Combat Zone one night, as if attracted by the lights.

The script was written by Mel Frohman, whose previous work included a movie about lady wrestlers called *All the Marbles*. Also given credit was Russell M. Glitman of the *Lawrence Eagle-Tribune*. His unpublished book, *The Ruling Passion,* was the movie's basis. Director Larry Elikann was best known for such TV fare as *Dallas* and *Remington Steele* but would later become the go-to director for TV movies about whatever case was hot at the moment (e.g., *Menendez: A Killing in Beverly Hills*).

Douglas's wife and children are not depicted in the movie, and neither is J. R. In fact, the movie makes a point of Robin working without a pimp. Strangely, a white actor appears late in the story as Robin's boyfriend, as if NBC feared a black boyfriend would somehow make her less sympathetic to the TV audience. In a similar vein, Robin's Trinidadian father was portrayed by a pale Irish actor, Sean McCann.

"It would have been a better story to have the pimp in there," Troy told the Associated Press. "Not only because it was true, but to show other young girls the dangers of falling into the clutches of these slick-talking sewer rats."

Meanwhile, the Benedicts appreciated Robin being shown as a cutie pie, but they felt Douglas was portrayed as too kind. They also felt the movie downplayed the violence of Robin's death. Produced for network television, it had to be discreet about the killing; the fatal moment was seen only in shadows. "The movie was made with a PG audience in mind," Glitman recalled.

Generally, *The High Price of Passion* was well received. (The *San Francisco Examiner* described it as "Almost good, and almost true.") The TV movie was also quite successful in the weekly Nielsen ratings, placing fifteenth. This showed that even a slicked-up, inaccurate version of the Douglas saga had legs more than two years after the fact.

Globe critic Jack Thomas described it as "not a bad movie," adding that despite many facts being ignored, the story was compelling, making us wonder if we all had "the same potential for obsessive behavior that destroyed Douglas."

How many others thought Douglas was the one being destroyed, not the young woman whose blood ended up on his bedroom wall?

63.

As authors and television producers struggled to tell his gruesome story, Douglas was adjusting to life in prison.

The reports on inmate W40457 show a fellow on his best behavior. An early summation by Douglas's case manager described him as "pleasant and cooperative," and aside from a bit of "heckling" during his first few weeks in prison, there'd been no instances of harassment. Douglas did express concerns "about a possible enemy situation," though he gave no details. He soon denied any problems in a letter that stated he could "live in general population without fear of my life." An evaluation of Douglas from July of 1984 states that he was "too polite, mainly because he is still scared."

Walpole State Prison was a frightening place with a brutal reputation. Even hardened cops and prisoners called the environment nightmarish. It was known for stabbings and killings and riots, with inmates having easy access to drugs. By the time Douglas arrived, the prison's image was being revamped. The facility's name was changed from MCI Walpole to the less ominous Cedar Junction, while newspaper articles depicted inmates enjoying Christmas festivities and rock concerts. Yet the place was still tense and overcrowded.

Douglas was assigned to work in the prison metal shop. He spent his evenings in the prison's law library. He told his advisors that he was interested in studying auto mechanics or carpentry, but the prison brain trust didn't know how best to handle a middle-aged professor. Having a PhD, he was miles above the prison's educational system. As the main figure in a highly publicized crime, he might attract trouble. Comments on his quarterly reports indicate the authorities considered Douglas to be unique.

"Inmate Douglas has not presented any management problems since his commitment," reported one of his case managers, "and it is not anticipated that he will during his incarceration. However, it was not anticipated that [he] would end up in Walpole State Prison serving time for killing a prostitute."

Since the prison seemed uncertain of how to manage him, Douglas took the reins. By January of 1985, he was teaching a prison course in horticulture.

Teaching was foremost in Douglas's mind. He clung to what was left of his old persona like a man grasping at a rapidly deflating life raft. In one of his last statements before being locked away, he told the United Press through his lawyer, "I hope I will be able to teach, perhaps high school equivalency courses, in whatever branch of the prison system I end up in."

Within months he had a full teaching schedule, giving lectures on everything from photosynthesis to the human digestive system. Though he also filled his days with more traditional prison assignments, such as clerical work and helping maintain the toolshed in the prison yard, it was his background in teaching that took up most of his days. Teaching also enabled him to earn time for good conduct.

Douglas also signed up for various substance abuse programs. He claimed to have had problems with cocaine and marijuana during his time with Robin; in the coming months he'd be counseled for narcotic and alcohol addiction. Though it was a bit late, he also took a course in anger management.

There's a sense that Douglas signed up for anything offered, whether he needed help or not. In the next few years he would actually take over the sessions and counsel other inmates himself; the same upward drive that had propelled him through Yale and Brown was getting him through prison. It may have also been Douglas's ego prompting him to usurp the position of the prison counselors and show he could do it better.

Though a bid for sentence reduction in 1985 was rejected, Douglas was making a strong impression on the authorities. A classification review from September of 1986 deemed him "a positive role model for other inmates to emulate." That same year, another evaluator regarded Douglas's adjustment to be remarkable, "unique in my career in corrections." One of his counselors commented that people didn't work as hard as Douglas *outside* of prison, never mind inside.

Douglas never discussed his past, though once he admitted to his case manager that he hated his "notoriety." Douglas was also upset that "they," meaning the state police, didn't believe his confession. While he agreed with what most people said about him, he maintained that he had killed Robin in self-defense and that Nancy hadn't been involved.

• • •

Douglas filled his days with work. He wrote articles for the prison newspaper, designed banners for prison events, and tutored inmates on the basics of reading and writing. In a rare interview from that time, Douglas told the *Herald*, "If I could go out that door right now, I would go back to my family—find a job teaching, or in research or maybe writing." Nancy visited three times a week; the children accompanied her once a week.

By the time *The High Price of Passion* began filming in Toronto, Douglas had been transferred from Walpole to a medium/minimum security prison in Gardner, Massachusetts. At one time a state hospital, the North Central Correctional Institution consisted of eighteen buildings where a thousand or so male felons were housed dormitory style, the perimeter manned by guards and K9 teams, plus chain-link fences topped by razor wire. As tough as it sounds, it was a relief from Walpole. While at Gardner, Douglas found himself profiled in the ultimate tabloid paper, the *Weekly World News*.

Known for stories about alien visitors and Bigfoot sightings, the *Weekly World News* had become by 1986 a sort of supermarket phenomenon. Douglas didn't make the cover of that week's issue—that lofty spot was reserved for a baby born with a tattoo and such headlines as "SHRIEKING DEMONS KILLED MY HUSBAND"—but the first inside page was dominated by a photo of Douglas and a headline reading, "MEET THE BEST EDUCATED CONVICT IN AMERICA."

After a brief recap of the infamous case, Douglas was described as a model inmate. Called "the pudgy professor," he sounded upbeat. "I just do my time by staying busy," he said. "I don't get lonely, I just stay busy. That way I go right to sleep . . . too tired to dream."

Whether or not the *Weekly World News* story was legit, it did seem Douglas was getting along in prison. Later that year, Douglas told the Associated Press that he had taken up a new fundraising project for ill children, and that other inmates had agreed to help.

"Men in prison are often viewed in very negative terms," Douglas said. "I'm just proud the men here are not focused on a negative image, but spending their time in useful and productive ways."

With Douglas at the helm, prisoners had contributed more than $1,000 to A Child's Wish Come True Inc., a national nonprofit group with an office in Worcester, Massachusetts. A group of twenty-four inmates even recorded a song that would be sent to radio stations in hopes of raising more money. That the convicts only made scant money at their prison jobs made their effort doubly touching, and with Douglas spearheading the drive, it was oddly newsworthy.

"I'm very happy to report that the phenomenon has caught on here at Gardner," Douglas said. "It's a very positive one."

He refused to discuss why he was in prison but instead focused on the fundraising drive and how it gave him "a great sense of good feeling."

"This is an opportunity to give the men here a feeling of accomplishment," Douglas said. "They are working toward a goal in an unselfish way. It can only boost morale."

The foundation closed in 1989 amid an inquiry by the Better Business Bureau of Central New England. But that wasn't Douglas's fault. For Douglas, his public rehabilitation was in full bloom.

A photograph of Douglas began circulating. In it, he wore a T-shirt with the message "I Helped A Child's Wish Come True."

• • •

What stands out in his quarterly prison reports is the amount of time Douglas spent on religious studies. Along with his volunteering at the Protestant chapel, he regularly attended services at the Catholic chapel. He took several Bible courses and even led a Bible study group. He was especially fascinated by a class called "The Life of Jesus" (another fellow who had a unique relationship with a prostitute) and sometimes mentioned it in his correspondence with prison officials.

Though it wasn't unusual for an inmate to find religion, Douglas impressed the right people. A letter written on behalf of the Chaplaincy Team praised Douglas for having "a faith that has sustained him and allowed him the strength to reach out and help others." Another letter from the chaplain's office that went into Douglas's file verified his new image. "He shows a tender spirit," the chaplain wrote. "I wish him the best as a man."

But had Douglas really tapped into his benevolent side, or was he merely showing the pseudo empathy of a narcissist?

During the filming of *The High Price of Passion*, Richard Crenna described Douglas as a man who lived by deception, a man who offered different personalities depending on the occasion. "He had to make people believe him," Crenna said. At the university he was one way, at home he was another way, and with Robin, he was yet another way. He was an ever-changing opaque prism, practically changing color to fit his environment. In prison, he'd become God's little man.

"The scary thing," Crenna said, "is this guy could be out of jail in just five years."

PEEK-A-
RAMA
MOVIE
HOUSE
PRIVAT
BOOTH
25

PEEP
X
XX
SHOWS

Part THREE

ROSTI-
SLAYER

64.

The case was everywhere during the summer of 1986. News of the NBC movie was beginning to spread, while Linda Wolfe's *New York* magazine article, "The Professor and the Prostitute," had been published as part of a true-crime anthology of the same name and was receiving much publicity, with Teresa Carpenter's *Missing Beauty* soon to follow. John Brady, editor of *Boston Globe Magazine,* had already published a lengthy recap of the crime in *Penthouse* and again in the *Globe*'s Sunday edition.

Another Hollywood movie went into production, slated for a 1987 release. This one was for the big screen, shot in North Carolina by the Dino de Laurentiis Entertainment Group. Called *From the Hip*, it starred Judd Nelson as a young attorney hired to defend a professor who had killed a prostitute with a hammer. Names were changed and the movie was a dark comedy, but its roots were clearly in the Douglas–Benedict story. There were also rumors that the case would be the basis for a major studio feature by multi-Oscar-winner Francis Ford Coppola, tentatively titled *Girl Under Glass.* Coppola was not only writing and directing, but he also planned to star as Douglas. The project fell through; he instead directed another story of obsession, *Bram Stoker's Dracula.*

The case's longevity had a sickening effect on Robin's family. There were anonymous calls to the Benedict home, with heartless pranksters speaking obscenely about Robin. People sent hate mail. They tore pictures of Robin out of newspapers and mailed them to the Methuen address, the word "whore" written across her face. Not even the priest who presided over the mass for Robin was spared; he received threatening phone calls.

"Robin's life is there in front of everybody," Shirley Benedict told the Associated Press. "It's bringing back the memories every day." She added that Robin's younger siblings had to live with the constant media coverage, "and it's hard for them."

Three years had passed since Robin's death. While Shirley was aggravated that the story wouldn't die, John Benedict was still baffled as to why his daughter became a prostitute. Sometimes he tortured himself with questions. If he hadn't objected to so many of Robin's boyfriends, would she have not ended up with a pimp?

"Maybe it was the good money," he said. "I don't know. I wish I could find out. I've asked myself a lot of times . . . short of chaining her up, what could I do?"

The ongoing repercussion against the Benedicts wasn't limited to trolls sending nasty letters. When the family approached the Dedham court seeking Robin's old address books plus transcripts of the grand jury hearings for use in pending civil trials, Judge Donahue inexplicably denied their request.

"I've wondered if some of the backlash was based on racism," said Russell Glitman. "I've never heard anyone say this directly, but I think about it. Robin's father was from Trinidad. All of Robin's high school friends that were interviewed for the *Eagle-Tribune* were Hispanic, and they had Hispanic names. There was an attitude about the Hispanics from Lawrence. They were stereotyped as maybe not the most upright, law-abiding people."

Shirley and John were weary of the way they continued to be depicted. They were going down in history as the clueless parents of a ruthless prostitute. John objected to the way he was portrayed as not wanting Robin to have black boyfriends, and Shirley was hurt by one journalist who described her home as "unkempt" without ever having set foot inside it.

Mostly, they were tired of reminding people that their daughter was the victim, not Douglas.

• • •

Meanwhile, the Benedicts continued to make mortgage payments on Robin's home in Malden and were said to have rented the place out. J. R. certainly had no intention of maintaining the home, not with his chief breadwinner dead and gone. He purportedly said he was scared to live there alone.

J. R. was said to have traveled to the South for a business endeavor and was never heard from again. There were rumors that he'd moved in briefly with his mother in Mattapan and then fled Boston because Dwyer wanted him dead.

"How utterly ridiculous," Dwyer wrote in his memoir, "but par for the course when dealing with the sleaze of the industry."

J. R. spent many years bouncing from one state to another but stayed out of trouble. There was, however, an incident in 1988 where phone calls were being made to Tennessee businessmen to raise money for an antidrug magazine. The callers said they worked for a "J. R. Rogers Talent Agency," which turned out to not exist. Was this another of his scams?

The role of Clarence "J. R." Rogers in this story is complex. He wept when he learned Robin was dead and cursed Douglas in the courtroom. Douglas even tried to frame him for the murder. Yet J. R. changed the details of his story as often as Douglas did, leaving investigators mistrustful of him. As Robin's brother Rob said in a 2016 interview, there is no comprehending a pimp. "He wanted to marry her? And he still sent her out at night to do these things? I don't understand that."

Many felt that J. R.'s actions, from hiring detectives, to befriending the Benedicts, to claiming his intentions were to marry Robin, were simply calculated acts to shed any suspicion of his own role in her disappearance. Once Douglas confessed, the Benedicts never heard from J. R. again. The bills he'd accrued from the detective agency went unpaid.

Dwyer noted that J. R.'s part in Robin's death was obvious: "Without Rogers, there was no way Robin Benedict would have wound up working as a prostitute at Good Time Charlie's. Therefore, Professor Douglas would never have met Robin Benedict. Do the math."

65.

Douglas's good conduct streak was snapped on January 1, 1987.

On New Year's morning, just a bit after 9:30 a.m., he was caught having a sexual encounter in the visitor's room. As described in the disciplinary report, a guard noticed Douglas with a female visitor. The guard saw the woman's hand "moving in the crotch area of Douglas," while a second guard "observed what appeared to be semen" on the visiting woman's fingers.

The senior guard shouted at Douglas. "Clean up your act!"

Startled, Douglas said that he would. The visit was immediately terminated.

For engaging in an unauthorized sexual act, Douglas received three days in isolation. The woman's visiting privileges were suspended for six months.

Her name was Bonnie-Jean Smith. She was a Connecticut woman in her midforties, divorced with two children. Short, pleasant in appearance, with medium-length brown hair, Bonnie-Jean was not just some random woman who rang in the New Year by pleasuring a convict. She was a respected member of her community. She had a background in nursing and was active in her local school system and at her church.

She had been corresponding with Douglas ever since learning about his case. In her first letter she explained that she felt sorry him. They had carried on a correspondence for several months; some sources claim more than a hundred letters were exchanged. As we know about Douglas, any attention shown by a woman was welcomed. In a short time, he seemed to forget about Nancy and put all of his focus on this new female admirer.

Women who fall in love with imprisoned killers are often depicted as somewhat damaged and delusional, or chasing their own sort of fame. The unpredictable nature of prison life also serves to keep these romances at an incredibly high pitch; the women never know if their men will be released or if they'll be available for a visit. With circumstances often keeping these couples apart, the relationships take on a Romeo and Juliet sort of drama.

Adding to the intensity was Bonnie-Jean's deep Christian background. It is common for religious types to send letters to convicted killers encouraging them to find Jesus, and Douglas was already heading in that direction. To quote Pamela Perillo, an inmate in a Texas penitentiary, "Prison without Christ is probably as close to Hell as one can come." Douglas had embraced the Christian ethos early on at Walpole. By accepting Jesus, a man's sins are not only forgiven, but he's promised eternal life. And Douglas was getting a girlfriend in the bargain.

Once the penalties were handed out for his sexual misconduct, Douglas contacted Gardner superintendent James R. Bender. Playing on his exemplary prison record, Douglas suggested the ban on Bonnie-Jean's visits be reduced to one month. Bender wrote back that Douglas's clean record was appreciated, "but unfortunately I cannot show favoritism and must treat every inmate the same."

Though Douglas's initial request was denied, the original six-month ban was eventually shortened to three months.

• • •

Tom Troy made a special announcement on July 16, 1987: Douglas had divorced Nancy and married Bonnie-Jean.

By February of 1988, Douglas was moved from the prison in Gardner to a facility in Osborn, Connecticut. Less than a month later, he was transferred to the state prison in Enfield, all to be closer to his new bride, who lived in Bolton.

Douglas was once again the star of a relationship. He'd been that way with Nancy, who had been content to stay in the background as her scientist husband received all of the attention and accolades. During his troubled year with Robin, it was Douglas who groveled and pleaded to be noticed. Now, in Bonnie-Jean's eyes, Douglas was probably a bigger star than he'd ever been: the reformed sinner, the fallen man who had found Jesus. To Bonnie-Jean, Douglas was the ultimate reclamation project, the definitive proof of Christianity's redemptive power.

Fortunately for the new couple, the Enfield prison allowed conjugal visits. They were granted one weekend together every three months. The encounters took place in one of the trailers that circled the prison, a romantic enough setting for a killer and his pen pal.

66.

As Douglas was relocating to Enfield, Teresa Carpenter's nearly five-hundred-page book, *Missing Beauty*, was released to impressive fanfare, including coverage on daytime talk shows. Carpenter and her husband, Steven Levy, were both authors specializing in true crime, and since each had a book coming out at the same time, the couple was often profiled together in newspapers, bringing her book even more publicity.

Carpenter was a glib and thoughtful interviewee, sure to portray prostitutes as just regular gals, even if some earned money by sticking pins into a customer's scrotum. She even joked about Douglas's new prison romance, saying women like Bonnie-Jean "want a guy who isn't going to step out on them. At least when they marry a guy behind bars, they know where he is at night."

Carpenter had built a reputation as a crime reporter years earlier with her coverage of the Dorothy Stratten case. Stratten had been a *Playboy* centerfold killed by her possessive boyfriend, who then took his own life. Carpenter's reporting for *The Village Voice* would later be the basis for the Bob Fosse movie *Star 80*, starring Muriel Hemingway as the doomed Playmate. In the story of Douglas and Robin, Carpenter had another tale of a sexualized young woman and the man who wanted to possess her.

Unfortunately, the book's release meant another round of discomfort for the Benedict family.

Not only did it bring the case back into the spotlight, but some critics suggested that Carpenter had fashioned the story to flatter Robin. Since the Benedicts had cooperated with Carpenter, there was suspicion that the author was in cahoots with the family to refurbish Robin's image. It was as if people couldn't remember Robin as anything but a scheming prostitute. To suggest anything else contradicted the public's collective memory.

Carpenter's book received a mixed reception in Boston. Dwyer disliked the book and regretted helping Carpenter with research. He felt her view of the Boston Police was unfair and inaccurate.

The book also reignited the old rivalry between the *Globe* and *Herald*. The *Herald* offered a five-day serialization of *Missing Beauty*, a total of twelve newspaper pages. It was an exclusive designed to draw readers still infatuated with the case. Perhaps smarting at having lost their chance to do something similar, the *Globe* mounted an attack. Book reviewer Bob MacDonald criticized Carpenter for some insignificant proofreading errors and a few gaffes with geography and street names. Shortly after, the *Globe*'s Jack Thomas scrutinized the *Herald*'s excerpts. Though MacDonald's review was mostly petty griping, Thomas's conclusions were interesting.

Though Carpenter had mentioned the *Herald* frequently in her book, including both the good and the bad of tabloid reporting, Thomas suggested there'd been an arrangement between Carpenter and the *Herald* that permitted the removal of quotes critical of the newspaper, along with, as Thomas noted, "the insertion of a line or two flattering to the *Herald*." In other words, the *Herald* was happy to excerpt the book if they could cut Carpenter's comments about the *Herald* being seedy. Thomas had liked the cheesy TV movie, which was mostly inaccurate, but he found it unpardonable that Carpenter's book excerpts appeared to glorify the *Herald*.

Thomas's column was amusing—he was one of the *Globe*'s aces for many years—but the double whammy of his story and MacDonald's review left *Globe* readers certain that Carpenter's book was one to be missed.

Elsewhere, the book received generally positive reviews. It helped establish Carpenter as a top name in the ever-expanding true-crime genre, a status she would maintain for years.

There was, however, a sense that the Douglas case was fading from the public's memory. Five years had passed since Robin disappeared. The story felt old. Karen Heller of the Knight Ridder News Service ended her review by writing, "A nerd murdering a tart doesn't make for a particularly fascinating story."

The case was bound to lose momentum. In Boston alone, there was a rising crack problem, with drug-gang warfare in the news almost every week. The 1989 Chuck Stuart case, where a young white man murdered his pregnant wife and put the blame on a supposed black carjacker, earned supersized headlines and added fuel to Boston's well-known racial tension. When his brother revealed to police that Stuart himself had done the killing, the guilty man jumped to his death from the Tobin Bridge in Chelsea.

On the national level, new serial killers emerged every year, each more heinous than the last. There was also a new brand of headline-grabbing crimes, everything from the "Preppie Murder" in New York's Central Park, to the nationwide "satanic panic," where devil-worshipping cults were popping up in every suburban neighborhood and daycare center, and teenagers were letting heavy-metal music drag them straight to hell. Additionally, there was a new vogue for gun-wielding psychotics opening fire on crowds, the likes of James Huberty and Patrick Sherrill becoming household names for a brief time in the mid-1980s. (Postal employee Sherill likely gave rise to the term "going postal.") In August of 1989, Erik and Lyle Menendez murdered their wealthy Hollywood parents, inspiring a new era of mammoth crime coverage centered on the rich and famous.

In comparison to all that was happening on crime pages, Douglas seemed a bit quaint and old-fashioned. He wasn't a satanist. He wasn't a Hollywood millionaire. He had killed only one person, not twenty-one customers at a McDonald's. The novelty of the professor had worn off. It was as if murderers were expected to change with the times just like pop stars.

The other issue that dated the Douglas case was the collapse of the Combat Zone. The neighborhood that had given the story its spicy backdrop was nearly gone, soon to be replaced by trendy cafes, overpriced condominiums, and office space. A new Boston mayor, Raymond L. Flynn, was credited with the area's overhaul. If you tried to tell a younger person about the bad old days on Washington Street, you'd be met with a vacant stare.

Good Time Charlie's was gone, too. Charlie's lost its liquor license around the time of Douglas's confession. Subsequent efforts to become a showcase for nude dancers were blocked by Mayor Flynn and the city's licensing board. By 1990, the barroom on LaGrange Street where William Douglas first met Robin Benedict was an art gallery and performance space.

Even the *Herald* had altered its tabloid style since the Douglas days, with new publisher Patrick Purcell veering away from the old scandal-sheet method. Suddenly, Boston newsstands seemed quieter. Headlines no longer screamed.

67.

As the Combat Zone dried up, Douglas was dazzling prison authorities with his Herculean workload.

Having been given an adjunct faculty appointment by the University of Massachusetts, Douglas taught college biology classes to inmates. He also edited books in braille for blind children. He had reorganized the prison library and remained active in the prison's substance abuse programs. He became a sort of father figure to other inmates, establishing a variety of courses, helping them with anything from quitting smoking to choosing careers.

He occasionally gave lectures at nearby high schools, warning teens about the criminal life. An armed corrections officer accompanied Douglas to these speaking engagements, though he once wrote to the Classification Board and described the guard as "an expense to the state of Connecticut" and unnecessary if Douglas was granted his request for furlough approval.

In keeping with his new image as a champion of grandiose causes, Douglas even wrote proposals and campaigned for African American History Month and Hispanic History Month.

He constantly wrote letters, reminding the board of his achievements. He'd provide carefully drawn charts and graphs, explaining the good behavior point system, reminding the authorities that he was indeed a good little man, and that the classes he'd taught and programs he'd started were adding points to his cause.

Sometimes Douglas got what he wanted. According to his Connecticut prison records, he was given a fifteen-day "release to home jurisdiction" in July of 1991, which was likely a supervised stay at Bonnie-Jean's home to celebrate their fifth wedding anniversary.

He'd also replaced the attention-seeking Troy with the far more subdued Damon Scarano, a modest forty-two-year-old attorney with a private practice in Boston. Scarano had worked briefly for Douglas in the past and seemed to fit the famous killer's new and humble personality. Compared to the bombastic Troy, Scarano was a church mouse. Yet Scarano did right by his client and was gutsy in his own way. In the summer of 1990, Scarano filed a petition for Douglas's early release.

Scarano proposed shortening Douglas's sentence and incorporating a "bracelet program," where he could work outside of the prison during the day, wearing an electronic bracelet, and return to a state prison at night. There was apparently a plan for Douglas to work at the University of Massachusetts as an onsite biologist in the aquaculture program to "provide food for the needy and impoverished Third World nations."

It appeared Douglas wanted out of prison in order to feed the world.

Showing incredible nerve, and perhaps a touch of delusion, Bonnie-Jean contacted an unlikely source for help in getting her husband out of prison: the Benedicts. The family reeled. Shirley told the *Globe* that she was "stunned that anybody could actually do that." Of course, the Benedicts had no intention of helping Douglas get an early release.

To the relief of the Benedict family, Douglas's bid was denied. At the hearing, Judge Donahue acknowledged that Douglas was doing good work at the Connecticut Correctional Institute, but there'd been no new evidence to suggest he deserved less punishment for his crime.

What was most surprising about the hearing was Douglas's physical appearance. When he took his seat at the old Dedham courthouse, he looked different. He had slimmed down, his hair was nicely cut, and his complexion looked almost ruddy. The ashen, tense look that had been so familiar to newspaper readers was gone. It appeared prison had been good for him.

• • •

Many had wondered how a professor would survive in prison. Surely, Douglas would be an easy target for abuse. Yet as legend has it, Douglas showed early on that he was not going to be bothered. A story had circulated during his time at the Dedham jail that a belligerent black prisoner awaiting his own trial had tried to put a scare into Douglas. Rather than be intimidated, Douglas stared the fellow down and made him back off. Within the prison culture, a white, upper-middle-class professor fending off a hardened black criminal was a rare occurrence and carried great significance.

Word got around. Don't mess with the professor. In prison, a murderer gets a wide berth. He's killed once, and he could kill again.

The irony was that Douglas had always presented himself as a frightened goofball, one who was constantly being mugged and harassed on the street, and that even Robin had attacked and bitten him. The truth was Douglas had a tougher edge than anyone knew. Douglas's size may have helped him, too. Up close he must've been something like a polar bear on its hind legs.

Another factor that likely helped Douglas in prison was his strange demeanor. Even the toughest cons are leery of someone who seems unusual. According to former *Globe* reporter Mike Frisby, Douglas's presence could make a person uneasy.

"Douglas struck me as weird," Frisby recalled. "He was the sort of guy you'd see on the street, and even if you knew nothing about him, you'd think something seemed off."

A large man. A murderer's reputation. A peculiar air. Douglas was fine in prison.

But he'd be out soon enough.

68.

Douglas was released on June 3, 1993. He'd served less than nine years.

For those appalled that Douglas was a free man, his new attorney had a quote ready.

"He's not a menace to society," Scarano said. "It was a crime of passion and he served his time."

In one of his final letters to a prison authority, Douglas wrote, "I am very sorry for the crimes I committed and I am extremely remorseful for these actions."

It was exceedingly rare for him to mention his past, but as was sometimes the case with Douglas, the wording is unusual—"crimes" is plural, as if he considered killing and stealing to be equal. The letter was simply another effort to have his good conduct time reviewed, and the *mea culpa* a bit of fancy trimming. He didn't even mention the woman he'd killed by name.

The Benedicts were furious that Douglas would be trading his prison togs for civilian clothes. Douglas's good behavior had shortened his sentence by more than three thousand days.

As for the *Globe* and *Herald,* Douglas was still a hot item. His release earned front-page coverage from both, but it was the *Herald* that really rolled out the red carpet. The *Globe* split the front page between articles on Douglas, President Bill Clinton, gun control, and a futuristic car being designed by Raytheon. The *Herald* gave Douglas full-on star treatment, devoting most of the front page to him, including a dynamic triptych of Douglas's face from different angles. As passersby saw the professor peering out from newspaper kiosks, it was as if the old tabloid king was coming out of retirement to defend his crown.

Shirley Benedict was in disbelief. She told the Associated Press, "We didn't realize he was just going to walk free and nothing else was going to be done about it." The man who had killed her daughter with a hammer would serve less time than if he had robbed a liquor store.

Douglas's freedom jolted the New England area all over again. William Delahunt called it "a disservice to the community and the system."

Politicians capitalized on Douglas's early release, making him a poster boy for new prison reforms, echoing Delahunt's cry that giving Douglas his freedom "sends a message that one has to be suspect of the criminal justice system."

The truth-in-sentencing law, where convicted criminals were guaranteed to serve no less than their stated minimum sentence, had been adapted in various states. The problem was that prisons were at a crisis point of overcrowding; there was always pressure to release inmates as soon as they were eligible for parole to ease the congested conditions. A 1991 study showed that nearly half of the inmates released that year in Massachusetts had served nothing close to their original sentences and were free on parole. Douglas was just one more example.

Massachusetts Governor William Weld proposed the state implement truth-in-sentencing and do away with automatic reductions based on good behavior. Weld cited Douglas and other convicted killers in a call for reforms. Weld's goal was to ask the legislature for nearly $600 million to create more than 4,000 new beds for prisons and county jails.

Within days of Douglas's release, a small but angry gathering at Boston's city hall rallied in support of Weld's proposal. A bimonthly meeting of a group known as Parents of Murdered Children felt the release of Douglas was an abomination. Marilyn Abramofsky, the aunt of a murdered child, suggested Douglas be "put in a landfill three-thousand-feet deep, instead of being given three thousand good behavior days. . . . Don't reward a murder; that just keeps murdering the victim."

Weld's bill was passed later in the year. It entailed a complete revamp of prisoners benefiting from good behavior credits. Weld called it "the most significant anti-crime legislation enacted in Massachusetts in the last decade. . . . At long last, a ten-year prison sentence in Massachusetts really is going to mean a decade behind bars."

Had the bill been in place when Douglas was sentenced, he would've served eighteen years instead of eight and a half.

Scarano stood by his client. He felt the critics were overreacting, especially the Benedicts, and that Douglas was being "discriminated against." Douglas had made the system work for him, and Scarano was impatient with those who felt he'd done something underhanded.

"A lot of people get out in eight years for manslaughter," Scarano said. "If he served two more years, would that make Weld and everybody happy?"

Douglas, now age fifty-one, had plans to resume teaching. He also planned to meet with the Benedict family.

The Benedicts had tried to meet with Douglas many times to discuss the discrepancies in his confession, but he'd always declined. It was also said that the Benedicts had bowed out of scheduled meetings for various reasons. At one point in 1984, Troy had tried to arrange a meeting between Douglas and John Benedict so the professor could ask Robin's father for forgiveness. The meeting was cancelled when the Benedicts realized Troy wanted it to be on TV to draw more sympathy for Douglas. Now, according to Scarano, Douglas would talk to the Benedicts and answer their questions. No cameras allowed.

"We're trying to curb the rage," Scarano said. "People have to get on with their lives."

• • •

The Benedicts were anxious during the days before meeting with Douglas. Shirley hoped for the best, but she was exhausted by years of not knowing the whereabouts of her daughter's body.

"You just never forget," Shirley said. "We go to an empty grave every Memorial Day. You know it's empty, but what can you do."

Douglas's confession had meant nothing to her.

"It just didn't give any closure, when you don't have a body. Sure, we've got the grave, but we know she's not there," Shirley said.

Robin's father, it turned out, refused to take part in the meeting, "because I didn't know what I might do with someone who killed my kid."

The other Benedicts were equally hostile regarding Douglas. "The court system shafted my family by letting my sister's murderer out of prison before he was even eligible for parole," Robin's older brother Ronnie told the *Herald*. "But all we want out of this is my sister's body. We want [Douglas] to tell us where he put the body. I'm ready to sit down with Douglas anytime, but he's promised us information before. . . ."

Ronnie believed Douglas received special treatment since he'd been a Tufts professor, not taking into consideration that Douglas had been disgraced at the school for embezzling. Robin's sister Rhonda was just as vehement, telling the *Globe* that Douglas had received preferential treatment, and that the Benedicts' lack of status prevented them from getting justice.

"We're a nobody family from a nobody town, so he walks with three thousand hours of good time," Rhonda said. "And now he and his wife are hiding so nobody can hassle him and they can lead a normal life? Why should he?"

It was decided that Shirley Benedict would represent the family. According to Scarano, Douglas was hoping to "ease her grief."

• • •

The long-awaited summit took place on July 5, 1993, at a restaurant called Woodie's in Ashford, Connecticut.

Anthony DiFruscia was there to mediate. Scarano was there, too, as well as DiFruscia's wife, Kathleen, also an attorney. DiFruscia would later recall the small gathering as "a tense meeting."

Douglas had only agreed to meet Shirley because of the $29 million lawsuit the Benedicts had filed against him; the meeting, along with paying $20,000 as part of the settlement, would squash the suit.

Shirley had waited a decade to hear details about her daughter's death directly from the killer's mouth. Observers noticed that Shirley was trembling, while Douglas was calm. At one point, Shirley's hand was shaking as she signed a document; Douglas reached over to hold the page steady as she wrote.

Unfortunately for Shirley, Douglas said nothing useful. In a deadpan voice, Douglas stuck to his story that Robin came to his home demanding money and that he'd killed her accidentally in self-defense.

"It was like he was reading something," Shirley said later. "He was talking like he hadn't done it."

It was hardly the revelation for which Shirley had hoped.

"We wanted the meeting to see what Douglas knew," DiFruscia said in 2021. "We wanted details about where he had dumped the body, but he was evasive. He wasn't very believable. This was disappointing, but it was what I'd expected from him. He was a liar, a weirdo. Not charismatic, that's for sure. But he never cracked.

"Maybe someday the truth will come out. But I think it will be a mystery forever."

Douglas apologized for sending the telegram on Easter to make it seem Robin was still alive. Then, claiming his attorneys had put him up to it, he apologized for saying Robin had introduced him to cocaine.

He wrote a letter of apology to the Benedict family and officially retracted his statements about the cocaine.

Douglas supposedly agreed that any money he made from book deals, or any newspaper or magazine articles he might write, would be split with John and Shirley Benedict. But it was a hollow promise. Douglas had no intention of discussing the case with anyone.

He was about to reenter society and leave his past behind.

69.

As 1999 came to a close, the *Boston Globe* ran a series of weekly articles focusing on the city's "Crimes of the Century." The case of William Douglas and Robin Benedict was mentioned along with the usual headline grabbers, including the Boston Strangler killings of the 1960s, the Brinks robbery of 1950, and the Chuck Stuart case of 1989. Douglas and Benedict were still enmeshed in the city's history, their names exuding a sort of grim nostalgia.

"Given all of the hoopla," John Kivlan recalled, "it's not a case you would easily forget."

The pair was even included in the Boston Disaster Tour, conducted twice weekly in the early 1990s by local café owner Daniel J. Holmes. The four-block walking tour covered some of Boston's most notorious ground, including the remains of the old Combat Zone, the site of the Cocoanut Grove fire that took nearly five hundred lives, and the spot outside the Intermission Lounge where Andrew Puopolo was stabbed. Then, before bringing the tourists back to his café for a lunch of chicken lasagna, Holmes would take them down LaGrange Street where Good Time Charlie's once stood and tell the story of the professor and the prostitute.

Douglas's name cropped up sometimes in relation to other cases. In 1995 a Maryland man named John Dickstein was sentenced to four and a half years in prison after harassing a prostitute named Blasa Valdes. Dickstein had read about Douglas in the 1985 *Penthouse* article. He copied Douglas's methods of stalking and using the phone to terrorize Valdes, whom he secretly loved.

Then there was Ronald Spiewak, a New Hampshire man convicted of murdering two Boston prostitutes, Gina Guarniere and Kathleen Rozier, shortly after the Douglas case. Likely inspired by Douglas, Spiewak pleaded self-defense, insisting that the two women had attacked him. He wasn't as lucky as Douglas; he was given two concurrent life sentences.

The Zone was waning. Many of the old businesses were now abandoned storefronts, neglected to the point where certain addresses looked like rubble after a wartime bombing. Some of the old shops had been turned into makeshift crack dens. A look into a shattered window might reveal a urine-stained mattress on the ground, a nervous crack user, sans underwear, standing by like a hermit at the mouth of a cave. The old Zone, with its peep shows and theaters, seemed like Broadway in comparison to the Zone of the 1990s. Yet the neighborhood was still a magnet for mayhem. In 1994, three men picked up a teenage prostitute named Sonia Leal in the Zone; when she argued with them over her payment, she was beaten, raped, killed, and hidden in the Granite Rail Quarry in Quincy. Her body was found wrapped in a blanket, weighted down with cinder blocks.

As late in the Zone's existence as 1995, computer programmer William Palmer picked up a preoperative transgender woman named Chanelle Pickett at an Essex Street gay bar called Playland, took her to his apartment where they smoked crack, and then strangled Pickett to death. Palmer kept his sexuality a secret. Even in its dying moments, the Zone was a place of hidden identities and occasional tragedy.

70.

The case found its way into various true-crime anthologies, usually with scant details, but always with Douglas cast as an "insanely jealous" man. With each retelling, the story became simplified. In Simon Schama's account of another crime, *Dead Certainties*, Douglas is briefly mentioned as having killed "his greedy whore," out of "desperation that he could no longer afford her."

Colin Wilson, the prolific crime historian, included the case in his 2006 omnibus, *Crimes of Passion: The Thin Line Between Love and Hate*. Amid such notorious characters as Sid Vicious, O. J. Simpson, Amy Fisher, and Pam Smart were New England's own professor and prostitute. Wilson and his team of writers recounted a century or so of such cases in a punchy, tabloid style. In the chapter on Douglas, the unknowable final details are described as "moot." To Wilson, all that mattered was the terrible end result: blood on the walls.

In his 2006 autobiography, *Brutal*, Whitey Bulger associate Kevin Weeks claimed to have issued a threat to *Herald* columnist Howie Carr that recalled the old case. Carr had made a career out of trashing Bulger in print. Weeks allegedly told one of Carr's colleagues, "We got a fresh dumpster out back waiting for him. Just like with Robin Benedict." Carr was so impressed that he included the story in his own book, *The Brothers Bulger*.

Not surprisingly, in a city fascinated by anything to do with Bulger and his cronies, a new urban legend was added to the Douglas story. Now there were murmurs about mob involvement, that Robin had learned secrets about the Charlestown drug scene. Now the story went that Douglas simply took the fall for a mob hit on a prostitute who knew too much. According to this version, the Bulger mob even helped arrange his early release. It was silly stuff, but it played well in barbershops and barrooms.

The case had always attracted alternate scenarios. Some wondered if it had actually been a botched murder-suicide, with Douglas turning chicken at the last minute. The favorite and longest lasting of the urban legends was that Douglas was a serial killer and that Robin was just one of many victims.

Kivlan had considered this idea early in the investigation. As soon as he had heard about the missing young woman who had last been seen in Sharon, Kivlan's mind turned to a recent unsolved killing of a fourteen-year-old Providence girl found in a sandpit near Sharon. There'd been four other young women slain in the years just prior, hitchhikers mostly, their bodies dumped near the area where the hammer was found. All of them, even the fourteen-year-old, had been prostitutes.

Douglas had traveled extensively before his time at Tufts, living in communities throughout New York and New England, making him a juicy suspect for cold-case investigations. There'd been a young woman in Plattsburgh who had been killed around the time Douglas had lived there. There'd even been a prostitute several miles from Plattsburgh who had been found dead in her apartment, her head caved in with a blunt instrument. It was all enough to fire up the imagination. One of the reasons Kivlan and Delahunt wanted to get Douglas off the street was their suspicion that he was a serial killer and might kill again.

Detectives tried connecting Douglas to various unsolved murders, even after he'd been sentenced. Connolly, in particular, believed Douglas had been involved in the murders of two other women. Douglas's fingerprints were sent to the FBI in 1987 for their files, but there was never any evidence linking Douglas to other killings. Robin was his sole obsession, and his sole victim. Despite the wishful thinking of many, Douglas wasn't Boston's version of the Yorkshire Ripper.

Yet the urban legends continued.

71.

Before the case was scheduled for trial, Tom Troy wanted to interview Lorna Johnson, a black Combat Zone prostitute who sometimes worked with Robin to entertain customers. When clients wanted a so-called "salt and pepper" lesbian act, Lorna and Robin were always available. The task of finding Lorna fell to Billy Dwyer. This was an easy assignment for a veteran vice cop. Dwyer tracked Lorna down in the Zone and brought her to the Dedham courthouse. But like most of the area prostitutes, she didn't know Robin well and had nothing useful to share.

Dwyer thought his day was done, but Troy wanted to speak to him. The brash attorney bluntly told Dwyer that he was too friendly with the local prostitutes. Dwyer was flabbergasted. He would note years later, "I had done them a favor and this is what I get in return?"

This wasn't the first time Troy had questioned Dwyer about his link to the local prostitutes. He'd previously told Dwyer that the state police suspected him of having had an affair with Robin. This was a startling thing to hear. Dwyer assumed J. R. had started these rumors, a parting shot before the pimp left the area.

The accusation that Dwyer had a special relationship with Robin is of less interest, however, than the rumor of a business partnership involving Dwyer and Douglas. This gossip has been at the fringes of the story and bears repeating. It stems from Dwyer's business card being found in Douglas's wallet during the first search of his home, and whether it was normal procedure for a vice cop to give his card to a prostitute's customer. Dwyer claimed to know Douglas fleetingly, and he attached no special meaning to him having his card. Yet others feel Dwyer giving Douglas his card was highly unusual. "Given the fact that it is a crime to solicit a prostitute, I would say it was odd," said Paul Landry.

The rumor is that Douglas and Dwyer had an arrangement where Douglas would provide information about Robin, or other prostitutes, in exchange for something. Granted, there was little Douglas could tell such a seasoned cop as Dwyer. Yet it is easy to imagine Dwyer and a john working this way in 1980s Boston.

Dwyer was the sort of detective who made connections wherever he could, with bar owners and even streetwalkers. Dwyer and Willie Moses, the manager at Good Time Charlie's, allegedly had a sort of understanding where Dwyer wouldn't arrest prostitutes onsite as long as Moses turned in the occasional pickpocket or petty crook. Is it far-fetched to think Dwyer might enlist help from a Zone regular such as Douglas? Of course, that would suggest a vice cop, in order to get tips, had inadvertently enabled a stalker. It is a horrifying idea, but some who worked in the city don't dismiss the possibility.

"The Boston police in those days was the picture of corruption," said Mike Frisby. "The number of prostitutes in the city was astounding. They weren't just in the Combat Zone. They were everywhere: Back Bay, Fenway, up and down Park Street, into Brighton, Chinatown, everywhere. They were in Good Time Charlie's, and they were working out of their apartments. There were hookers on every block. How does that happen? Because the police were being paid off. The mob owned a lot of those old strip clubs and bars, and the mob knew how to work with the police. Hookers brought business to those places. Remember, these were the prime years of Whitey Bulger; it was a corrupt city."

In his confession, Douglas claimed he was thinking of bringing Robin's corpse to Dwyer, just to "get it over with." Dwyer later addressed this, laughing at the absurdity. "I often think about that," he wrote, "and what my reaction would have been."

Dwyer has defended himself by saying his accusers know nothing about the life and methods of a Boston police officer during the 1980s. As for tales of police corruption in the city, he insists they are greatly exaggerated.

But it is also true that Dwyer seemed friendly with the area's prostitutes. Shirley Benedict claimed to have even seen Robin playing with Dwyer's collar at the police station. Still, Dwyer denied that he knew the girls well. Once, when Robin's father called him with some questions, Dwyer brusquely told him, "I barely knew your daughter."

Dwyer self-published a lengthy memoir in 2016. Though he seemed to recall every arrest he ever made on the Boston vice circuit, he spent only a few pages on the Robin Benedict case and revealed little of interest. The most to be gleaned from his book is that he disapproved of the way the investigation was handled. He'd wanted to help but was "irritated" with Landry for not returning his calls. Dwyer felt that ignoring the city cops was "a big faux pas," since the "accepted protocol" for state troopers was to contact the local municipality.

If Dwyer is guilty of anything, it is that he sends out a mixed message. On the one hand, he has an old Bostonian's sense of pride in his turf and feels that those who weren't there should just shut their mouths. On the other hand, he'll tell you he doesn't know much. As the years passed, Dwyer grew uncomfortable with his role in the Douglas–Benedict case. In Dwyer's own words, he's misunderstood. As for journalists, he has little faith in them. According to Dwyer, "Most would trade their next born for an important exclusive."

72.

Was the search for Robin's body called off too soon?

Even as the district attorney lamented the cost and the unlikelihood of ever finding the body, some felt that there was something suspicious in his ending the search before it had even started.

Trooper Howe was given the task of researching dumpsites. He reported back to the DA that approximately four hundred trucks per day deposited refuse at the Johnston landfill, and no records were kept of exact locations. Finding the body would've been a daunting task. Yet landfill searches do turn up bodies. In 2004, Salt Lake City police found the body of a Utah woman who had been killed by her husband. Using nothing more scientific than cadaver dogs and garden rakes, they'd sifted through 4,600 tons of garbage over thirty-three days until they found the body of twenty-seven-year-old Lori Hacking. In 2020, a Florida woman's remains were found in a Folkston, Georgia, landfill. With the FBI and local investigators in charge, as many as ninety people moved 7,300 tons of trash to find the skull of Susan Mauldin. The next day they found the rest of her.

Even forty years ago and earlier, bodies were found in landfills. Just a few years before Robin's body went missing, police in South Carolina found a fetus in a dumpsite. If a decomposed fetus could be found, so could the corpse of an adult woman in a blue comforter. Yet Delahunt quickly accepted Howe's word that searching the landfill would be expensive and pointless.

The explanation, if one thinks about it, may not be complicated. It could be that in 1984 the Norfolk DA's office simply didn't care about finding the body. They already had a confession, and Douglas was going to prison.

"It was unfair," recalled Landry. "Robin was a prostitute, but she was a human being and deserved better."

Delahunt had a long and important career, but he had his critics. To some, he was a typical Boston public figure of his time, a gadfly who smiled a lot and paid attention to social issues, while living a lavish lifestyle. He allegedly billed pricey vacations to his political campaigns and drove expensive cars repossessed from drug dealers by his prosecutors. And before anyone had ever heard of William Douglas, Delahunt had already been accused of everything from paying witnesses to interfering with investigations. The gossip around the city was that Kivlan and other assistants handled the hard work of prosecuting criminals, while Delahunt enjoyed power lunches and swooped in at the last moment for a nice photo op.

There's no evidence that Delahunt was cavalier in his decision, but one wonders if the search would've taken place if Robin Benedict were something other than a prostitute. All we know for sure is that while the search was being contemplated, Delahunt was thinking about his future in politics.

Delahunt had once served in the Massachusetts House of Representatives and would later serve as a U.S. congressman. He was part of Boston's long tradition of Irish political players and knew how the public reacted to his every move. Months before Douglas's confession, Delahunt was being questioned on another matter—the death of a *Patriot Ledger* journalist killed in a fire at her home—when he purportedly asked for his comments to not be recorded. He feared they might damage his political ambitions. As the *Globe* and *Herald* reported, Delahunt knew the deceased woman and had been to her house but was ambiguous in an interview with arson investigators.

"I may be running for another office in another three or four years," Delahunt purportedly said, concerned that "someone may just take your report out of the file and use it against me. I have to worry about this possibility."

Delahunt later denied that he'd wanted his comments struck, but it is compelling to know he was already thinking about his career in Congress. When it came time to find Robin's body, Delahunt knew what any Boston politician knew: Nothing plays worse at election time than having spent state money on the search for a dead hooker.

Kivlan agreed that Robin's profession might have influenced Delahunt's decision. The search might have happened, he admitted, had she not been a prostitute.

"There would've been some effort," Kivlan said in 2022. "Families always want closure. But I don't want to blame Bill Delahunt. Even if the search would be costly, it could've happened if the Benedict family had pushed for it."

If the family didn't insist upon a search, it could've been because Shirley Benedict never believed her daughter's body was in a landfill. Whether it was because one of her psychic friends had suggested it or because she'd read about the Harvard case from a century earlier, she believed Douglas had disposed of Robin in a Tufts incinerator. That Douglas had been dismissed from the university for two months at the time of Robin's disappearance didn't matter to Shirley. She simply didn't trust Douglas's confession or the landfill story.

She wasn't alone. Some didn't believe that a five-foot-four-inch body passed from a dumpster to a truck to a landfill without being noticed. Landfill workers were known to turn up bodies as they moved debris around with bulldozers, and there was speculation that Robin's corpse would've been found in that manner. At the least, the makeshift burial garment Douglas allegedly made from a comforter would've unraveled, and the body would've spilled out.

One who doubted a body could escape detection was Albert Dumont, owner of an Attleboro landfill. "I spread every load of rubbish myself," Dumont told the *Globe*. "Everything is broken open and spread out by my machine. If there's even a piece of copper wire, I'd pick it up. I go through everything very carefully."

There was nothing to suggest that Douglas did any mutilating, but the body could've gone unnoticed if it had been chopped up, perhaps, and sprinkled along various locations. Douglas's winding trip on the night of Robin's disappearance took him all over Massachusetts and into Rhode Island. Was he dropping body parts along the highway as he traveled, leaving bits of her in different dumpsters, or tossing them from the Starlet window like a fisherman throwing chum to the sharks?

Paul Landry remains skeptical that Douglas disposed of Robin's body in a dumpster. Landry reasons that Douglas would've kept Robin as close as possible, even in death.

"I think he buried her somewhere," Landry said. "That way he could visit her."

73.

What part did Nancy Douglas play?

Douglas admitted in his confession that he had told Nancy about killing Robin. Yet Nancy's exact role was always the subject of speculation.

A popular theory had Nancy engineering the entire bloody event. Realizing Robin was destroying her marriage, she simply ordered Douglas to get rid of her. *I'll take the kids out tonight . . . you will be alone with her . . . do what has to be done!*

Charles Balliro, one of the many lawyers to handle Douglas's case before Troy took over, once proposed that Nancy herself had dealt the fatal hammer blow. His scenario had Nancy coming home to find Douglas and Robin together. In a fury, she was supposed to have attacked them, which would've explained the injury to Douglas's head. It was fanciful, but Balliro thought it would get his client off the hook for murder. Douglas rejected the idea. Nancy began calling around for a new attorney.

An enduring urban legend around the case involved Douglas trying to coax Robin into joining him and Nancy for a *ménage à trois*, but when Robin was repulsed by the idea of a threesome, the couple turned violent and killed her. Since many of Douglas's pornographic books featured scenes of lesbian torture and sex slavery, some wondered if Robin was a victim of a porn scene gone wrong, that she may have been killed accidentally during some rough sex play with Nancy. It was idle talk. The case inspired a lot of morbid thinking.

Matt Connolly suspected Nancy knew about Douglas's "initial murder plans," but he doubted Nancy would do anything that might endanger or involve the kids. Yet her own brother, Steve Boulton, had raised suspicions about Nancy when he spoke before a grand jury just prior to Douglas's arrest. According to Boulton, Nancy had contacted him just after Robin's disappearance to say she and Douglas needed a lawyer and that her husband had a lot of problems to address, including his possible involvement with a "missing girl." As far as her alibi about going to New Hampshire, Boulton said before the grand jury that some of his sister's story was "outrageous and unbelievable."

One of the most hard-to-believe details from Nancy's statement to Landry was that she just happened to pick up Pammy that night. The girl was supposedly walking home from babysitting and Nancy happened to see her. If that was true, and Nancy hadn't spotted her at the right moment, Pammy could've walked in on her father killing Robin. With so many parts of the story hinging on dumb luck, it is no wonder Nancy refused to cooperate with the investigation. She may not have believed her own story. "There was always a question about her involvement," Kivlan remembered. Her baleful stare before the grand jury may have been Nancy's way of telling the world, *You figure it out*.

"She had clothing in her closets that were covered in blood," Anthony DiFruscia said in 2021. "That always struck me as odd. I think she certainly knew more than she revealed. I think she played a big part in the cover up."

"She had to know more than she was telling," Landry recalled. "She knew all about Robin. I think Douglas may have sent her to New Hampshire on the 'shopping trip' for a reason, so he could be alone with Robin and kill her. But that is only my theory." DiFruscia added, "Nancy was smart and manipulative. She was hard to know. And she remained that way through the entire ordeal."

The fact that Nancy often referred to Robin by her street name, Nadine, was significant. It suggests she and Douglas discussed her more than casually.

Douglas's account of killing Robin, cleaning up the mess, and departing with the body within an hour was also hard to believe. Could it be that Nancy returned home to find Douglas frantically trying to wipe up Robin's blood, and in her no-nonsense manner told him to get the body out of the house, while she stayed behind and mopped up? Was it something they had arranged? Had he killed Robin in the bedroom, rather than the living room, so the children wouldn't see anything, including blood spatter? (In his confession, Douglas said he took Robin to the bedroom because the living room featured a large bay window overlooking the cul-de-sac; he didn't want the neighbors to see that he had a woman in the house who wasn't Nancy.)

Then there was the mysterious voice on one of Douglas's tape recordings. Though Landry believes it was simply Douglas trying out different voices, it could have been Nancy. The voice has been described as "androgynous," neither male nor female. Is it possible that Nancy was sitting with her husband as he made the tape recording, offering suggestions as to how he might solve his financial trouble at Tufts? But even more compelling is the notion that Nancy accompanied Douglas on his trip to the Providence dumpster.

Though not picked up on by his interrogators, Douglas's confession alluded to his not being alone when he drove to Providence. He said "I drove," and "we," as if he had company. While under a hypnotic trance, Douglas had said, "It's not me by the dumpster."

Who was by the dumpster? Is it possible that Nancy went with him to dispose of the body?

Douglas's intermittent phone calls home during his journey were allegedly to check in with Nancy. But it is absolutely possible that she had gone with him to Providence. Maybe she would ask him to pull over so she could call home and check on the children. Is it possible that the kids stayed behind when she left with Douglas? Maybe she was calling to tell them, *Mom and dad are out on a little trip . . . we'll be back home soon . . . and don't answer the door for any pimps. . . .*

Why would Nancy go with Douglas? It is possible that he simply needed help lifting and moving the body. He was, as Billy Dwyer once said of him, "as unathletic as a guy could be." Could he have hauled Robin's body around all by himself? Nancy, a stout woman, could've helped. It is also likely that Douglas was falling apart mentally on this night, and Nancy may have gone along to keep him calm. The simplest answer could be that he needed help. Being the dutiful wife, Nancy obliged.

And though Douglas purportedly parked Robin's car in Providence and then took a Bonanza Bus back to Foxborough where Nancy picked him up, it could also be that Nancy was with him all the way, taking the bus home with him. Once in Foxborough, they could have simply called a taxi. It is only a fifteen-minute ride from Foxborough to Sharon.

Another possibility is that the oldest of the children, Bill Jr., accompanied dad on his journey to dispose of the body. This is a long shot, but worthy of consideration. The boy was nearly sixteen, somewhat athletic, with an interest in schoolboy hockey. If dad needed help hoisting a body around, why not bring Bill Jr. along? This was all the more reason for Douglas to fear his children having to testify, but as most of the investigators believed, it is doubtful that Douglas or his wife would've involved their children.

There was an investigation into the Bonanza Bus out of Providence on the morning of March 6. By looking at Douglas's phone records, it was possible to calculate which bus he would've taken and when he would've arrived at Foxfield Plaza, the Sharon stop. A trooper asked if anyone had gotten off the bus at that particular time and location, and the driver replied that only one person did. Oddly, the driver said the departing passenger "looked like a professor" but couldn't identify Douglas from a photo. (Douglas, with a wool cap pulled over his bloody forehead, probably didn't look much like a professor after driving all night. Of course, it was ridiculous to think a bus driver could remember who got off at a particular stop a month after the fact.)

Another possibility is that Douglas and Nancy may have been traveling in separate cars, with her following. Once he dropped off Robin's Toyota in Providence, he could have gotten into Nancy's car and gone home with her, the bus story another of his lies.

The prosecution didn't pursue Nancy as Douglas's accomplice, though an investigation into the family phone records indicate Douglas had called his wife at her job several times on Friday, March 4, possibly to discuss something else the investigators had learned: The $200 check Douglas had given to Robin that week had been canceled by Nancy. It is possible that she was putting her foot down on her husband's affair, though that still doesn't put her in the car with him.

Yet there was a moment that nearly convinced DiFruscia of Nancy's participation in her husband's crime.

"Nancy knew I was a smoker, and one time she offered me one of her cigarettes," DiFruscia said. "It was the same kind of cigarette found in the ashtray of Robin Benedict's car."

Granted, Douglas may have smoked that cigarette in Robin's car. Douglas had been a smoker but supposedly stopped when he met Robin and went on his crash diet. In 1983 it wasn't uncommon for people to smoke under times of stress, even if they weren't regular smokers. Douglas might've grabbed a pack of Nancy's cigarettes just before he left the house, knowing he'd need a smoke as he nervously drove around. For that matter, Robin or one of her friends could've smoked it.

These days, forty years later, the butts in the ashtray could be used for DNA analysis. How would the investigation have changed if Nancy's DNA was found in Robin's Toyota? It is a tantalizing thought.

"Her giving me that cigarette makes me think Nancy was in that car just before it was abandoned," DiFruscia said in 2021. "But what do I know?"

74.

"How could you throw your wife, your family, your profession away for a girl in a bar?"

So said one of Douglas's colleagues to the *Miami Herald* at the height of the media storm.

The killing notwithstanding, it is an oversimplification to dismiss Douglas as a man who threw it all away on a barfly. Douglas's quest for unrequited love may have erupted from the greenest jungles of his psyche.

The literature on stalking has grown since Douglas's day. J. Reid Meloy's groundbreaking 1998 anthology, *The Psychology of Stalking: Clinical and Forensic Perspectives* lamented the pop culture's playful spin on the subject, with so many songs and movies dedicated to the positive outcomes of obsessional love. "Stalking is the dark heart of romantic pursuit," Meloy wrote, in hopes that his study would deromanticize any sort of harassment and obsessive behavior.

The book delved into various case studies, including the "preoccupied" stalker, a term explored by Dr. Kristine K. Kienlen. With a poor self-image and a positive view of others, the preoccupied stalker constantly seeks approval and validation to feel good about himself. When rejected, the person stalks to restore his sense of self. Variations of Douglas's behavior can be found throughout the book, particularly in a section by Dr. Glen Skoler devoted to stalkers who have "rescue" fantasies, where they create an atmosphere of danger with the intention of saving the woman, who is often a prostitute. Once rescued, she would recognize her stalker as her savior and fall in love with him, a theme "readily recognized throughout Western culture, modern American media, and our collective unconscious."

Douglas would certainly fit this idea, especially with his penchant for calling the police on Robin, breaking into her trick pads, and getting her fired from her job. He wasn't doing it face to face, but he *was* terrorizing her and then comforting her. The studies also address a stalker who felt so "psychologically tormented by his love obsession that he attempted to obtain a restraining order on *her*." That echoes Douglas's report that Robin was extorting him and, of course, his claim that she tortured him in the hospital and attacked him in his home.

Meloy's book suggests the mindset of a stalker is from the melding of five key psychosocial factors: social incompetence, isolation and loneliness, obsessional thinking, pathological narcissism, and aggression. To varying degrees, Douglas displayed all of these traits.

Along with being maladjusted socially, stalkers often suffer from serious mental illness. Douglas, however, was not psychotic—he didn't hear voices or believe he was guided by invisible forces—though he showed symptoms of obsessive-compulsive disorder, which has also been linked to stalking behavior. The public perception of OCD usually involves a fear of germs, but OCD can also manifest in endless phone calls and letter writing or in recurring thoughts. There are differences between OCD and obsessive behavior. A person obsessed with something doesn't necessarily have OCD. And a person with OCD isn't necessarily going to stalk a person and become violent.

It isn't known if Douglas was ever diagnosed as having OCD, but his behavior in prison suggests someone who has sought help in curbing an obsession. Therapists suggest that a patient suffering from obsessive behavior engage in activities to provide distraction. Douglas stayed extremely busy during his prison years, but his goal to get out early through good behavior may have served a dual purpose. The idea of his workload was possibly to keep his mind focused to override the old thoughts. According to psychotherapists, the obsessive person's mind is reinvigorated by staying busy and becomes strong enough to dominate the darker thoughts that come back on occasion. One can never conquer an obsession, but one can manage it.

The general consensus is that obsessive behavior such as we saw in Douglas stems from unresolved episodes of childhood shame or guilt. One obsesses over a subject or person to help keep painful feelings at bay. Obsessions also develop in depressed people who feel life has become meaningless, and the object of their fascination temporarily fills a void. The person becomes tense to a painful degree, and fastening onto someone else serves as a kind of release valve.

It sounds a bit touchy-feely to think Douglas's fatal fixation on a prostitute was simply a way to stifle some long-buried emotional trauma, but that's how some therapists might interpret his case. Others might determine that being isolated in his childhood left him with a fragile sense of self-worth, which led to a profound attachment disorder. His academic credentials and family life could not fill the gap that led to his overdependence on Robin. Longing for the unavailable person is in itself a form of escapism. What we know now about sex and pornography addictions, and the insidious effects of each on the brain, would also figure in any contemporary analysis of Douglas.

Douglas had traits and symptoms that played across a wide range of conditions. Add to that a psychopath's tendency to lie and blame the victim and, despite Douglas's professional competency, an extreme lack of maturity. Though Douglas had no past record of violence, he was a selfish, impulsive man who felt he could do as he pleased. When he was hungry, he stuffed himself with junk food. When he needed money, he stole it. When he was angry, he yelled and threw things. When he was horny, he went to the Combat Zone looking for hookers.

Robin may have been the accelerant, but Douglas had long held the ingredients for a disaster.

• • •

New York magazine's Linda Wolfe couldn't resist ending her coverage of the Douglas case with a flourish. "In my mind's eye," she wrote, "I kept seeing him wrapped with Robin in their final embrace, arms and legs tangled together on the king-size bed, the hammer over their heads, and I thought Douglas had killed, not someone he loved, but someone he had loved having created."

Wolfe's poetry of the damned was effective and invited others to treat the case in a similar way, with Douglas as a man driven to madness by his obsessions.

Yet the scenario follows Douglas's confession too closely. It relies on the notion that he and Robin struggled for the murder weapon. If we don't accept Douglas's accusations of "she hit me first," such writing is mere fantasy, proof that Douglas's backroom confession worked on even the most well-intentioned of journalists.

Foremost, Douglas's claim that he struck Robin only "two or three" times in self-defense simply doesn't wash. It can take many blows to kill a person. A handful of serial killers have used hammers on their victims, and many of the women survived. Some killers have actually commented that the hammer wasn't enough, and they had to resort to a knife or strangling. To kill someone with a hammer takes effort. The autopsies of some hammer victims show skulls so horribly damaged that coroners couldn't determine how many blows had landed or what sort of instrument had been used. We can assume Robin's head was in a similar condition.

Though only a small percentage of stalking cases end in murder, forensic psychologist Glen Skoler has written that when violence does occur in stalking cases, "it can be shockingly vicious and uncontrolled." Recalling police reports he'd read during his time working in a maximum-security prison, Skoler noted the "narcissistic rage" that takes over during these "cases of violent attachment. Often it was not psychologically 'good enough' for the offender to 'merely' kill the victim; rather, there was an attempt to psychologically and physically annihilate the 'beloved' by primitive means such as stabbing, strangulation, and burning. In two cases perpetrators sodomized their victims *after* killing them." (This reminds one of Douglas promising there'd been no "monkey business with the body.")

More feasible than a struggle for the hammer is Douglas hitting Robin from behind, stunning her, and then bringing the hammer down ten or twelve more times. A two-and-a-half-pound sledgehammer is also unwieldy. Even such a large man as Douglas would have trouble swinging one with precision. He said in his confession that he hit Robin "in rapid succession," like he was using a ball peen hammer to drive a nail. But a sledge is heavy, the weight at one end; he'd probably need a two-handed grip, and he'd need solid footing. If they were tussling, as he claimed, he would've failed to land a clean shot. It is far more plausible that Robin's back was turned, or perhaps she was lying down, which allowed Douglas to grip the hammer with two hands and swing it like a baseball bat. Then he probably stood over Robin, hitting her as many times as it took to kill her.

Douglas wasn't defending himself from her. He was seizing control.

And despite the way he was depicted, Douglas wasn't a man "just like us." He didn't transform overnight from a normal suburban hockey dad to a hammer-wielding maniac. He didn't "snap." He simply realized he wasn't calling the shots anymore. He may have felt it was his right to kill Robin, since he'd spent so much money on her. The public shies away from understanding the deeper origins of certain murders, preferring to say some fellow just "lost it." Some men, once they've run out of money or drugs or whatever means they'd used to control their victim, turn to violence. A murderous urge doesn't merely appear one day like a pimple. It usually follows a sustained period of controlling or manipulative behavior. It simmers.

Dr. Elizabeth Yardley, one of the United Kingdom's top criminologists, has written often about violent crimes against women. For Yardley, men like Douglas usually find their motivation in simple misogyny. She writes: "For a man to kill a woman he needs to believe that he has the right to do so, he must have a sense of entitlement to behave in this way. This is built upon a value system (that) sees women as inferior. Women are not equals to be respected, they are subordinates to be owned, possessed, controlled, and violated."

The story of William Douglas and Robin Benedict had many layers, but it was merely another example of a man trying to control a woman.

Douglas's claim that he blacked out and couldn't remember how many times or exactly where he'd hit Robin was likely another attempt at control. He'd given his confession, he'd played his last card, and all that remained were the final details of the murder, details he kept for himself.

75.

Tom Troy died in 2000. He rarely spoke of his infamous client once the case was closed, but he said one last thing about Douglas in the late 1990s. "I don't think he knew what he was getting into," Troy told the *Globe*.

"He's a different kind of man, not the same kind of man that the Robin Benedicts of the world are used to."

"He had formed an attachment," wrote Linda Wolfe, "not to an actual girl, but to a figment of his imagination. No wonder he felt he could erase her, wipe her away."

This mixture of glibness and pop psychology may be as close to the truth as we'll get. But it ignores the collection of attributes that made Douglas dangerous. He was a man of prominence, with genteel manners and a soft appearance, yet he harbored a roiling anger and irrational yearnings. With what he knew about prostitutes—their murders went largely unsolved—he was probably confident he'd get away with killing Robin.

He was a perfect candidate to kill a woman. Douglas was such a textbook fit that the phrase "psychopathic narcissism" could've been created with him in mind. From his earliest days, he was told that he didn't belong with other people. In an upscale community, his dad was a mere plumber, his mother a part-time maid. Status was all-important, and Douglas bore that burden.

Yet there was no way a chubby, average boy could somehow lift his family name beyond the trailer court. He excelled at science, but he married an average woman and had an average family. He had kinky interests: bondage; women with whips; sex slaves and prostitutes. His head was swimming with insecurities and pornography, and a long-standing desire to be noticed. The academic achievements weren't enough; he wanted a beautiful woman. That he was twice as old as Robin made no difference. In his own mind, he was still a lonesome teenager wanting to be accepted.

He began his life in isolation. He learned a routine with his mother, where he'd make her angry and then grovel for forgiveness. When he was old enough to not need her, he was rude to her. He would always be slightly smug, never quite understanding how to deal with people, offering a surface politeness but never developing his own personality. Instead, he perfected the façade of the academic dynamo, intimidating colleagues with his intelligence.

For most of his early years, Douglas was in a vacuum. The fellow who finally emerged rose to a respected position at Tufts, but inside he was a cruel child, taking what he wanted and blaming others for his problems.

It isn't a surprise that he favored prostitutes. He didn't know how to charm women. But he could put money in a prostitute's hand and they'd feed his craving for attention, a craving that couldn't be satisfied. He married Nancy, and later Bonnie-Jean, because he recognized they would be subservient to him. It is significant that both were nurses; each marriage supplied him with an underling who would admire his genius. In between he tried his luck with hookers, and that turned out horribly. It was better to stick with nurses who would put him on a pedestal.

It must've enraged Douglas when he couldn't get Robin to fall for him. It was enough to fill his mind with murderous thoughts. Yet there was something in Douglas's letters to Robin that makes one wonder if there was more going on, something the chroniclers didn't dare touch. Were they actually closer than anyone realized?

"As you know, the truly wonderful times in my life this last year were those times I spent with you," Douglas wrote in one of them. "You shared so much with me . . . our thoughts, our lives, and we had so many special meaningful times together that can only happen between friends. I cherish those memories and look forward to the time when we are together again."

Douglas goes on to describe Robin as a "treasure . . . something that is precious, a one-of-a-kind possession, something that is priceless and must be protected at all costs."

The language is right out of a stalker's manual. But Douglas's fantasy world was built with Robin's help. Even J. R. had said Robin had respected Douglas at first. Robin's simple show of respect may have been enough to encourage Douglas that something special was happening.

Douglas's comment that Robin had "shared so much" is intriguing. The eyewitness accounts of them together are few; no one was privy to how they'd behaved with each other. We don't know what went on in the trick pads or during their many dinners together. Did they talk in some personal way?

What we do have are a few notes from Robin. Among the mess of Douglas's office was a birthday card from her, a jokey thing about too much sex being bad for the eyes. How many prostitutes send birthday cards to clients?

Tucked inside one of Douglas's books was a short note from Robin, one that suggested theirs was more than an arrangement born at Good Time Charlie's. In it, Robin described Douglas as a "wonderful person . . . finally getting what he deserves. And I'm glad and grateful that you're letting me be a part of it all."

In another, she wrote, "May our friendship grow more wonderful as time goes on. Let's keep it strong as we help each other to achieve all that we've talked about.

"Friends always, Robin."

Then there was J. R.'s initial concern that Robin and Douglas had left together for the Virgin Islands. Was J. R. talking nonsense, or had Robin discussed such a trip?

What was overlooked in the mythmaking of the case is that Douglas and Robin were in business together. Their business involved embezzling from Tufts. Both Douglas and J. R. told the investigators that it had been Robin's idea to steal from Tufts, which made her the de facto boss of the Douglas–Benedict operation. Douglas's infatuation was tolerated, because no other tricks were coming up with $67,000 in a year, which was roughly twice the average salary of an associate professor in those days. And even if Robin had instigated the embezzling, Douglas had happily obliged. He was showing Robin that he had a touch of larceny in him, that he was just as daring and rebellious as her.

It is possible that Douglas intended to enact a similar swindle at SUNY but, to Kivlan's point, something must've happened in Plattsburgh.

The general theories that Douglas killed Robin over money or, as he put it, in self-defense, feel stale. Their relationship had been complex. It stands to reason that his decision to kill her was every bit as complex.

76.

As Kivlan prepared to prosecute Douglas back in 1984, Matt Connolly sketched out a detailed scenario of what he believed happened. In it, he surmised that Robin was invited to Douglas's house for some kind of payday. Kivlan never believed Douglas's story about Robin bringing slides over. It was a money deal, nothing else, though Douglas's backup plan was murder.

"I cannot see Douglas whacking her with the hammer as soon as she walked in," Connolly wrote in his notes. "He is still madly in love with Robin."

Referring to him as "the donkey," Connolly wrote that Douglas made a final effort to declare his feelings for her and was frightened by her response. Connolly believed Robin was going to blackmail Douglas, perhaps by bringing "pictures, tapes, or letters" to Douglas's wife, kids, the *Globe*, or his potential employers. This threat revealed that Robin was "no more than a hardened whore." When she did this, Douglas realized what he was up against. "Douglas tells her he'll get the money," Connolly writes. "He gets the hammer and raps her on the head. She falls down either dead or unconscious."

It is a reasonable scenario, but Kivlan and Connolly were reasonable, educated men, trying to get into the minds of a Combat Zone prostitute and the desperate man who killed her. They may have been effective prosecutors, but this scenario is like something out of old Hollywood, with Douglas stopping short of saying, "If I can't have you, no one will!" That was the theory favored by many, including Sharkey and Dwyer. It was the sort of thinking that came from watching late-night detective movies and *Perry Mason*.

"I think he was planning to rape her," said Paul Landry in 2021. "I think Douglas invited her to his house with the intention of raping her and killing her. By that time, he was angry with her. He was thinking, 'You're gonna dime me out to Tufts? I'm gonna put an end to this, and get my revenge.' But when he tried to rape her she fought him; that's when he took the hammer and hit her."

Rape was never part of Douglas's methodology, but Landry's scenario does account for the wound to his head. Connolly's theory overlooked Douglas getting hit.

Though he claimed Robin had hit him with the hammer, the wound was not from a blunt object. From the photographs taken when he was first questioned in March of 1983, Douglas's wound looked more like a cut down his forehead. It is possible that Robin picked up something to defend herself and whacked him, though it is unlikely that they, as Douglas described, brawled in his bedroom. It is doubtful that during Robin's education as a prostitute she was instructed to grapple with 300-pound clients.

If Douglas had thoughtfully planned to murder Robin, would he have done it in his home? Why leave blood all over the place? Connolly's treatise stumbled over this part of the case. "Why," he wrote, "does Douglas decide to do her in at his house? Is it [so] he can better commit the [murder] if he does it this way?" It is sensible to think Douglas might feel more comfortable in his home rather than in a strange hotel room or on a deserted stretch of highway. But would it be smart to kill Robin in his house when Nancy or the children could've walked in to catch daddy hovering over a dead woman?

There has never been a general consensus on Douglas as a killer. Sharkey once described him as a chump, "with his arms sewn on backward," while Connolly insisted Douglas plotted Robin's death carefully and that his soft demeanor was a scam. "He wanted us to think he was just a wimp," Connolly told Linda Wolfe, "but I think he planned her killing, and that he planned it cleverly."

Just a few days after Robin's disappearance, neighbors in the Back Bay apartment building thought they heard flute music coming from her place. It could've only been Douglas, making noise to convince the neighbors that Robin was there. Who else could it have been? He had keys to her trick pad, and troopers later found Robin's flute in his closet. He'd probably let himself in searching for evidence that might incriminate him. How did he get the flute? It is doubtful that she had the flute in her trick pad, but possible. The flute may have been in her Starlet, too, and Douglas had kept it after disposing of the car in New York.

Getting a reasonable sound on a flute is very difficult for someone who lacked musical training, so one can only imagine the odd noises Douglas produced. Stranger still, people reportedly heard someone singing in the apartment. Douglas's voice was often described as womanish.

That Douglas kept the flute in his possession was just another of his quirks, though he may have been like many killers, wanting a keepsake to remind him of his beautiful victim. After all, she'd once played for him on one of the special nights they'd shared.

But whether he had cleverly planned anything is unclear. He may have been thinking about killing Robin for a while. His attempt to control her had failed, and he was angry. His strategic and organized method of stalking was the work of a man whose goal was damage, perhaps obliteration.

Yet Douglas was shrewd. Had he planned to kill her, he wouldn't have done it on a night when her friends knew she was going to his house. Or was he doing as he'd done with the police, tipping them off that Robin was a prostitute while he was right there with her? Was part of his method to hide in plain sight? Did he think no one would suspect him if he seemed too obvious?

A call had been made to Robin and J. R.'s answering service at 10:07 p.m. on the night she disappeared. The message was allegedly from Robin saying she was leaving Sharon for a party in Charlestown. Though the Americall operators interviewed couldn't recall that specific call, there were statements that someone, believed to be a man disguising his voice as a woman, had left messages as "Nadine" that weekend. This was most likely Douglas creating a diversion, but it was never proven. (In his confession, he said he left the message just to "tease" Robin.) Kivlan had hoped to use one of the operators as a witness before the grand jury, but she was unreliable and couldn't remember taking the call. Had Kivlan been able to prove Douglas had left the 10:07 p.m. message, it would've been more evidence that he had planned the murder and was creating a false impression that Robin was in Charlestown.

The quick and explosive violence, the scramble to clean up, and the long erratic drive around Massachusetts and Rhode Island are the marks of a spur-of-the-moment killing. The long drive wouldn't have been necessary if he'd planned things. He would've picked out a dumping ground well in advance. According to most forensics psychologists, murders by hammer are usually spur of the moment, the weapon picked up because it's handy, within reach. Hence, the manslaughter verdict may have been appropriate, even if Douglas's confession sounded sketchy.

Kivlan agrees, forty years later, that if the killing was premeditated, Douglas was intelligent enough to have never been caught. Regarding what exactly took place, Kivlan can only speculate.

"It was an escalation of everything that had been going on," Kivlan said. "Douglas was in over his head. And he wasn't streetwise."

As for Douglas's own wound, Kivlan offered a possible solution.

"He was such a big, clumsy ox that he probably did it to himself."

77.

His spot assured in the pantheon of killers, William Douglas shambled out of the cold spotlight and into the pleasant warmth of obscurity. He'd shed his past like a skin.

He and Bonnie-Jean were devout members of their local Catholic Church and were helpful in their community. She worked for a local doctor, and many would tell you she was as kind and caring as anyone you'd ever met. They'd tell you her husband Bill was perfectly matched to her, a gentle soul with a big heart. For a while he was employed by a rehabilitation center in Hartford, Connecticut.

In photos of Douglas and Bonnie-Jean together, he looks relaxed, contented. He was no longer William Douglas, the perverted professor. He was just good ol' Bill Douglas, happily married and working a respectable job.

But had he really overcome his obsessions? How did he leave such a pronounced part of his life behind?

"It is possible to commit one crime and figure out a way to move on," said Dr. Katherine Ramsland. "Especially with religion. Cognitive-behavioral therapy can address it, as can a prison sentence." Ramsland, one of the premiere forensic psychologists in America, believed Douglas could ease back into society with a minimum of problems. "It doesn't surprise me. Lots of killers who get released don't kill again."

Eight years in prison may not have been enough for Douglas in terms of punishment, but those years did serve as a kind of cold-turkey treatment. Away from the Combat Zone, and with Bonnie-Jean's talk of Jesus and eternity, it seemed the darker aspects of Douglas's life drained away. Douglas had always had an addictive personality; perhaps he traded his old addiction to prostitutes and porn for a new addiction, one that involved the Holy Spirit.

Was Douglas ever tempted to sample the new era of internet porn and a new generation of sex workers who advertised online? Perhaps he was something like a recovering alcoholic in AA leaning on the Bible when temptation hit.

"Obsessive thinking is complex and incompletely understood," explained Dr. Alex Lickerman, who has written extensively on the topic. "The short answer is that obsessions *can* come back and re-establish a hold on a person. It's also possible for someone to think about a past obsession without becoming obsessed again."

Douglas became a humble, near-invisible member of society, a loyal husband who took his wife on yearly trips to New York. Bonnie-Jean's churchgoing, forgiving nature seemed to work on him. Perhaps, as Douglas had once dreamed of rescuing a prostitute from the streets,

Bonnie-Jean had fantasies of lifting a fallen man up from damnation. His fantasy ended in tragedy. Hers resulted in a happily-ever-after scenario. Life is very odd.

It could also be that Douglas was simply exercising his need to be seen as a kind and gentle man. With each passing day, Douglas was showing the world that he was one of God's lambs, a good little man who would never do anything wrong again. *See how nice I am? That mess back in 1983 was really the hooker's fault. . . .*

The blissful marriage ended in 2002 when Bonnie-Jean died at age fifty-eight of cancer. Douglas stayed by his wife's side during her final months, looking after her.

The funeral home's online guest book was filled with comments from her friends and family. No one from Douglas's family wrote in it.

What is astonishing about these online homages is the way Douglas added to them on every holiday, even six months after her death, signing them with incredible embellishments, such as "All My Love Eternally, Your Loving Husband, forever, Bill."

At times, though, as he slathers on the compliments and tells the deceased Bonnie-Jean how special she was, there's a vague similarity to the letters he'd written twenty years earlier to Robin. The wording, the excessive praise, is all the same. It appeared Douglas celebrated the women he loved in more or less the same way, whether his treasured, Bible-thumping wife or the sex worker he'd killed with a heavy carpenter's tool.

The difference is that Douglas's notes to his dead wife were loaded with references to God and Jesus and Heaven. In one of his entries, he imagines seeing Bonnie-Jean in the afterlife, running into her arms "with Jesus and Mary by my side."

Douglas also makes mention of Saint Gertrude, a thirteenth-century German Benedictine nun who was the self-proclaimed "bride of Christ." He mentions that he was reading about her during his saddest days just after Bonnie-Jean's death. There is significance here, because Saint Gertrude's role was to say prayers for those in purgatory. One of the prayers attributed to her ended with the line, "for all the Holy Souls in Purgatory, for sinners everywhere, for sinners in the universal Church, for those in my own home and in my family. Amen."

From her mouth to the ears of God, Douglas was probably hoping Saint Gertrude had some clout. He may have wondered if an old sinner like him really stood a chance of seeing Bonnie-Jean in Heaven.

• • •

Though the funeral home's guest book was filled with condolences to Bonnie-Jean's family, not everyone was so sympathetic.

One entry reads, "Will Miss You."

It was signed, "Robin Benedict."

78.

During the 2010s, the Investigation Discovery channel began producing an avalanche of quickly made documentaries. The network specialized in hour-long programs about unfaithful spouses, stalkers, and online dating gone wrong. Some of the programming was of high quality, but much of it was cheaply assembled entertainment for the Roku generation, as if the made-for-TV movies of the 1980s and '90s had been reduced to their most basic plot points. The crude dramatizations by actors were interspersed with comments from actual detectives and journalists who may have worked on the cases being profiled. The network's search for content eventually led to Douglas and Benedict.

The case was first featured on *Scorned: Love Kills* in a 2014 episode called "Teacher's Pet." The actor playing Douglas, Mark O'Neal, was a tall, athletic fellow with a neatly groomed beard. This was Douglas reimagined as a CrossFit stud, ripping his shirt off to dive into bed with Robin. (He wore glasses so viewers would know he was a professor. Otherwise, he looked like a Banana Republic model.) Melissa Saint Amand was cast as Robin. Though attractive, Saint Amand played Robin as bedraggled, skanky; she was apparently directed to stare into the camera with a bug-eyed look, like a demonic cokehead. The program was laughable; details were smudged or ignored and characters were dropped. For the sake of political correctness, a fictional female detective was added to the story. Predictably, those old spotlight hounds Billy Dwyer and William Delahunt made brief appearances. They offered only banal comments that seemed to be read from a teleprompter.

Dwyer would later write that he "deeply regretted" taking part in a television production that was "not particularly accurate" and "minimized the real story." Boston TV reporter Ron Gollobin also recalled "awful experiences with incompetents from Investigation Discovery and other true-crime outlets who took up a good swatch of my time and then botched the telling of the story."

Two years later, Investigation Discovery resurrected Douglas and Benedict for a program called *Married with Secrets*. The episode, "Obsession Has Its Price," was a slight improvement on "Teacher's Pet," but details were still glossed over. The Investigation Discovery channel seemed determined to cast women who were not as appealing as Robin, while everyone else in the cast was much more attractive than their real-life counterparts. Showing that little had changed since *The High Price of Passion*, Robin's black pimp was portrayed by a young white man. Robin's brother Rob appears in the program to offer a few touching comments about his sister, but this hardly makes up for the show being slipshod.

Also glaring was the omission of Douglas's fascination with porn and prostitutes. Both Investigation Discovery programs made it appear he just happened to meet Robin the first time he'd ever walked into a bar. In short, the channel took a groundbreaking case full of quirks and kinks and watered it down until it was a corny daytime drama. There was no indication that the case had been a nationwide phenomenon.

Such a simplified presentation does no justice to a story that dominated the news for so long. Douglas's extreme weirdness may be beyond the grasp of any pay-TV network.

Douglas didn't get to see how his story fared on *Married with Secrets*. He had died a year earlier at seventy-three, a fragile old man in a New England nursing home. The family kept quiet about his passing, the final secret they'd have to keep.

79.

None of those who knew Douglas were surprised that he sank back into anonymity. Paul Landry assumed some New England college hired him, since most schools "wouldn't care that he was a murderer."

After Bonnie-Jean's death, Douglas's own health began failing. There were rumors that he had moved to England or had stealthily moved into a

Massachusetts suburb. Enough time had passed that Douglas's new neighbors may have had no idea about his past. Like any public figure from an earlier generation, he was of no significance to anyone under a certain age.

Douglas had lived long enough to see the tabloids replaced by internet news feeds and websites where amateur sleuths discuss the crimes of serial killers like baseball fans arguing statistics. The old splash pages that he'd once dominated were now reduced to flickering images on a mobile phone or a laptop. He'd lived to see events that dwarfed his own, from the unsolved murder of JonBenét Ramsey to the carnage of high school massacres. These were terrible stories, but his own story had been terrible—indeed, Douglas was one of the people with a reasonable claim to having kicked off the modern tabloid era, for better or worse.

• • •

The informant on Douglas's death certificate was listed as his "sister." Yet Douglas was an only child. The woman was merely one of his Connecticut church associates, a so-called "sister in Christ."

Long after Douglas's death, his "sister" was contacted.

"I can't talk now," the old woman said. "God bless you and your family."

The informant's role is to provide personal information for the funeral director. The informant is usually a relative who can provide details in the event of legal situations. One of Douglas's children might've served in the role rather than a friend from church. Furthermore, a "sister in Christ" wouldn't qualify as a relative and shouldn't have been listed as Douglas's sister.

Curiously, some of the document is left blank, including the names of former spouses, as if the informant simply knew no details of Douglas's life. Not surprisingly, the one space that is filled in bold letters is the one for "occupation." The word PROFESSOR is clear.

It wasn't unusual for a murderer to pass away in such a secretive fashion, said a representative of a Connecticut funeral home. "We get that all the time: murderers, pedophiles, Catholic priests who may have been in a scandal."

The few investigators who are still alive knew nothing of Douglas's whereabouts or his death. "The people in that nursing home probably had no idea who he was," said John Kivlan. "I wouldn't be surprised if he spent the later part of his life as a complete unknown."

Yet a spokesperson for the home said Douglas was not entirely anonymous. "Some of us knew," she said. "We looked him up on the internet. Sometimes you'd hear nurses talking about him, saying there was a murderer on the floor. Of course, he wasn't the only murderer we had."

80.

William Douglas never attained iconic status. The 1980s did not begin or end with his case. By the time of his sentencing in 1984, the nuclear accident at Chernobyl and the explosion of the Space Shuttle Challenger were still two years away. Compared to the crumbling of the Berlin Wall or the debut of the Macintosh computer, his killing of a young prostitute was merely a speck on the timeline. It is inaccurate to say Douglas somehow represented the era. Bernard Goetz, the New York subway vigilante, was more fitting, as were the variously named preppie, yuppie, and cheerleader murders of the period. And yet the future of crime coverage seemed to originate right there in the professor who prowled the Combat Zone. Was there ever a clumsier walk on the wild side?

It is hard to think of Douglas and not remember downtown Boston at night, rain-swept streets, blasting car horns, and the glare of neon; the barroom touts on the sidewalk, men who looked well-dressed but up close were unshaven and smelled of alcohol, promising us tons of illicit fun if we stepped inside. This was the Combat Zone, a hungry neighborhood. It was the Boston of Larry Bird and Ray Bourque, of Governor Mike Dukakis and the gang at *Cheers*. Douglas didn't embody his time. He was more like a cheap ornament dangling from the edges of an era. Yet he captivated the public for a while.

Whenever we grow fascinated by a killer, it's not because we hate him. We want to stare at him, like gawkers at an old-time carnival, staring at the wild man in the pit who eats live chickens. We want to look him in the eye and see if, perhaps, we recognize ourselves. We wonder if we could ever sink so low. What would it take?

With Douglas, as with carnival sideshows, we stared long enough that some of us started to pity him. A woman actually married him for that very reason. But imagine him hiding the body. Imagine him sneaking into his victim's apartment and playing a flute, the sound of evil wafting away on each dissonant note.

Looking back on Douglas and the killing of Robin Benedict, one wonders how the case would play nowadays. Much has changed in the years since, and women would be more firmly on the side of Robin, regardless of her lifestyle. It is doubtful that Douglas would particularly fascinate women, as Tom Troy once claimed; he'd be recognized for the malignant creature that he was. And with so many liars, hypocrites, and sex addicts existing in the pop culture, the professor and his secret life might not be such a national headline. Yet Douglas would still grab our attention, if just for a while, for a generation of true-crime podcasters and bloggers would always find room for a madman with a hammer.

• • •

Douglas didn't love killing. It is wrong to think he was a bloodthirsty sadist. What he loved was control.

Jealousy was part of it, too. But Douglas wasn't jealous of other men. He was jealous of Robin.

She was everything he wasn't. She was young, attractive, and charming. He tried to copy her—he used cocaine, watched *The Rocky Horror Picture Show,* and sat through an Air Supply concert; he stole from Tufts to prove he was as crooked as her; and he even bought a car like hers, anything to make him feel closer to her, to prove he was just like her.

Since he couldn't seem to gain Robin's approval or validation, it was integral for Douglas to keep her down and destroy her self-image. But she was tougher than he'd ever realized. It is likely that during the final moments of what had turned into a battle for dominance, he understood that he couldn't win. As he stood in front of her on their last night together, he was reduced to being the clumsy and friendless boy from the trailer court, while she was still attractive. And she didn't need him.

Chances are they argued again, because that was what they'd been doing lately. But something was different on this night. It's not that he finally realized she was a hardened prostitute, because he'd known that since their first meeting. But something happened to make his rage glow redder than hot coals.

Douglas had a history of punishing Robin for things she had done. When she'd been unpleasant during one of their sessions, he broke into her trick pad and stole from her. When she'd ignored him on New Year's Eve and said she no longer wanted to see him, he made the phone calls that cost Robin her job. But those were covert movements, done without her knowing. Whatever happened on this night pushed him into immediate and violent action. It may have been that he'd finally realized that he wasn't smart enough to control a simple Combat Zone hooker. The revelation was more than his dark little mind could handle. Maybe he grabbed her or tried to hit her. She may have defended herself, which left the mark on his head. Then, as she tried to run out, Douglas picked up the hammer. The anger that he'd been holding down for months suddenly heaved forth like a tidal wave.

Or consider that the key item in the story may not have been a hammer, but a flute. Robin's pocketbook, flute, and other items were found in Douglas's closet. Is it possible that Robin saw them? Did it dawn on her that Douglas had been the one to break into her trick pads and steal from her? With his cover blown, did Douglas panic and kill her? Or were these items what Robin had mentioned during their argument on his front lawn ("Give me what belongs to me . . ."). Had Douglas, in a childish mood, stolen her flute? And to get even, had she stolen things from his briefcase?

Maybe that's what happened. Or maybe not. It makes more sense than *She hit me first. . . .*

The killing was not the work of a criminal genius. No, Douglas's masterwork was his confession. Because of it, the public remembered Robin as a coldhearted prostitute who encouraged a man to embezzle, then came to his house and attacked him over money. Douglas hadn't been able to control Robin, but he'd controlled how the world saw her.

81.

Douglas spent the last seven years of his life in the Catholic Memorial Home, an assisted-living facility in Fall River, Massachusetts. According to the brochure, the home provided a "holistic approach," along with twenty-four-hour nursing care. The home offered a special focus on patients with Alzheimer's disease who were unable to care for themselves. That he was admitted while in his midsixties suggests he was succumbing to the same problems that had plagued his mother at roughly the same age. Such things are not always passed on genetically, but sometimes they are.

It is also significant that in one of Douglas's old letters he apologized to Robin for constantly repeating himself and promised to stop. (Reading his letters one can notice him repeating things, including certain phrases and even suggestions of things they might do for fun, sometimes within the same page.) Colleagues at the medical school also recalled that Douglas was forgetful. Obsessive behavior, short-term memory problems, and repetition are often preludes to dementia.

His files have long since been shredded, per the home's policy. Talking about him in 2022, a representative of the home said that she barely remembered Douglas but that he likely had cognitive problems and required daily care. "There were nuns here," she recalled. "And he would've had access to twice daily Catholic mass, depending on how badly he was impaired."

In late February of 2015, Douglas was taken to the nearby Charlton Memorial Hospital where he was treated for a urinary tract infection and other bacterial conditions—problems often associated with bedridden dementia sufferers. One day later, at 10:20 p.m., on February 27, Douglas was pronounced dead of septic shock.

Douglas's body was shipped to Connecticut. A private memorial service was held. The body was then taken to a Windsor crematory and placed in a special container designed for easy burning. It was then put in a cremation chamber. An attendant cranked the furnace to 1,800 degrees Fahrenheit. The body curled as the heat increased, like a piece of metal held over a flame. Within four or five hours there was nothing left of Douglas but his bones; they were allowed to cool, then crushed into bits.

There was no death announcement. No obituary. Records were destroyed, until it seemed William H. J. Douglas had never existed.

If he indeed suffered from end-stage dementia, it is possible that he spent the last years of his life with no memory at all of Robin Benedict.

SOURCES

If you want to know more about this case, I recommend Teresa Carpenter's book, *Missing Beauty*, and Linda Wolfe's collection of articles, *The Professor and the Prostitute*. Both were incredibly useful during the writing of *Boston Tabloid*. However, those authors ended their coverage of the case with Douglas going to prison. For me, the story continued beyond 1984.

I would also like to mention the late Carol Horner of the *Philadelphia Inquirer*. She wrote about this case as well as anybody. Maybe better. I must also praise the reporting of Joe Starita of the *Miami Herald*.

Books

Carpenter, Teresa. *Missing Beauty: A True Story of Murder and Obsession*. New York: W. W. Norton & Company, 1988.

Dwyer, William C. *On the Stroll: A Detective's Thirty-Two Year Journey in the Boston Police Department*. Self-published, 2019.

McPhee, Michele. *A Professor's Rage: The Chilling True Story of Harvard PhD Amy Bishop, Her Brother's Mysterious Death, and the Shooting Spree that Shocked the Nation*. New York: St. Martin's True Crime, 2011.

Meloy, J. Reid, ed. *The Psychology of Stalking: Clinical and Forensic Perspectives*. Academic Press, 1998.

Schama, Simon. *Dead Certainties: Unwarranted Speculations.* Knopf, 1991.
Singer, Peter. *Ethics into Action: Henry Spira and the Animal Rights Movement.* Rowman & Littlefield Publishers, Inc., 1998.
Wolfe, Linda. *The Professor and the Prostitute: And Other True Tales of Murder and Madness.* Houghton Mifflin Harcourt, 1986.

Newspapers and Newswires

Arizona Republic
Associated Press
Baltimore Sun
Boston Globe
Boston Herald
Boston Phoenix
Detroit Free Press
Miami Herald
Philadelphia Inquirer
Providence Journal
United Press International

Magazines

Boston
Penthouse

Most of Rob Benedict's quotes come from the Investigation Discovery channel program, *Married with Secrets: Teacher's Pet*, first aired 2016.

Various website articles were also useful in understanding some of the behavior described in this book.

"Anti-Mothers, Uber-Mothers, Passive Mothers and the Making of Murderers." Dr. Elizabeth Yardley. Huffpost.com. May 13, 2017.

"Control Through Destruction: Stalking as Righteous Retribution." Dr. Elizabeth Yardley. https://www.elizabethyardley.com/blog-1/control-through-destruction-stalking-as-righteous-retribution.

"An Expert Reveals the Psychology Behind Women Who Love Men Behind Bars." Taylor Bell. March 7, 2016. https://archive.attn.com/stories/6268/why-women-fall-in-love-prison-inmates.

"Flirtation or Fixation? When Valentine's Day Is Far from Romantic." Dr. Elizabeth Yardley. https://www.elizabethyardley.com/.

"How to Escape the Grip of Obsession." Darlene Lancer. Medium.com. March 10, 2020.

"I Thought God Could Never Love a Convicted Murderer. I Was Wrong." Pamela Perillo with John T. Thorngren. May 18, 2018. Christianity Today. https://www.christianitytoday.com/ct/2018/june/pamela-perillo-salvation-death-row.html

"Ten Views of the Combat Zone (Boston 1976)." William Landay. Esquire.com. January 30, 2008.

ACKNOWLEDGEMENTS

The following people were helpful in the writing of this book. Some talked a lot. Some talked a little. I present them in alphabetical order.

Kelley Bartlett
John Brady
Teresa Carpenter
Anthony DiFruscia
Mike Frisby
Russell M. Glitman
Ron Gollobin
John Kivlan
Paul Landry
Lawrence P. LeFebre
Alex Lickerman MD
Shelley Murphy
Dr. Katherine Ramsland
Joseph Starita
Sean Sullivan
Dr. Alex Williams
Dr. Elizabeth Yardley

There were people at various prisons, funeral homes, and record centers who insisted they were merely doing their jobs and didn't wish to be thanked. Still, I would like to mention a few of the institutions that were helpful in my research.

The Catholic Memorial Home, Fall River, Massachusetts
The Connecticut Department of Correction
The Windsor Crematory, Windsor, Connecticut.
Massachusetts Registry of Vital Records and Statistics
Massachusetts State Police Museum and Learning Center

There were many obstacles to writing this book. The main one, obviously, was that the crime happened so long ago that many of the people involved have died. Some passed away fairly recently, such as attorney, Damon Scarano, who died during the first wave of Covid-19.

Another obstacle was that many people contacted simply didn't wish to take part. Some initially agreed, but at the last moment decided to remain quiet and canceled our scheduled interview. I'm sure they had their reasons.

ABOUT THE AUTHOR

DON STRADLEY is the author of *The War: Hagler–Hearns and Three Rounds for the Ages* (one of *The Progressive* magazine's "Favorite of Books 2021"); *Berserk: The Shocking Life and Death of Edwin Valero; Slaughter in the Streets: When Boston Became Boxing's Murder Capital*; and *A Fistful of Murder: The Fights and Crimes of Carlos Monzon*, all from Hamilcar Publications. *Slaughter in the Streets* was named by CrimeReads in 2020 as one of "The Classics of Boxing Literature." Stradley's work has also appeared in *The Ring*, Cinema Retro, and on ESPN.com. He lives on Boston's North Shore.

Boston Tabloid is set in 10-point Sabon, which was designed by the German-born typographer and designer Jan Tschichold (1902–1974) in the period 1964–1967. It was released jointly by the Linotype, Monotype, and Stempel type foundries in 1967. Copyeditor for this project was Shannon LeMay-Finn. The book was designed by Brad Norr Design, Minneapolis, Minnesota, and typeset by New Best-set Typesetters Ltd.